Conquerabia

The Struggle For Identity

Diane M. Hinds

Contents

Dedication i
Acknowledgements ii
About the Author iii
Introduction iv
Real characters: v
Chapter 1 1
Chapter 2 25
Chapter 3 35
Chapter 4 48
Chapter 5 54
Chapter 6 78
Chapter 7 91
Chapter 8 111
Chapter 9 122
Chapter 10 129
Chapter 11 145
Chapter 12 154
Chapter 13 160
Chapter 14 196
Chapter 15 205
Chapter 16 210
Chapter 17 222

Chapter 18 234
Chapter 19 241
Chapter 20 263
Chapter 21 277
Chapter 22 288
Chapter 23 293
Chapter 24 299
Chapter 25 320
Chapter 26 334
Chapter 27 339
Chapter 28 346
Chapter 29 349
Chapter 30 367
Chapter 31 375
Chapter 32 384
Chapter 33 393
Chapter 34 419
Chapter 35 427
Chapter 36 437
Chapter 37 447
BIBLIOGRAPHY: 454

Dedication

This book is dedicated to

F. Holly Gibbons and John Louis Gibbons,

who are the lights of my life.

Acknowledgements

Fr KAL and Mrs Lenore Hinds, my parents whose move back to Trinidad with the family on the 15 November, 1975, inspired this story.

Anne Perry, one of the best people to have entered my life. You helped make me a better person. I cherish the conversations we used to have and I thank you for encouraging me to pursue my Masters.

Further thanks go to Richard Huzzey, Alec Ryrie, David Charnick, Andy Regan, Chris Silk, Tom Stiles. John Rawlinson, Gail Chipperfield and Mia Gibbons.

A special 'thank you' to a wonderful woman and close friend Hanley Kanar who has helped to edit this book, of which I'm immensely proud.

Author photo © Edward Taylor of Digital-Flow.co.uk.

About the Author

DianeHindsWrites.com

"Conquerabia" draws inspiration from author Diane Hinds' life on the island from 1975 to 1979. Her father, Rev. Kenneth Hinds, and her mother, Lenore Dottin, emigrated to the UK for Kenneth to train at a theological college. After his ordination at St Albans Abbey by Archbishop Bob Runcie, the family returned to their homeland, where Kenneth served as a Clerk in Holy Orders. This vibrant four-year chapter deeply influenced Diane, fuelling her creativity.

Diane Hinds is an accomplished entertainment publicist whose career could be a fascinating story in its own right. She is also a mother of two adult children and lives with Sickle Cell Disease.

Introduction

A New World opens up for trade and the demand for a cheap form of labour is necessitated. A barbaric business exploiting Africans and those of a darker complexion begin as those Europeans with colonial interests around the world search to enrich themselves. So began more than four hundred years of The Slave Trade.

The inhuman business advanced by the use of weapons of mass destruction, the indigenous found themselves at the mercy of their usurpers and owners. Guns and canons that would cause mass devastation, loss of life against primitive weapons. No one was free from the whims of these plantation owners and those determined to find wealth, at whatever cost to others. To witness the immediate death, slaughter of your fellow human as bodies are eviscerated combined with greed make most of us fearful.

The West Indies had long been a battleground for colonialism between Britain, France, the Dutch and Spain. The first European to land on the Spanish Antilles was Christopher Columbus in 1498. It was ceded to Britain in 1797 and was, over the years, populated by the Dutch, French, Spanish, Indian as well as Africans.

Upon the abolition of slavery indentureship became another form of slavery and this took place between 1845 and 1917.

Trinidad is a true melting pot of cultures, creeds and races, and is the inspiration for the authors' story, inspired by her life there between 1975 and 1979.

Real characters:

- Governor Thomas Picton
- Rosetta Smith
- Luisa Calderon
- Sir Ralph Abercromby
- Rear Admiral Don Sebastian Ruis de Apodoca
- Governor Jose Maria Chacon
- Captain Gabriel Sorirodo
- Saint Hillaire Bergorrat
- John Nihell
- Rosalba Carriera
- Captain Woodriff
- Mary Wollstonecraft
- Dutty Boukman
- Philbert Francois Rouvle de Blanchard
- Anthony Benezet
- Lord Chief Justice Ellenborough
- Catalina Calderon
- Benacia Calderon
- Maria Calderon
- Metro Ruiz
- William Dowding
- Sir Edward Raleigh

- Christopher Columbus
- Elizabeth Heyrick
- Captain Henry Harvey
- Samuel Hood
- Dr William Smellie

Chapter 1

Antwerp, Belgium

1777

The latest bi-annual report from Diego Manancala arrived by courier. Johan Dottin hastily spread the pages on the ornate mahogany desk. With his left hand he lifted one page about a foot from his eyes and adjusted the monocle to help him read the copperplate writing better. He did the same with a few more pages. Then he looked down at the papers spread on the table, eyes trained, hmm. Back to the page on the right. Again to the left. His attention focused on absorbing all the figures.

His wife came in. She was always interested when the plantation reports arrived since her husband's moods were so closely intertwined with the state of his investments.

"Well?"

"Diego recommends we expand the cotton and sugar." A smile grew across his face. "We're going to need more slaves."

-o0o-

For Mabel Dottin, née Van Hoebeek, this life of privilege and high finance was very different from the life of relative penury and emotional privation of her youth. Her father Henck, a clerk for a local firm of solicitors in Antwerp, known for his to-the-last-penny accounting, was, true to form, a parsimonious and unemotional warden who lauded his patriarchal and financial power over his dependents.

Mabel's mother Greetje was like most women of the time who, though from good families, had only modest dowries to offer. Thinking a clerk's prospects promising and eager to avoid a life of spinster-hood, she married the first man that made eyes at her, swiftly giving birth to two daughters within one year of marriage. Too late she realised she was married to a version of her own stingy father.

Greetje struggled to live with this secretive and miserly man who kept his income locked away and his heart even less available. Unlike her peers of their social status, who had outside help to keep their homes in order, Greetje was little more than a maid to Henck, and an ill-treated one at that. Henck expected the floors were scrubbed, the clothes boiled and pressed, and everything in place. He commanded order.

The caustic soap ruined her hands, her housemaid's knees ached. Henck often returned home at night and imperiously ran his index finger along the window sills or counter tops to test if she had cleaned to his impossible standards. Her slightest complaint or reproach was immediately silenced with Henck reminding her how lucky she was, the envy of every other wife. But she knew this was not true. She knew she was pitied.

Henck was also mercurial and withholding with his daughters, and he further added to the misery in the home by pitting them against each other. He cruelly told Mabel she was less attractive than her older sister Eloise, and made no secret expressing he felt Mabel would not find a suitable husband, as she had little by way of looks to attract someone of standing and wealth, unlike his favourite Eloise. In truth they were both attractive young women but first born Eloise was blond and blue eyed like Henck; Mabel was not the son he wanted and her hair was auburn. She favoured her mother. It was his way of insulting them both at the same time.

Though he was still as stingy with the girls as he was with his wife, Eloise's situation was presently the best. Both girls had all their clothes made by Greetje, coarse cotton dresses as plain and as cheap as was possible to make, but Mabel's were always her older sister's hand-me-downs. Their only "nicer" dresses were saved for Sundays and infrequent high days, but these were not made of the fine brocades or highly ornamented fabrics worn by stylish women of the time. The Van Hoebeek women's clothing bore more than one patch, different from the original fabric. Sundays were a source of humiliation, but at least a coat provided cover during colder months. Summer shawls barely hid the patchwork of repairs.

Like their mother, both girls knew marriage was an inevitable social step and necessary to avoid the dreaded spinsterhood, but with their mother's misery as an abject lesson they were more strategic than romance driven. Since she was favoured and told she was beautiful, Eloise was a confident young lady. She knew how to attract eligible bachelors, strategically tossing her blond hair and smiling beguilingly with her impossibly rose coloured Cupid-bow lips, bitten in company to enhance their colour. She turned heads wherever she went. Her shabby clothes were hardly noticed.

Eloise had her pick of handsome young suitors, but it was an older man, Pietr Koek, on whom she set her sights. He was from a well established family that had status and wealth, both of which were more attractive than the husband with whom it all came. She envisaged a world utterly removed from the present drudgery of constant cleaning, sewing, cooking, tasks for which affluent households had help. After years of shabby clothes, Eloise craved the latest Paris fashions, and a manor decorated with French furnishings. It was her desire to be written about in the newspaper as the Lady of the Manor who threw the most sought after and entertaining soirées, society's way of affirming her arrival and an affront to her miserly father and her colourless and subservient mother.

While her older sister craved a life of excess, filled with the gaiety absent in their childhoods, Mabel craved different things; loving affection and a quiet life where she had time to paint and read. Despite their apparent differences, though, Mabel, too, knew a marriage for money was the fastest escape route.

Within seven months of Eloise's marriage, Mabel met a fastidious and foppish clerk of the bank, several years older than she. Johan was comfortably off, because he was ambitious and inordinately devoted to his job. For him, marriage was functional. He was able to satisfy his manly desires elsewhere without the complications of marriage, but he knew he needed a wife to move ahead in society and an heir to achieve the financial empire he envisioned. Mabel fit his financial plan.

Equally ambitious, Mabel saw Johan as a man whose appearance was less important to her than the welcome escape from the poverty and subjugation her poor mother endured. Johan was a pleasant enough man, and though he smelled, mostly of tobacco, he seemed no more prone to manly foibles than other men. She set her sights. She had learned a lot from Eloise. Johan fit her financial plan.

Marriage was imperative for both, but not just for financial reasons. For Mabel? The significant gratification of proving her father wrong about her prospects for finding a prosperous husband and the immediate escape from both emotional and monetary privation. For Johan, marriage was not just a necessary step toward achieving his standing at the bank for appearances and to handle hostess duties, but she would bear the heir necessary to ensure his name and financial dynasty. And together? Their match was surprisingly companionable, despite the one possible obstacle - they were of different faiths, with Mabel Catholic and Johan the unusual Protestant in Belgium. But no matter, Johan agreed that any children would be baptised Catholic, and Mable was free to worship wherever she chose. Both were content with their arrangement.

Mabel thrived outside of the dour conditions of her family home, and she found her wifely duties an unexpected pleasure. She craved the affection and loving attention of a man. Johan found having an affectionate wife enhanced his well-being and Mabel was very attentive to his every desire, both physical and fiscal.

The first few months of marriage for Mabel were about finding an equilibrium living with Johan's eccentricities. He was a study in contradictions. He was fussy and fastidious in dress and manners at home but utterly fearless and driven in business. Mabel learned how to massage Johan's ego without patronising him. And she did not let him get the better of her when things were difficult at work or when he came home angry and moody after one of those late night meetings he sometimes had. Good thing, too, because the further into the marriage the more capricious he became. It was hard work, social climbing.

One thing was certain, Johan loved the bank and he moved ahead with a Machiavellian skill at steering the stodgier members to what might look to be risky foreign investments but were proving to be wildly lucrative. These investments, Mabel learned, were lucrative in more ways than fiscal for her. When Johan made the bank more wealthy, he made money on bonuses and commissions on those earnings, and his lust for money often translated into amorousness at home.

Despite worshipping the kronenthaler at work, at home he exercised a calculated magnanimity. He made generous enough provisions for Mabel to enhance their wardrobes and the beauty of their home, making it more inviting and impressive for their guests. Johan believed that appearances were almost everything. Mabel knew she not only had to continually defer to Johan's desires to move up in society and enhance his reputation among his peers, she had to enhance it so she could be part of it. She was not going to end up like her mother.

They both settled into a routine. Once they added a young maid, fourteen year old Flossie, and a strapping young handyman, Job, whose family was in the area, Mabel found a sense of independence she had never experienced before. This freed her to use her artistic abilities to decorate their Antwerp home, masculine and unloved until Mabel's arrival.

When Mabel announced she was pregnant Johan was ecstatic. The heir he wanted was coming, and provided it was a boy, Johan felt that his long planned dynasty was beginning to manifest. But this child also added to his responsibilities and his urgency to acquire more money and status to pass along. His happiness was overwhelmed by his ambition. And this was when he started drinking more than his usual and his other idiosyncrasies became more pronounced.

Unsurprisingly, it was their young maid, Flossie, who struggled most to adapt to his behaviour, due to her tender years. Mr. Dottin was so particular about just everything that she was nervous all the time. She would finally get used to all the rules when he'd change them after he'd been drinking. She just tried to be invisible to her master. She focused on her mistress and the child.

Devoted to habit, Johan started each day at the circular table in the hall collecting the newspaper from the silver salver he insisted it be placed on. Then as the elegant grandfather clock in the entry chimed the early hour, in a well practised one-handed movement, he pulled aside the left half of his day coat, retrieved and glanced at his Verge pocket watch, and deftly replaced it with a satisfied exhale. The watch and clock synchronised. It was 7am.

Next in his routine was breakfast in the beautifully appointed dining room, with its elegant mahogany table and Dutch Baroque style chairs. On the mantle sat an elegant bronze Louis XV clock, gently ticking away the morning, a gift from his employer in gratitude for his services at the bank. It took pride of place on the marble mantelpiece, a showpiece for guests to admire as they entered. Something else that took pride of place in this room were two of Mabel's paintings, landscapes of the countryside. He had not expected it, but his wife turned out to be a surprisingly fine artist, adding to his prestige.

This morning there were three place settings prepared, one of them used. Johan took his place as the sun's rays illuminated the deep crimson red-striped silk wall covering.

Flossie, dressed in her usual white cotton cap, nodded and curtseyed a 'good morning, sir' to him as he arrived in the breakfast room. She silently poured his tea. Johan did not like to be disturbed when reading and the maid knew, to her cost, not to upset his morning.

"Oh Flossie, I see Florian has already eaten, where is he now?" Mabel asked, walking into the room and sitting across from Johan. Flossie nodded and curtseyed before her mistress, whom she highly regarded.

"He's upstairs in his room playing, Ma'am."

"Good morning, My love. I trust you slept well?" Johan enquired. As per usual, Mabel prepared a bid to wrestle some of his attention away from the business news. Flossie poured Mabel's tea and quietly retreated, her employer's morning rituals being private.

"I did, Johan. Thank you." Mabel replied. "Did you hear the wind howling last night? I was most concerned the roof would be blown away." Johan did not respond.

Mabel had blossomed into a striking woman. Considerably younger than her husband, she too enjoyed the fashions of the time now that Johan was rising in society, She wore the tete de mouton hairstyle, which accentuated her strong cheekbones.

"Do you have a busy day ahead?" Mabel tried for his attention again, frustrated to be competing for his time. She was all too familiar with Johan's morning rituals, but she longed for conversation and attention. It was so rare. After so long a bachelor, Johan was set in his ways and used to his own company.

Before marriage Johan's only urgency was to adhere to an almost caricature banker's schedule. First make a set amount of money. Accomplished. Then marry a suitable woman to produce an heir that would keep the family name alive and to leave his legacy to, and who could perform the hostessing duties the wife of a successful man must perform. He was pleased with his progress. Marital perks and Mabel's agreeable company were a pleasurable surprise but he was not compelled to entertain her, especially in the morning. Besides, she had a child for that.

"I'm sure I will have to go and inspect after breakfast to see if there is any damage outside." Mabel offered. She looked towards

Johan to see if he would engage. Without glancing up from the paper he replied, “It’s best that Job be instructed to look instead.” Silence.

“I’m wearing a new perfume. Do you like it?” Mabel playfully teased. Johan finally looked up, catching the scent. Success. “Lilies is it? It’s lovely.” He looked back at the paper.

“Thank you, Johan.” She would try again. “Is that something interesting that’s caught your attention, my dear?”

Johan was slightly annoyed by the questions but finally he placed the paper down on the table next to him, took a long sip of tea, and he tried, again, to explain it all to Mabel.

“Just reading more about the West Indies, Dear. I know I have mentioned that we at the bank have been interested in these islands. Timing is everything, Mabel. As I have said before, Dear.”

“I know, Johan, but every day, even at breakfast?” Mabel was weary of vying for his attention, constantly.

Johan sighed. “The Seven Years War never really ended, it only slowed enough for Spain, France and Great Britain to refill their coffers. No one ever really stopped racing each other to expand into the most profitable open territories. These islands have great potential for producing cash crops like cotton, indigo, nutmeg, coffee, sugarcane and rum. The key for the bank now is to figure out how to profit from investing in these islands. Look here.” Johan pointed to his paper. “Spain has just passed The Royal Cedula and they are getting a new Governor in the Spanish Antilles. This is potentially fantastic news. The news about the Royal Cedula is complicated but the main points seem very favourable for new Catholic settlers."

Mabel nodded her head but she didn't really understand. Royal Cedula? What could this have to do with God? And Johan wasn't Catholic. He continued, explaining the early history of the Antilles area to her, that the Italian Columbus discovered it and dubbed it La Trinita upon seeing three peaks when they came into view. Awfully literal, Mabel thought, but evidently he saw this trinity of peaks as a sign from God that he was on the right course on his search for El Dorado. A worthy goal, Mabel thought. And Johan also said Columbus' patron, Queen Isabella of Spain, wanted him to find a route to China and India to find gold. Also worthy goals, she thought. But he didn't find gold or China, and Johan said all the natives died!

"Johan, you said Columbus failed to find anything he set out for, and you said all the natives got the plague! How do they know if the farming is as good as they hope? And even if crops do grow well there, who will work the fields?"

"That happened a long, long time ago, my dear", he was growing weary of this conversation with Mabel. "And Columbus did find gold, only the gold Columbus found wasn't in the ground, it was those islands themselves! I believe I mentioned to you how the current reports about the yields of land worked by the imported labour shows the land to be quite fertile and worth exploring. The Spanish solved the labour problems by importing heathen slaves from Africa and converting them, so it is a blessing for them."

"Well, how do they know it is safe to explore? Those diseases could still be there. And how on earth can you trust the godless savages not to kill the farmers?" The thought of those black savages was repellent to Mabel, and those disease riddled jungle islands sounded dreadful, Mabel knew that all those natives died of some sort of plague. She heard stories and had seen depictions of the plagues earlier in the century. They were horrifying, And yet they were all that Johan was interested in, even though he was making plenty of money here without having to deal with those pestilent islands.

Johan raised his head to look at his wife, unsure of what he just heard.

"Nothing is without risk, dear, but I am sure it is safe enough. Now you are sounding like those nay-sayers at the bank, afraid of trying something new, afraid of risk. If Columbus hadn't risked it we wouldn't even know the Spanish Antilles existed. And Mabel, Spain is prospering there with all those savages. This Royal Cedula seems to lay out the strategy for new settlers and I told you about encomienda. They simply convert the slaves to Catholicism, show them the superior ways of their Christian masters, save their souls from damnation and give them useful work to occupy them. I will have to learn the details more, but this alone proves the islands are safe, sanctioned by the Pope, and more importantly, financially viable!" Johan stood. "With that, I need to go to work. We have a meeting and it would not give the right impression for me to be late." He leaned over Mabel, kissed the top of her head, and he walked off. Truth be told he had no particular meeting. He just wanted to get away from Mabel's silly worries.

Mabel felt belittled and wrung her handkerchief in her lap, upset by how small she now felt. Johan shook his head, got up from the table and headed off to work. To Johan, the promise of the great riches to be had there made it worth the risk and Mabel's fretting annoyed him. To Mabel, despite how righteous Johan made all the expeditions and expanding into far places sound, she wasn't so sure. Johan thought that just occupying these places reflected God's blessings on the acquisitive desires of European kings, but Mabel couldn't imagine why God would bless killing all the savages or dragging them away from their jungle homes where God had put them in the first place. Why not just bring the gospel to them and save them from damnation there?

-o0o-

At the bank, Johan continued pursuing his obsessive interest in the Antilles, making further enquiries, reading reports and developing the bank's interests. It was a slow process. All investing and banking concerns had to be handled through Spain and had to have a whiff of catechism. This Royal Cedula was complicated but it changed everything. He had a lot of analysis to do on the terms and conditions, and he also had to contend with the island laws put in place by the new Governor there, but the gist seemed to be that Spain wanted more Catholic settlers to spread God's word, to bless their acquisition, and raise taxable crops. The dictates of this document gave land as an incentive - just gave it free to Roman Catholics brave enough and avaricious enough to move to this uncivilised jungle. It sounds daft but also intriguing.

They also encouraged slaving by offering the carrot of giving Catholic settlers land contingent on them bringing more slaves! The taste for slave labour was waning on the continent but on these islands and in the newly formed United States? Slaves were essential to progress. Johan didn't understand the problem. Those African brutes were closer to apes than people. The newly written constitution in the upstart United States even assessed them as being valued only ⅗ of a white man. The banks in Catholic Belgium needed only to position themselves, if they would only get over their fears, and that was Johan's role, to lead The Prussian Bank to what he felt sure was the best investment they were ever going to make.

Johan was a shrewd banker, no doubt, but he also knew how to play a good hand of cards. He took advantage of what he learned while pursuing the bank's interests to purchase a plantation he had learned of outside of the bank's purview. Conquerabia.

Through his weekly card game meetings, he learned the previous owner had died from some island disease and his young wife wanted to return to Spain with their children. She wanted to leave as quickly as possible and her agent, for a few, was willing to forgo many of the legal formalities and wrangling, hoping that the transaction could be accomplished quietly during the switch to the new Governor and laws. The simple deed transfer would be signed over without switching almost anything but the names, so the fact that the previous owner was Catholic would be as if conferred upon the new owner simply by transferring money between banks in Europe, no questions asked in the Spanish Antilles. And by chance Mabel actually is a practising Catholic, an aspect of his wife's background he never imagined would be a financial asset. Catholic God was clearly blessing these islands for all Catholics so why not follow what seems to be God's plan, unorthodox as it may be? He would even keep on their head manager, Diego Manancala, to make it even more seamless. Under the terms of the Cedula, within only the slightest surreptitiousness, their plantation would be seen to be Catholic owned.

Regardless of Johan's justifications he knew this was an irregular manoeuvre and conflict of interest that the bank could not be involved in or even know about. This wasn't really cheating,

Johan reasoned, because he would certainly make the best possible deals in the bank's interests. And to Spain and their interests? The plantation would comply almost completely with the Royal Cedula's Catholic requirement and more importantly, Johan figured, it would increase the size and profitably over time and send to the crown what the crown was owed. To all intents, constructions and purposes, Johan's slightly irregular purchase of Conquerabia would appear no different from any property sale. His bank would be none the wiser nor the poorer and he would live up to the intent of the law, if not to the exact letter of it. As he always thought, no harm looking out for one's personal interests. It stretched Johan's finances, but this was the opportunity of a lifetime and he would make it work.

-o0o-

As Job pulled up with the carriage outside the bank, Johan wondered why the Bank chairman called him in for the unscheduled meeting. When he entered, the florid Mr. Jacobs bid him sit down.

"Dottin, we are well pleased with prospects you have directed the bank to explore in the Spanish Antilles, so much so that to proceed we require a man there to act as proxy establishing the bank's interests. We see you as that man."

Johan was rather taken by surprise and asked what it would entail on his part.

"We wish to get ahead of our competitors, so we need to move swiftly and this requires the transport of sealed documents and official signatures in situ. I'm sorry, that it will mean we have to send you away from your lovely wife, but this is your territory, and we can only trust you to follow through on these matters. I am having the necessary visas and permits arranged, scheduling your meetings with our men in London and booking your passage. I do hope you can get your house in order quickly?"

Johan understood the urgency of the request and knew he could not refuse, not that he wanted to. It was not simply a request. He knew his future at the bank and his long term social standing depended on this test of his loyalty to the bank and the veracity of this investment he procured for the bank. Mr. Jacob apologised for sending him, but to Johan this was pure luck. What Mr. Jacob did not know was that instead of it being a hardship, this excited Johan. He knew that by sending him the Bank was approving his strategy, and he longed to see more of the world at another's expense.

It also meant that while there he could see in person how his own investment was developing, under Diego's deft hand. His last communication from Diego was very encouraging. He said that the unbelievably generous provisions of the Royal Cedula were true! Spain was so eager to populate these islands with Catholic settlers that it made the terms of the Royal Cedula very generous. As an incentive to leave the comforts of civilised Europe, the Cedula provided that commensurate with any increase in the number of slaves working their fields the more land they would be given to develop! Catholic or not, Johan chuckled to himself, it would surely be a sin not to get in on this land windfall.

Calculating in his head, once he brought in a base population of slave labour, the savages just multiplied on their own. Yes, Johan thought, God would surely think it a sin not to stretch a bit for this opportunity.

Pending the approval of the papers by the bank, Johan would board a vessel in a few week's time, arriving in the Antilles after about eight weeks at sea. Virtually buzzing with anticipation, he closed his ledgers early for the day.

He was excited to share his news with Mabel. She always seems to be as excited as he is when he has good news to share. This was more than news, to be sure, but she may even like this better.

Mabel, in the garden tending her flowers, was startled at hearing the dogs yapping about something around the front of the house and she got up to investigate. They weren't expecting company. When she came around to the front of the house she was surprised to see Johan's carriage in the drive. What on earth? He rarely came home early.

Mabel rushed inside, searching him out. Not finding him in the common areas she went to his study. His door was partially closed. Ordinarily she knew never to bother him here. In fact she was not even allowed to enter his study but she was startled by him coming home early like this. She tapped on the door.

"Johan, why are you home so early? Are you ill? Johan?" She kept tapping.

There, reclining in his chair, chewing tobacco and contemplating what he could do with his wealth, Johan finally heard Mabel at the study door.

"Johan?"

"Come."

When she opened the door she was about to rattle off questions but he playfully motioned to silence and he beckoned her to enter into his usually prohibited study.

"My dear, do take a seat. I have some important news. Come, sit down."

"Please Johan, just tell me what's going on?" Mabel gently lowered herself onto the padded arm of the Chesterfield chair by the unlit fireplace. Johan looked at Mabel, trying to appear serious and a bit sorry, though his blue eyes were glistening with excitement.

"My dear, my duty demands that, as proxy for the bank, I attend to the signatures and other formalities in our island acquisitions in person." Johan watched as the implications set in. Mabel rose to her feet.

"You're leaving us?" This had been her fear ever since he told her about Conquerabia.

"Temporarily, my dear."

"What will I do without you Johan? How long will you be away?" So many questions left Mabel's lips he knew answering them would do no good, she was so anxious. He tried not to be irritated.

"I know it will be a hardship for a while, my dear, but the bank's involvement on those islands are entirely under my purview. There are legal issues and documents for the bank that must be attended to, and we can't ignore the opportunity to expand our family investment there, either. There are the labour issues that impact both the bank and us, and documents for both banking stakes and land holders that must be signed in person. I'm afraid I must present myself."

Johan could see that Mabel was not convinced. He decided to read the latest letter from their overseer. Picking up the correspondence with an overly dramatic flourish, he read, "Dear Mr Dottin, I take great pleasure in writing that the additions to the workforce have arrived and you have been allocated the promised additional acreage, equal to the amount of negroes purchased. However, your signature will be required to develop the land for cultivating the new crops. The demand for tobacco, coffee and sugar cane is increasing. The local Alguida is happy to allocate the land provision as you are entitled, but require that you provide identification and signature to secure the additional land. This is apparently normal for new owners and is only required once."

Johan placed the paper on the desk and went to his wife's side. "You can see that this trip is essential to my position at the bank, and for our investment, too."

Johan could see Mabel was barely listening. She was nearly frantic at the prospect of being left alone while Johan took the dangerous voyage to those godforsaken, vermin infested islands.

"And, my dear, although I trust our overseer, at this point it is essential to take actual stock of the imported labour, upon which our financial future depends. Those brutes are necessary to the functioning of the entire economy. They increase on their own like rabbits but without importing more to start, expansion is limited, and the future of the bank's dealings there depends on this increase in landowner profits, so you see my presence is essential to us all."

Johan stopped for a moment, drawing his hand gently up and down her arm, anticipating her arousal, then added. "And can you believe there are those who oppose employing them altogether?"

Mabel shook her head, trying to listen but also comprehending a threat to the income she was enjoying more and more.

Johan flattened the map on the desk and pointed around the area Mabel knew to be their plantation. "This area is the land we will be allocated according to the Royal Cedula with the latest slave acquisition. If the natural increase of that population goes apace, by the end of a few years from now, the plantation will be profitable three times over, and the bank's profits even more than that, since the scale of their operations are so much larger and they add to their profits through shipping interests and settler profits owing to their transport of African slaves."

Mabel listened to his emphatic tone and saw his animated countenance, arguing a point that she had no power to refute, about a decision he had already made. The whole idea of an island filled with diseased savages and ague appalled her, and the thought of Johan going there to be among them terrified her. How could he want to go? Still, she had to admit she loved how happy Johan had been, and of course the flow of money made everything better at the Dottin household.

"And for our interests and those of the bank, I must look into the rumblings about slavery being inhumane! Inhumane! How absurd! That new Governor has made the ill treatment of slaves virtually illegal. There is no more slave beating so severe it causes injury. Besides, they are an investment! Why would we do anything to damage them? Furthermore, it is almost a moot point. Haven't they seen pictures? If that Hottentot Venus that has been travelling around like a circus animal doesn't prove they are a different species, I don't know what would!"

"But Johan, we have never been apart for more than several days. I don't think I will cope without you here for weeks, let alone months on end." Tears welled in her eyes.

"The time will pass quickly and you have Florian to attend to. I will write to you every week. Flossie and Job will be here." He wiped the tear tenderly away from his wife's cheek. He had never seen her looking more beautiful. Her delicate porcelain complexion flushed from emotion, her lips now full and red from biting them. She was so delicate. He patted the paperwork on the desk.

"This proves that expanding and adding those darkies to the workforce is the right thing to do." Johan added. "It will be our nest egg, Mabel. Our nest egg. You, I and little Florian will want for nothing! He stood, indicating he was through discussing it. "Let's retire upstairs, shall we? He put his arm around his wife's slender shoulders. This was the first time Mabel was unable to enthusiastically return Johan's lucre related ardour.

Chapter 2

After their marital relations, Johan swiftly dressed and left, saying something vague about preparing for his voyage. Mabel collected herself and went downstairs.

The house was quiet. She couldn't hear Florian or Flossie about and there was no sign of Johan. Feeling entitled after learning of Johan's plan to leave, she braved his possible wrath and went into his precious study! She wanted to see what had triggered his oddly demanding lovemaking. Since her marriage, and learning of her husband's tendency to feel more amorous when financial gains occurred, she found money and the things it provided aroused desire in her, too. Her beautiful home and lavish clothing filled her with satisfaction. She loved having servants.

She pushed aside some random documents and notes payable, just bank papers, she thought. She spotted the letter from Diego Manancala, and started reading furtively, listening for the frenzied King Charles spaniels who would become excited by their master's return. Reading quickly, it said that Diego is especially pleased with the number of breeding females they had acquired. Funny Johan hadn't mentioned that. And what was this part about signing the Catholic documents?

Returning the letters as she found them, she then picked up the paper Johan had brought into the study from the breakfast table. She was particularly interested in learning about the British government's new Prime Minister, William Pitt. An editorial raised concerns about his youth and his being in favour of the abolition of slavery and all that it meant for the colonial workforce. How inexperienced and foolish he must be, indeed! To abolish slavery would be an act of idiocy! Posturing, perhaps? How ridiculous, she thought to herself, to even consider removing the workforce. And besides, Johan said those savages are better off in Christian households doing productive labour.

Then she turned the page and saw a long article explaining the Royal Cedula Johan had been going on about. She didn't usually care much about Johan's breakfast reading, other than it seemed to interest him more than she did. But he was especially elated about the terms of this decree so she decided to read more about it. Maybe now she would be able to understand all his excitement about a place so far away from everything they loved.

-o0o-

Despite her fears, after Mabel tearfully waved off his carriage and Johan was on his way, she found she was less lonely than she imagined she would be. She set about filling her days with the management of the house, entertaining or lunching with the wives of other bankers who worked with Johan, and the wives of local dignitaries with whom she became friends. Her social life without Johan included concerts and shows to which she was invited. She also loved spending time painting landscapes, portraits and cameos.

Soon she began to gain a reputation amongst her social circle and church, and was invited to paint cameos for the local gentry who took pride in setting her portraits on mantle pieces and pianos, a testament to their own wealth. Over the next few months she was invited to teach porcelain and cameo painting at the church hall.

-o0o-

Johan first travelled for the bank to Spain then London for meetings at The Royal Exchange to set up the formalities for cementing its interests in the Spanish Antilles. A London office would be hugely advantageous to them. London was recognised as one of the main ports for trade with sugar and rum at the top of trade from the West Indies .

This is the area where Johan excelled; development. His vision and ability to make the abstract actually impressed and instilled admiration from his colleagues. They found him something of a visionary, which is why he received promotions with ease.

Johan left on this important trip thinking he looked every bit the sartorial gentleman in his bespoke French suits. On his first day in London to meet clients at The Royal Exchange, he saw nothing but men in dark coloured worsted coats and leather boots. Surely these successful men could afford apparel more demonstrative of their station than such drab attire?

The next day he had a meeting with the financiers in a coffee house frequented by the banking crowd. It served up fresh, ground coffee made in urns for an audience, and the aroma could be smelled down the street. It also doubled as a receiving location for mail sent onto the West Indies on Packet Ships like the one Johan would join in just under two weeks.

By the time Johan walked in the place it was already heaving. He stood for a while searching for his colleagues but it was they who found him as his attire suggested he was not local. His newly purchased peruke with long hair tied so the remaining curls rested down his shoulders and his gold jacket were far too elaborate to look serious and too colourful against the navy blues, blacks and greys of his peers. The two men whom he met teased him about his dress sense, said he was too foppish, and let him know that his effete French fashion was not the preferred business uniform. For the first time Johan felt overdressed. How could he be so wrong?

Every so often someone would come in, seek directions to the sacks with locations printed on them, and drop in a small parcel or letter, the recipient left to pay the receiving bill in order to accept the correspondence.

With his meetings completed, Johan went for a walk. He had been sitting for hours and he relished the opportunity to stretch his legs, plus he was curious to see the Tower of London, a landmark he had heard about but had never seen. With directions from his new colleagues, he headed out. Looking above him, Johan noticed how closely the buildings were to each other and the convex centre of the cobbled road he traversed.

The streets were busy with many people offering their wares for sale including two dubious looking prostitutes Johan made sure he crossed the road as not to encounter them. With the taunt from his last meeting about his attire, Johan was now eager to walk with purpose.

He passed The Monument on Pudding Lane, its fluted doric column was erected to commemorate The Great Fire of London in 1666. Johan paused at that thought. The column standing some 200 feet tall was adorned with an urn layered with a decorative gold coating. There was a viewing platform but it had over 300 steps and he wanted to see the River Thames, so he continued his walk towards St Magnus The Martyr. He followed the road until he saw the famous Tower of London in the distance, sitting majestically beside the river.

Along the way Johan's eye caught a wagon, bobbling along in the cobblestone street, precariously loaded with household items, what looked like a chest of drawers, two large armchairs and a table, upended. A yeoman class family moving? When it came into better view he was surprised to see the driver was a negro with a young negro boy beside him. They seemed completely at ease going about their business. This scene was not something he would come across back in Antwerp.

Johan thought, with a jolt, he may have just encountered a free negro in London. He had heard of them but he was surprised. These were not savages, they weren't even shabby. Perhaps these were a different breed than the ones employed on his plantation? Then he laughed at himself! But of course these had to be in the employ of some wealthy family who needed some muscular men to hoist their furniture.

He was aware of the growing movement for the abolition of slavery and the London periodicals addressed it on a regular basis, but he thought that it was more posturing than anything and therefore disregarded it. Seeing those negroes on the wagon reinforced his thinking that the best thing for freed negroes was the same as for protected slaves, manual labour and service.

Johan spent a short time viewing the Great Tower then meandered along the river bank on his way back to his residence. Perhaps one day, he will bring his son and Mabel and enjoy a tour of The Tower of London and the Bridge. Tonight, though, his mind was on nothing but the next stages of his travels. Tomorrow, his coach will trek over 10 days to Falmouth. He felt this part would pass quickly, with the scenery and interesting towns along the way. Much more daunting, however, was the 40 days or so voyage to the islands he knew only on maps and ledgers.

Early the next morning, Johan made the easy walk from his inn, Swan with Two Necks on Cheapside, to where he was to board the stagecoach. It was already bustling outside as the coachman readied the four horses.

The wooden coach had hard leather cushions and was far from comfortable. Three fellow travellers boarded the coach with Johan: a surgeon and his wife and a ship's chaplain, assigned to another ship heading to Barbados. The surgeon's wife was offered an extra blanket to sit on. They all made polite introductions, Johan patted his pocket for the comforting feel of the bank portfolio. The whip cracked and the coachman navigated them into the busy cobbled London streets.

Each passenger went into their own thoughts as they bumped along. Johan, still thinking about the free negroes he saw in London, thought about his imported labour force. He had servants, but he had never seen a black man before, much less had one do his bidding. He knew he owned them as part of Conquerabia, but they were abstract to him, as void of identity as livestock. How would it be, he wondered, to interact with these beings whose entire lives he controlled?

The days on the road were exhausting. Every town began to look the same and the overnight accommodations often left a lot to be desired. When they reached Falmouth, he was more than ready to get off the stagecoach and swiftly made his way to the Custom House to check on his voyage. It was still fairly early, and with no business to attend to, Johan enjoyed a tankard of ale then ventured out to explore the harbour before he lost daylight. Tomorrow he will set sail to see his investment for himself.

It was a lively place, this harbour, different from London. There was less frenetic industry, fewer people scurrying about to disparate places for different reasons. No, here everything moved in a sort of rhythm, like the tide, now heading out with the departure of a ship. Methodical workmen loaded victuals and the methodical crew went about readying the ship to set sail. Johan, a man of methodical preparation, saw the scene as a good sign. That there were a few strong backed negroes hoisting huge containers up the loading plank gave him a moment of pause, wondering how the white men felt about them, but he quickly categorised them as more beasts of burden than mates.

-o0o-

Johan finally arrived at his cabin on the Gallant, a packet ship of 120 tonnes. Along with the ship's captain, James Garrett, and a crew of 13, aboard were a couple of Johan's fellow coach companions, a priest, two teachers, an ambassador and a physician. In time he would get to know them.

Most of the cabins were double berths, but at considerable expense to his employers, who wanted to keep their most valued employee healthy on the arduous journey, Johan commandeered a cabin for himself. It had a sleeping area for one, opposite a shelf coupling up as a desk and dresser. Despite being such a privileged cabin, it was clearly not luxurious. It lacked a porthole so the only light came from above during the day, but when it was dark, the lant horns helped to illuminate his journaling and change of attire. The premium of £30 included some captain's discretionary privileges: dining, alcohol and access to roam where others were not permitted.

Unpacking, Johan set aside the official documents that he was to deliver to key individuals within the government. These he would keep on his person.

When he boarded he noticed two curious leather portmanteaux hanging over the side of the vessel. At his first formal dinner with the Captain, two days after the ship departed, he learned those portmanteaux contained a range of important and diplomatic letters, and the leather protected them from the elements. With the rise of piracy in the West Indies, they could swiftly be cut loose into the sea, to prevent such important documents getting into the wrong hands.

Johan contemplated whether he should have added his documents to the bags. Would they be safer there or with him, should danger arise? He reasoned that there was nothing of such diplomatic worth to be concerned about and that they would be lost with him, should the vessel be attacked. Safer with him, he figured, since he knew nothing of the crew or his fellow passengers. Who knew what form a thief might take? A banker at heart, he knew the value of private accounts, he knew everyone has a secret life where self interest supersedes all else.

After several days, Johan became used to the undulations of the sea. At night, when the weather was calm, it was a comfort to him. He missed Mabel: the touch of her skin against him and the gentle smell of her favourite lily scented perfume. He could almost conjure the scent even at sea. He missed Florian too, and the jolly way he greeted him when he came home from work. With so much idle time at sea these thoughts both comforted him and tortured him, so to keep himself busy Johan kept a journal of his voyage. Occasionally he would join the captain at his table for a friendly game of cards, along with the surgeon and priest, if all was quiet.

Chapter 3

The sun was beating down as the passengers alighted the Gallant. After the long voyage and a few wobbly moments adjusting to stationary earth, it felt good to be on land. He was excited to be here, finally. Johan stood, taking in the sights of the main road. The long sea voyage was monotonous and not as relaxing as he anticipated, especially in his windowless cabin. Now, here, everything was like a dream. Nothing familiar about it. The heat felt like clear steam. The flora unimaginably odd, colours brighter than any at home and trees with spiky umbrellas of leaves atop long bark-less trunks. The various shades of people, with a range of differently shaped facial features, dressed in a mosaic of fabrics, from thin and woven, to bright, quilted and embroidered, to twisted and draped cotton cloth. His eyes felt unable to open wide enough to take it all in.

While the stevedores unloaded the luggage and cargo from the ship, Johan was directed to a local tavern. He saw it in the distance. It looked busy. After more than 40 days of galley food and rocking tables, he was peckish and ready for a motionless meal.

A young woman, with broad interesting features and dark olive skin greeted him. Pretty? He was undecided. She had warm brown eyes and plaited long, black hair that hung down over her left shoulder almost to her waist. There was a purple hibiscus behind her ear. Her dark hair accentuated the whiteness of her blouse and her caramel coloured skin. She showed him to a table. He sat and fanned his face with his panama hat. As she turned to get the beverage he ordered, she smiled. It was friendly and Johan noticed that as she did so, her whole face lit up. He studied how she swayed between the tables, intrigued. When she returned with cutlery, he realised she must be what was referred to as a mulatto; a woman of mixed race. Neither one thing, Nor the other, but fascinating, especially as she seemed happy and, by her demeanour, free. He also witnessed something he would not see happen regarding a negro women in Belgium. The white men here seemed to be attracted to her and they were chatting with her in a friendly manner. She was mesmerising.

"What is your name?" Johan was uncharacteristically forward but he had to know. He had never seen a woman like her, so confident about her place in the world, unperturbed by the attention of the ogling men. "Mirian is what I am called. Welcome to my tavern." And she set off to her duties. Her tavern?

She returned with a tankard and as she placed it in front of him she spoke in a rapid sing-song dialect of Spanish, too fast and too peppered with the local patois for him to fully understand, but he recognised a word or two and nodded in acknowledgment. He couldn't help but notice her high, taut breasts framed by the white blouse she wore. My, he thought, and smiled inwardly. He gave the local quaff a try. Some sort of ale. It tasted different from what he knew, but it was refreshing. He drank the cooling beverage and returned to fanning his face. He had finally arrived.

Mirian returned with a platter of colourful, grilled vegetables, many he did not recognise, nestled around a whole roasted fish, eyes open, mouth agape. He took in the exotic sight. It wasn't what he thought he'd ordered but what a happy surprise. It smelled wonderful. It tasted better. The ale went quickly. He wondered if most inns were like this….He made a note to stop in here again on his way home.

Sated, he had a moment to settle into his new reality, this strange inn in this strange land. He sat for a while, looking out onto the busy street, so fantastically different from the ordered streets at home. Brown-skinned women in white skirts rimmed with the red and brown dirt from the road, moving with an unfamiliar sway, clearly not wearing the tight and restrictive undergarments of the women at home. Children without hovering nannies were all about, but these were not street urchins like in the Antwerp and London slums, ready to rob you. These children were simply playing outside. There were professional businessmen in the attire of their European homeland looking out of place and miserable, losing the war against the heat and dirt. Working men of every shade moving about intently.

The street sounds, an unfamiliar combination of languages, animals, vendors, and, if possible to hear, humidity, were very different from what he was used to. Even the harbour had an unfamiliar odour, different from the last harbour in Falmouth. He could almost taste the dust from the road, and a sickly sweet smell hung in the air; perhaps from the impossibly coloured flowers that seemed to be everywhere, fuchsia, yellow and persimmon, or maybe it was the sugar cane which he saw being transported in a horse driven cart.

Refreshed, Johan was excited by the prospects at hand, both professionally and personally. First, he needed to hire a horse and acquire a map. He had to get to the administrative offices in San Jose de Oruña to attend to the bank's business. He planned to stay in Portes des Espana for the next five days, to shore up business before he travelled to Caroni, but first that horse.

By the time he made the short walk to the paddock, Johan was wiping away sweat with an already saturated handkerchief. A young lad, with dark hair and almost black eyes, took him to the stall where the horse was tied, and stroked its nose. It snorted. Johan noticed that to the back of the stable was an older man, sitting in the shade. He looked at Johan, dripping with perspiration, and said, "Mon Dieu! Monsieur! You need a light coat, not a heavy coat." He pointed to the jacket Johan had slung over his arm. "Go to the tailor. He can make you a nice coat. Light weight coat. See, over there is his shop." Johan turned to where the man was pointing. He could see a sign next to the open top of a split door.

Johan paid the young lad for the hire of the horse and buggy and the lad, who had said nothing at all when Johan arrived and to whom Johan had been using hand signals to communicate with, surprised him by writing a receipt in a fine copperplate hand. Yet another lesson about how much Johan had to learn about this place and the people here.

"Thank you, young man. I will go and see the tailor now."

Looking through the top of the door, Johan watched the tailor, head down, carefully stitching together cloth for a jacket, his needlework small and precise. With him were two other men and a lady also sewing garments by hand.

"A-hem." Johan coughed. It went unnoticed. "Excuse me!" Johan raised his voice.

"Ah, Buenos Dias señor! I am sorry, I did not see you standing there. May I help you?"

"The older man over there recommended I come and see you. The tailor looked the sweaty, overdressed Johan up and down, nodding. "Yes, señor." He opened the lower half of the door and invited Johan in, and in doing so made a mental note of Johan's height and build. "What do you need?

The tailor took out a piece of string and signalled for Johan to stand by the wooden post. "I think I am in need of a light weight jacket, possibly some trousers. A shirt, perhaps?" The tailor nodded in agreement.

"I can see sir is not comfortable in what he is wearing. I can make you anything you require."

"I am here for a few weeks and will be traveling around. Perhaps I should invest in at least two jackets and two shirts to keep me presentable? I like the look of this." Johan touched a jacket awaiting its owner: a light brown fabric with matching trousers, the hand stitching superior to what he ordered from his own fine tailor back home. It was plain and uncomplicated, unlike the ornately embroidered Parisian-inspired coat he was carrying. Johan was so miserable in the heat he didn't care about the cost. "How long will it take?" The tailor was already assessing Johan's arm length using string marked with guides, and chalking the measurements on a well-used broken remnant of a piece of slate.

"When do you require them, Sir? I can get you one suit in four days, if it is urgent. Both will take seven to ten days. Depending on the fabric. I charge fifteen reales per suit, nine reales per jacket, if you don't need trousers." Johan mentally calculated the exchange rate and found it to be a favourable price.

At the back of the store Johan spotted a young lad, no more than about fourteen, ironing a pile of clothes.

"I am happy to request one suit for collection in four days. I have some business to conduct here and can collect the others towards the end of next week, when I return from Caroni, or could you arrange for them to be sent on?"

"Yes, I can. Very good, señor. I will require a deposit of ten reales and payment at your final fitting. Before you depart. Please have a look at these bolts of fabric and choose which one you would prefer and, if you don't mind, I need to take more measurements. What is your name please?"

"Of course, Johan Dottin. And thank you." He shook hands with the diminutive man.

"My name is Carson. Carson the tailor they call me." And he smiled at Johan who noted the happy disposition of his new outfitter. With payment down for two new suits to accommodate the hotter climate, Johan returned to the paddock to collect the horse and head to San Jose de Oruña.

The young lad was waiting for Johan and presented him with horse and buggy as Johan loaded what luggage he had into the buggy, climbed aboard, tipped the lad, nodded and rode off. He was excited at his new adventure and as he followed his map along the dirt path, he passed men, women and young people, many free negroes, others more olive skinned, all transporting goods on their heads or bumping along in rickety old carts, all carrying produce, such as pineapples, mangoes and fruit he did not recognise, some on their way to the capital, others returning having traded their wares, all seemingly happy, no one looking like an owner. Lining his route, verdant vegetation: palm trees, shrubs and a rainbow of colours from an impossible profusion of blooming flowers, so random and wild. Portes de Espana soon faded into the distance.

Occasionally he would see a buggy or carriage driven by black men in shabby clothing transporting wealthy passengers who were carried in glib opulence. Who surprised Johan the most, though, were all the well dressed and haughty free negroes and mulattoes, just going about as though they were white.

It was not long before he saw the white-washed Cabilda building, the seat of government, and confirmed he was in the right place. Johan was relieved to have arrived. The heat and humidity were like nothing he had experienced, and he was sweating profusely. Despite his discomfort, there was something thrilling about being in the Spanish Antilles. He dismounted and walked in, taking in the size of the building and the well tailored grounds.

It was bustling. He reasoned that the uniformed men were officials. Johan walked up the few steps onto the verandah and made himself known to a burly, ruddy faced Spaniard, who sat behind a large wooden desk. Around him, people were milling about. There were desks inside the building where people queued, seeking official confirmation for whatever they needed: licenses, negroes, land and visas.

In the centre of the wall was a large painting of the King of Spain, his uniform decorated with two sashes crossed over his torso in the style of the Royal Marines' white crossed belts. His left hand gently leaned against a pillar and the vivid red sash around his waist billowed out behind him.

"May I help you, señor?" The burly Spaniard enquired.

"Yes sir. I have an appointment with the Chief Justice at two of the clock." Johan checked his pocket watch again. He had five minutes to spare, and suddenly felt self-important.

Johan presented his business card and the Spaniard snapped his fingers at an attendant, who ran to the side of the desk, standing as erect as he could. The card was passed to the attendant on the small silver salver with considerable pomp, and the attendant, with equal drama, turned on his heels, off to present the card to notify the Chief Justice his next appointment had arrived. Soon Johan was ushered into the majestic office.

Once seated in the elegant room, Johan happily enjoyed the gentle breeze from an overhead fan, swaying from side to side. It made the room comfortable despite the oppressive heat outside, thanks to a negro boy sitting on the floor outside, whose sole job was tugging and releasing the rope. Things were very different here. Johan was impressed.

The meeting went well and Johan was inspired with the efficiency of the Chief Justice whose manner was no nonsense and official which enabled Johan to return to Portes Des Espana before dusk. For the next two days or so, he would remain in town attending to the bank's business before setting off to Conquerabia but right now he needed to rest, so was eager to check into the Inn, perhaps another meal at the tavern, in hope of seeing the young lady once again. What was her name? Maria, or something like that. He was to be disappointed as Mirian had finished work for the day and a burly woman without the charm served him.

Dinner was therefore a hurried endeavour as Johan climbed into bed, satisfied with today's business affairs.

The following day Johan had to meet with one of the three Commissary of Population to be given his additional quarries of land. With business concluded in Portes Des Espana, Johan headed off to the plantation with a mixture of trepidation and excitement. It was a huge unknown, being almost on the other side of the world in an island he was unfamiliar with, yet visually it was striking with many pleasant odours from food to vegetation. The combination provided an enlightening experience which thrilled him.

Leading the buggy into Caroni, he saw on the horizon his plantation Conquerabia. The ironwork arch with the name and its access, framing the house and gardens was picturesque. Yes, it was hot but the abundance of sunshine was welcome. He noted an improvement in his demeanour and pondered if it was due to the weather or because he was somewhere different.

Inside the grounds Johan halted the buggy to take in the impressive view of his plantation and saw a number of negroes at work; women in the field picking cotton, men in the distance with carts of cut sugar cane. It was busy. As instructed in Diego's letter he was to meet his overseer in the plantation office, a separate building off to the left of the plantation. A building he saw as soon as he entered the land and the sweet smell of processed sugar hit him.

Diego, was a slight man around the same age as Johan who was delighted to meet his new employer and prepared a light meal of cold cuts and fruit which Johan found most welcome. It allowed Diego to present Johan with some of the paperwork, just enough to show him how the plantation was working and after Johan refreshed himself embarked on a tour of the plantation. It was vast.

Johan remarked to himself about how the process of manual labour was very different to the luxury of sitting behind a desk most of the day. He lost count of the amount of slaves Diego said he had working on the land as he was overwhelmed by what he saw. It excited him too, especially when Diego showed him the profit and loss ledger which showed the profit the plantation was making on an annual basis. He longed for Mabel.

Impressed by Diego, he asked if he would stay on as his manager to which Diego agreed. He enjoyed his job and was saddened when his previous boss's wife sold up, fearing he'd lose his valued position.

Diego left him alone on the verandah, enjoying the gentle breeze blowing whilst he trawled through the paperwork until a young house slave of interesting colouring came to him, clearing away the dishes.

Late afternoon brought a cooling breeze to the land as he and Diego further explored the land, the condition of the machinery and what needed urgent attention. The previous owner had left the plantation in decent repair; there was nothing pressing he needed to do other than stay on top of the exports and payments. Johan could not believe how lucky he was to buy the plantation in such good condition and profitability.

Diego suggested they return to the house as dusk was creeping towards them. Johan realised how famished he was, despite the platter of cold cuts he had for lunch. They arrived at the house where the table inside had been laid with a delicious smelling array of plates. He invited Diego to join him and the two tucked into what he was later informed was goat meat. It surprised him as the meat was so tender.

The young slave girl returned and Johan studied her as she poured him a glass of ale, taking her in as he raised the glass to his lips. She too looked delicious.

Diego bid him good night and left to go to his dwelling. Johan was free to do as he pleased. Johan sat out on the steps of the verandah, sated with a delicious meal and enjoying a shot of rum. Fireflies danced in the air as a soundtrack of cicadas and crickets brought the evening to a close.

Johan was very happy with today's proceedings. He liked what he saw in the figures. As soon as his head rested on the pillow, Johan was asleep.

-o0o-

Johan returned to Portes Des Espana with another visit to Mirian's Tavern. He wanted to delight in seeing this strange, exotic vision once again before he departed, not knowing when he could return.

All his business affairs were successfully tied up and this celebratory dinner would ease his journey back to Belgium in style. He was not to be disappointed.

Chapter 4

It began with symptoms he thought were the beginnings of a cold or an adjustment to the tropical environment, but then the symptoms exacerbated. He developed a fever, sweats and joint pain in addition to a cough, then vomiting and delirium. Johan had never felt so ill.

The ship's doctor thought it to be ague and gave Johan a tincture made from the cinchona tree, a native Indian remedy, but the medicine did not seem to ease any of Johan's symptoms.

It was late August when Johan finally arrived back in Antwerp, still suffering the illness he developed shipboard. They had to carry him from the ship to home. The local doctor diagnosed Johan as suffering from a noxious miasma he caught in the humid climate and island diseases, he said, and he prescribed a series of head steams with eucalyptus oils. Being back in the cold, damp European weather didn't help either.

Mabel was beside herself seeing Johan so sick. More proof that the diseases never left those awful islands, she thought. Maybe this will get his mind off them and they could go back to the way things were.

Despite his aversion to idleness, Johan was bed ridden, too sick to worry about his position at the bank, his obsession before his trip. He was listless. Even as he slowly regained his health and adjusted to his home again, his mind was elsewhere. Eventually, his energy level and strength returned and he was able to enjoy breakfast downstairs and read the papers. After another month he was well enough to begin playing cards with his friends.

One evening he came back late, flush with cash and fervour, and he found Mabel in such beautiful repose he could not wait until she awoke, and he roused her, urgent and apologetic but finally passionate again. Mabel, confused at first, soon understood. Her husband was finally well. Her husband was back from those damnable islands.

It was not long after that Mabel announced to Johan that she was once again with child. She was elated to be giving Johan another child. She didn't care what she had, but Johan hoped it would be a girl. Then Florian would inherit his estate without challenge, and a girl could be an asset down the line by being married into another powerful family. This is how dynasties are made. Plus Mabel might like a daughter, a little girl, a lovely reflection of her mother.

Mabel was shopping in Antwerp on a very warm day when she started feeling unwell. Thinking she should take it easy she decided to return home. As she climbed into the carriage she felt a sharp pain in her stomach which was so severe she gasped in pain. It took her by surprise. As passersby showed concern, Mabel assured them it was nothing. Such contractions at this stage of pregnancy - some six months - were not uncommon. She was trying to reassure herself as much as them.

But Job understood the urgency to head back home. He helped Mabel down from the carriage, calling out for Flossie. Florian arrived with her but Job, eager for him not to see his mother distressed, took the boy in the buggy, and headed off to the stables placing him next to him in the driver's seat in the carriage.

Flossie helped Mabel up the stairs to her bed. "Shall I call for the doctor?" Mabel felt better just lying down.

"No, I don't think that's necessary. I just had a strong contraction which winded me." But when another strong contraction took hold and Mabel screamed out in pain, Flossie called Job in from the stables. When he saw Flossie at the front door, he knew immediately he had to go and fetch the doctor, and he also knew he had to keep the boy apart from the dire situation. "Well Master Florian, I guess you and I are going for a ride. Wanna sit back next to me and drive?" He smiled at Florian.

"Oooh yes please Job, I'd like that?"

"You can even help me hold the reins." Job replied as he assembled the horse and smaller buggy. He rode with tempered urgency so as not to distress Florian. "When we get to the next house, I need you to sit patiently for me here in the wagon. I'll be quick, but you have to wait. Do you understand?" Job dismounted and tied the horse to the stand, next to the doctor's own horse. Florian nodded, excited to be fingering the leathery reins. "There's a juicy red apple for you, if you do as I say." Florian beamed at the prospect.

The Doctor, understanding Job's discretion in turn knew not to draw attention to his movements, not wanting to alarm the boy. As he left the cottage he greeted Florian, tousling his hair, unharnessed his horse and rode off towards the Dottin's house.

Job watched Florian eat the fruit, pretending to fix the spokes in the wheels, giving the doctor enough time to get a lead on them, then Job decided to take a different route, along the river towards home, stopping intermittently to draw Florian's attention to the fish in the water, or the birds in the trees.

Mabel was in so much pain she could not stop moaning and clutching her abdomen. She knew something was terribly wrong. This was no normal contraction. Where is the doctor? Flossie mopped her brow and sat by.

Finally the doctor rushed in and examined the terrified woman. This baby was coming, too soon, but it was coming. and there was nothing he could do but ease the pain with a little laudanum. Its bitter taste made Mabel feel sick, but it helped relieve most of the pain.

The provision of laudanum was still fairly new in the treatment of pregnant women and the Doctor, an admirer of the Glaswegian

Dr William Smellie, was keen to use it since previously he'd had nothing to offer.

Three hours later and one large final push Nancy came into the world. It was Saturday, April 28, 1778. Mabel held her in her arms too distraught to let go. Her daughter had no breath and lay lifeless. She looked like a fragile porcelain doll, with her features so perfect and still.

Flossie, assisting the doctor, cried gentle tears. She had held the little girl to help clean her up after the birth. It was the first time she held a newborn, but it was a dead child.

When all was clear Johan arrived in the bedroom to see Mabel holding the bundle in her arms, tears streaming down her cheeks. The doctor placed a reassuring hand on his arm, and gave a sombre look to Johan, knowing no words were needed, and he left the sad scene. Johan walked towards the bed and sat down next to his weeping wife. "Our poor baby, Oh Johan, I'm so sorry." She offered her husband the child to hold.

Johan abruptly stood up. "I can't. I can't!" I'm ... " Johan's voice cracked and he left the room. Mabel momentarily registered Johan's weakness and abandonment, but then she returned to cradling her lost daughter, tenderly stroking her face and head. In the hall the doctor advised Johan that Mabel would never survive another pregnancy.

Job went to inform the priest about the death. Mabel stayed in bed until the morning of the funeral, and returned to it soon after. Johan could not comfort her, did not comfort her. He did not comfort himself. He did what he knew to do; he went to work.

Chapter 5

The success in the Spanish Antilles bought Johan a significant promotion at the bank. This pleased him enormously. It meant more money and prestige, which would in turn give him more autonomy wielding the bank's power over trade deals involving the increasingly profitable sale of slaves, whose cheap labour was essential to the success of the sugar cane, coffee and cotton plantations increasingly called on to satisfy the world's growing demand. Even more important to Johan was his increased private leverage as an ambitious plantation owner.

Mabel was not recovering at all well from her loss and Johan, who was unused to failure, was a failure at helping her. He did not know how to deal with such grief or any strong emotions. His emotions were always redirected toward endeavours he knew could be successful.

He also knew he eventually would have to break his promise to her to remain in Antwerp. He knew he would have to travel back to the island again. This is why he decided that it might cheer her up if they moved to a larger house. He tried to consult with Mabel but so consumed with grief she did not understand why Johan worried about such things as moving.

Two months later they moved into a stately house in Peutie, with several bedrooms and land with separate gardens, its own river and orchards. It was picturesque and secluded. Johan hoped it would take her mind off the lost child. Mainly Johan hoped it would assuage his guilt about having to leave her soon, but he couldn't stay holding her hand when there was so much important to all of them to attend to. And like he always said, no harm looking out for one's personal interests. Surely Mabel would want him to secure their financial wellbeing if she were in her right mind?

The new house was in need of repair. Florian could have the entire top floor for his nursery and bedroom. Fortunately it had a circular window which Florian immediately likened to a ship's porthole. His room where he could look out over the make-believe sea, the river.

Florian was playing with Flossie one afternoon. Mabel was in bed. She heard Florian's laughter, a loud thud, then a scream. Flossie cried out. Mabel rushed to where the sound came and found Florian at the bottom of the stairs with an utterly stunned look on his flushed face. Flossie was at the top, rigid with fear. As soon as Florian saw Mabel he started screaming.

"Miss Mabel, he tripped on the floorboard. It gave way under him and he caught his foot!" Flossie was hysterical.

Mabel rushed to him. His breathing hitched and shuddered in the way only children's sobs do. It was impossible to know the extent of his injuries. Mabel gently ran her hand over his legs and his arms. "Where does it hurt, my love? Here?" Florian pointed to his leg. Fortunately he was wearing shoes which had taken the brunt of the scuff when the floorboard gave way. Due to the speed at which he was running, Florian had fallen down four stairs. The shock caused more pain than the grazing to his leg and arm. In that moment Mabel realised a love she had not experienced with Florian in some time. It marked the turning point in her rehabilitation.

She looked up at her maid. "Flossie, don't worry. I think the scare you both experienced is worse than what happened. He appears to be fine. Even now you can see he's calming down. It's fine. We'll watch him, just to make sure, but he was just being a playful little boy, and scrapes and scratches are expected."

"Oh, thank you ma'am, thank you. I'm so very sorry I let you down." She was emotional and sobbing. "I'm, I'm sorry ma'am. I'll collect my things and leave in a week, that should give you time to find my replacement."

"You'll do no such thing Flossie. There is no need for you to leave us. Florian is fine. By this time tomorrow, we'll probably be laughing about this. It's not your fault." Flossie looked at her mistress and began to calm down too. Florian was quietly sucking his thumb in his mother's lap, then, distracted by the toy he was originally playing with, he sat upright, got to his feet and ran off, his scrape forgotten. Mabel got up too, with a realisation that it was she, not the apologetic Flossie, who was most to blame for the accident. Had she been doing her job, the repairs to the house would have been completed and it would have prevented the whole incident.

Shocked into action, Mabel got to work refurbishing and redecorating the house. Job, handy with carpentry, was able to do the repairs, and she found she had a flair for selecting what fabrics looked best with specific items of furniture, and she was good at choosing soothing colour schemes for each room. As the manor house transformed, so did Mabel.

Johan noticed the improvement in Mabel's demeanour, though he thought better of mentioning it. He was happy she was returning to the woman he married. He hadn't had the heart to tell her that another child was verboten, and he assumed that neither did she wish to go through something like that again, so she should remain focused on decorating the house. He would have to satisfy himself in other ways. They would both have to content themselves with their individual interests.

As the house rehabilitation and decorating took shape, Mabel's focus returned to raising Florian. She was able to enjoy the bucolic setting and, finally, she was growing fond of her new home, once just a place to escape the memory of her loss.

When he turned 10, Florian had been put in the care of a governess, freeing Mabel to return to her first love, painting. Mabel took her paint and easel to the river to paint, or packed a lunch to the summer house where she could paint all day or read, undisturbed. The only things she missed about their old home were all the art jobs, like teaching porcelain painting, and being commissioned for the occasional cameo, or even selling a landscape now and then. And she missed the friends she made when Johan left her for that damned island.

On a chance trip into Peutie to run household errands and buy more paint and canvas, Mabel came across a gallery that had not been open the last time she had been in town. As she walked in, the smell of oil paint and canvas hit her. It was intoxicating.

On the right hand side of the gallery, a number of landscapes, and in the back Mabel caught sight of a portrait of a glamorous woman rendered in a style she did not recognise. She walked to it for a closer look. Mabel could not identify the medium.

A tall moustachioed man noticed her interest. "Good morning madam. It's beautiful, isn't it? It's been getting a lot of attention. It's called Spring by the Italian painter, Rosalba Carriera."

Mabel scrutinised the painting more closely. "The artist isn't using paint to get such fine detail and gentle textures. It's not even water-colour by the looks of it."

"This is something new. She used what they call pastels. From your question I take it you're something of an artist yourself? What's your medium?"

"Yes, something of one. Cameos mainly." Mabel was unwilling to disclose her hobby next to these professional works.

"Let me show you why these are so interesting." He moved to a table on the side, beckoned for Mabel to follow, and he produced and opened a slim box of the pastel crayons. On a sheet of paper he drew several strokes across the page with one crayon. Picking another, he added a stroke here and there and voila! He quickly created a likeness of her. He smudged with his fingers and layered the filmy colours, making the cheeks more rosy, the eyes more blue. He could see Mabel's keen interest. "Here, why don't you try?"

Mabel sat and drew Florian's head from memory, detailing his blond curls and deep set blue eyes, naturally blending and shading as her instinct guided her. "This is marvellous. How much for the crayons?"

Within a few minutes Mabel left the gallery with the portrait of her son, a new purchase in her bag and ideas for new works of art.

Whilst going between shops, Mabel ran into the widow Rayne Jansen and her daughter, Cicely. Rayne managed the church office for the local priest. She was a kindly woman who, by dint of her employ, was privy to most of the town's business.

"So lovely to see you, Mrs. Dottin. I am so sorry for your loss. How are you?" Mabel felt an internal burn at the reminder. News had obviously travelled upon arrival and it surprised her that Rayne obviously knew what had transpired. Of course, Rayne had been at the funeral several months earlier.

"Thank you Mrs. Jansen." Mabel wasn't used to speaking about the death of her baby, but the inquiry seemed genuine, even kind.

"Yes dear, we were concerned not to have seen you in church, but I must say you're looking very well."

As the two women good naturally prattled on to Mabel about various goings on in the parish, Mabel relaxed a bit and found the conversation welcome. She was amused at Rayne's benign gossip, nothing too private but just spicy enough to be interesting. Rayne was deeply involved in the duties of the church, administering the arrangements for weddings, baptisms and funerals, but she also stayed engaged with the social aspects of the church and parish life, even staying abreast of the dances of the day, particularly the waltz. Mabel easily warmed to her.

The conversation proved a good antidote to Mabel's solitude and she noted how much better she felt, tittering at Rayne's little, harmless indiscretions about the parishioners.

Cicely was prim, pretty and adored her irreverent mother. She also played a role within the church, leading Sunday School. On the cusp of womanhood at 17, she let it be known she wanted to be a teacher. Secretly she also had a crush on a handsome young missionary who had just returned to town. Willem.

Rayne, noticing how much the three were enjoying their chat, extended an invitation to Mabel to join them soon for an afternoon tea at the rectory, where she worked. The local priest, not that young, enjoyed Rayne taking the lead organising the odd afternoon tea or lunch as his unofficial social secretary, and so Mabel arrived at the rectory on the allocated Tuesday afternoon. It was overcast and cool but pleasant, nonetheless. She brought a cake she made herself and Rayne was just cutting into it when the priest arrived.

"Father Maxwell, look, Mrs Mabel Dottin is here and she brought a lovely lemon cake. Have a slice? It looks delicious." He had distinguished features. A prominent nose, large brown eyes and a recently cut head of dark wavy hair with just a few wisps of grey.

"Pleased to see you Mrs. Dottin. That's a Dutch surname, isn't it? I do hope I'm not interrupting?"

The priest pulled up a chair, joined the ladies, and tucked into his slice. "Mmm, yes, it's very good. We don't see you in church?" Maxwell lacked the finesse usually reserved for those absent from services due to grief, but since she ventured here to his private quarters he hoped to give her the opportunity to unburden herself.

"Yes, Father, I regret it's been a while since I was last in church. As you may know, I lost a child just before we moved here, and I have not been myself since."

"Yes, we know about that dreadful loss, and I am so sorry, Mrs Dottin. We cannot know God's reasons, but God is always there to help, as am I, His servant. I'm delighted to see you're out and about and with us today, and you've brought such glorious sunshine and delicious fare."

"Grief impacts us in different ways and it's not something you can rush. Just let us know if you need anything, at any time" Rayne added.

"I know that I've neglected my God. Mr Dottin travels a lot so it's just me with my boy, Florian, and my numbing relentless grief, however I do feel I'm coming to terms with it now. But Father, I would not have been able to venture here a year ago. It feels a relief to be able to say that now. I feel like I can face up to losing my precious child and get back to Florian and put the house in order."

"God heals all, Mrs. Dottin. We're pleased you have made such progress." The conversation continued in a congenial manner as Mabel found herself relaxing more. She was enjoying having a conversation once again, realising how much she had missed being social. It was also a relief to begin talking about her loss. A weight was lifted from her shoulders.

"On another topic, I read an interesting article in today's paper about something called a steam engine, invented by a fellow named James Watt." Fr. Maxwell stated. "He says it can speed up all manner of operations without extra hands. He plans to use one in a cotton mill in England. They say it could help increase the speed at which cotton is processed. What remarkable news this is, don't you think?"

"But what about jobs?" Rayne knew people in the fabric business. "Could people lose their jobs with something like this?"

"That's interesting." Mabel added. "If it could speed up processing, then more cotton will be needed." Mabel knew cotton was one of the main cash crops of their plantation, though she didn't want to disclose her personal interest. "I've read in the paper the greatest cost for European mills, processing cotton, is labour. Slaves provide free labour in the fields, so if machinery can cut costs in the production, isn't that a positive thing?"

Rayne was appalled that her new friend seemed to approve of that awful practice, slavery, but she didn't want to cause an issue and quickly changed the subject. "Mrs. Dottin, the Rosary Altar Society is working on a Summer Fair in August to help raise money for the church's missionary work overseas, aren't we Father? Would you like to join us?" The question has the desired effect of distracting Mabel, who was momentarily taken by surprise at the kind invitation.

"Oh my goodness, I've never done anything like that before. What would it require?" Mabel asked.

“Ideally I need someone to help with the decorations for the day and the cake stall. I can help provide the introductions. I have two other ladies, whom I know would welcome some help.

“Yes,” Mabel said, surprising herself and suddenly realising how much she missed being amongst other people. “Yes, I’d very much like to join in, if you’ll have me? I think it will be good for me to have something else on which to focus, other than Florian.”

“That’s wonderful. The ladies will catch you up on the decorations. We have three months to plan and I can guide you if you need help.” Rayne was buzzing with excitement once again. “We're due to meet exactly one week from today, here at the Rectory. How is midday for you? If you can bring a plate of sweets or savouries for us to share, that helps with the planning.” Rayne smiled and winked, putting Mabel at ease.

“I would really like that, if you’re sure you think I can do it.” Mabel said hesitantly.

“I know you can, otherwise I would not have asked.” She gently nudged Mabel.

“Well, there’s no turning back now Mrs. Dottin. Dear Rayne can be very persuasive.” Father Maxwell folded the newspaper, took another bite of the cake and sip of tea and buried his head in the newspaper again.

"Good afternoon!" A warm baritone voice announced himself. Mabel almost choked on her tea. Who was this handsome man who just burst in the door? Surprised at herself, she blushed as she politely returned the greeting.

"Brother Willem, this is Mrs. Dottin, wife of Johan who heads up The Prussian Bank in Antwerp. She's just joined the Rosary Altar Society to work on the fair in August. Would you like a slice of her delicious lemon cake?" Rayne loved making introductions.

"I'm certain her cake is delicious, but sadly I must decline. I am only just in time for my appointment with Father Maxwell, here. We have plans to do some future projects for the Parish. Father, shall we?" The men made their apologies and went to the office. Rayne smiled and shook her head.

"If only I were a bit younger. A Christian widow could dry her tears on his shoulder, couldn't she?" She winked at Mabel, who smiled back in agreement, but then she felt guilty.

Just then Job arrived with the carriage to collect her, and Mabel escaped without continuing on that topic. She was a married woman. On the ride home she pondered all that Rayne had asked of her. She was unexpectedly excited at the prospect of getting involved in the organisation of such an event, and apprehensive at the same time. She doubted herself and felt that she should withdraw, however, when she got home and walked into the beautiful parlour she had decorated and then thought of all the work and time she spent on renovating her home, she knew she could take on a new challenge.

Mabel later sat down and was starting a list of ideas to share with the ladies when Johan walked in, back from another business trip. He greeted his wife with a perfunctory kiss on her forehead. "Hello, my dear. How is our son?" He was distracted. "I need to eat, join me in the kitchen?" Mabel obliged.

"He is well, Johan. I think it's too late to see him. Flossie put him to bed over an hour ago. He's growing into a fine young boy. He looks so much like you." Johan nodded, sat down and bit into some cold chicken.

After satisfying his hunger, Johan looked around. "I like what you have done with the house, Mabel. it's looking fine. Perhaps we can start to host dinners or a party soon? I'm thinking we can host dinner for my work colleagues and bosses?" Mabel didn't relish the prospect of hosting a dinner or party at home, just yet. The thought of it overwhelmed her.

"Dear Johan. I know you would like to entertain more, and I'd like to again, but it's been such a long time. I need to work my way back to such an endeavour. And I'm starting to. Today I agreed to join the Rosary Altar Society and help organise a fair for the church's missionary work overseas. I'll be one of a whole group. If I can get through this, with all the people and duties, then perhaps we can consider a dinner party this autumn?"

“Congratulations and I understand my dear, and that makes perfect sense.” Johan was short, but Mabel was used to this manner by now. He was always cordial, but so distant. Even the promotion and his success at the bank didn’t seem to have the same effect as it used to have, and she missed it.

“How was your trip, Johan?” Johan was reading a report or something, but he looked up.

“Ummm? Oh, good. We are looking into industrialisation, and I’m getting more involved in the wider Caribbean region.”

“Industrialisation? I think I might know something about this. I was talking to Father Maxwell today and he mentioned James Watt and his steam machine. He said he was going to try it in one of the cotton mills in the north of England and it will take the place of employees. Johan, will people lose jobs?”

“Yes, potentially, but progress demands it. You can’t always worry about individuals, Mabel. Business needs progress for everyone’s benefit. There will always be a need for workers and business owners to do their best to consider their workforce. It will be good to take a lot of the drudgery out of factory jobs.”

Mabel wondered about it being progress if workers lose their jobs, but at least Johan discussed it with her. He was so difficult to communicate with when he was so preoccupied. He was more engrossed in his papers than conversation so Mabel let him continue reading undisturbed. She felt particularly hurt when he got up and left, without remark, preferring the solitude of his study.

-o0o-

Mabel's friendship with Rayne and Cicely, plus her involvement with the Rosary Altar Society, prompted her to attend Sunday services again, and she always brought Florian along. Soon Mabel had a circle of friends in Peutie, and an active social life, and Florian had friends too, with whom he attended Sunday School. This made all the difference in Mabel's outlook.

The solitude she needed to paint was part of her recovery, and with it she had tangible results to show. But her renewed sense of wellbeing was the direct result of her new friendships. She hadn't realised how lonely she had been and would still be if not for that chance meeting in town when Rayne extended her that simple invitation, Johan's frequent traveling and reduced interaction with her she excused as the price of his success, his shortness she attributed to fatigue, but they had left her depleted until her new friendships.

With just a few days before the August Fair, Mabel ventured into town to check up on the preparations. The ladies in the group were so impressed with Mabel's artistic abilities that they put her in charge of the decorations, and she found a sense of purpose she had been missing since she finished decorating the house. The late afternoon sun was bright despite the time of day. The trees drew long shadows on the grass of the church grounds where Mabel saw Father Maxwell, Brother Willem and several other men erecting temporary structures for booths and tents. Rayne, there to oversee her brainchild, spotted Mabel and went to fill her in on the schedule.

"The ensemble will be coming on Friday evening to rehearse. They're very good. I came across them at the Mayor's daughter's wedding earlier in the year. They had everyone on their feet," Rayne was enthusiastic.

"I'm really looking forward to the music. I've never been to anything like this before, especially one which I've helped to organise. I do hope it all goes well." Rayne smiled encouragingly.

"The ladies would never have put you in charge of the decorations if you hadn't proven yourself. You've got an eye for this. And when you offered one of your landscapes for auction? We can never thank you enough."

The two women busied themselves with the flowers and decorations until they lost the natural light.

Mabel joined Rayne, the Paster, Willem and Cicely for dinner at the rectory after which Rayne and Mabel went over last minute plans and preliminary figures.

"Nothing left to do but pray." Father Maxwell jokes, offering them a glass of sherry as the group ended their evening, satisfied there truly wasn't anything but praying left to do.

Outside it was still warm and Mabel wanted to walk back home but Rayne insisted she take the carriage. Her footman was called to take her and bring it back. Secretly Mabel was grateful as she realised how tired she really was.

"Will Johan be joining us for the fair?" Rayne enquired. Mabel shook her head.

"Sadly he is in Paris on business so it will just be me and Florian."

"In that case, you and Florian are more than welcome to stay the night with me. I'm not too far from the rectory." Mabel considered the offer. It would be a very late night and she knew she would be tired, and Florian up far past his bedtime.

"Then you won't have to worry about having to take him back home. It's the least I can do to say thank you for your hard work. Darling, please say you'll both stay?"

"Rayne, that would be lovely and would certainly prevent me from having to leave early and organise a carriage to take us back. Yes, I'd love to. That's such a kind offer." Mabel felt flattered. She hugged Rayne and left. Saturday will be a long day.

Job met the carriage when Mabel arrived and helped her down. "Good evening Ma'am. I hope you had a good day?"

"Oh yes, I truly did. Job. I'm going up now but please ask Flossie to bring me a jug of water?" Mabel took the taper from Job and lifted her skirts as she climbed the stairs.

Bed was a blessing. She was happily exhausted and within moments she was fast asleep. Even Flossie bringing the jug of water didn't stir her. As she left, Flossie looked back to check on her mistress and closed the bedroom door.

-o0o-

Florian bounded into Mabel's room excited at the prospect of that day's upcoming events. She stretched herself awake and wanted to cuddle him but he was determined to pull her out of bed.

Mabel looked at her son adoringly and ran her fingers through his uncombed hair. He was a lot like Johan. He had so much energy. Today she shared his excitement. She looked forward to seeing the results of their efforts.

At two o'clock, Rayne's carriage arrived to collect them. Job loaded their overnight bags, Mabel's carpet bag and vanity case, onboard. With Florian singing at the top of his voice in excitement, they set off. Soon, in the distance, Mabel could see the rectory and its grounds coming alive with music and fair goers. She could make out the children dancing around the maypole with the ribbons glinting in the light.

People were lined up at the Coconut Shy stall, all wanting to prove their skill, three balls at a time. Others were busy at the Shove Groat game stall, hoopla and other skill and chance games. Children with fluffy balls of candy floss in all colours paraded around the lawn, pulling and tugging their sticky treats apart. As soon as Florian saw a young girl with some he begged his mother to let him try the sugary confection.

To Florian, the festivities were exciting. He entered a world of bright lights, colour, music and dancing and he could not think where to go first. And there were other children. He pulled Mabel this way and that, and then he saw all the boys at the shooting gallery. There was a colourful rocking horse for the boy who could shoot three toy bullets in the centre of the bullseye. He watched a young lad, about two years older than himself, try and fail, Florian was eager to try his hand. But Mabel was unhappy that it was the guns which attracted Florian's attention and tried to draw him away.

"Look Florian, there's the circus tent. Why don't we go and see what's going on over there?" Florian sulked but agreed to go, picking at his candy floss. On the way they passed a side-stall where Father Maxwell was locked in stocks. Parishioners could buy three tries to hit the Pastor with a wet sponge, and when they did he would erupt into a highly dramatic diatribe about slings and arrows or sometimes he'd sputter and pretend to be hurt. It was comical. The priest was drenched in water and, laughing, was still encouraging those watching to see if they could hit him, too, telling people they could repent tomorrow. It was one of the most popular stalls as parishioners and locals enjoyed his mock ire when he was hit. It was raising a lot of money too.

Rayne was by the drinks stall, helping to serve hibiscus tea, chilled lemonade and apple juice for the more delicate, hard cider and ale for those so inclined. She waved to Mabel.

Johan had left Mabel some money to treat herself and Florian at the fair. She allowed him to play a round of stall games but what he really wanted was the shooting game. Mabel tried to distract him with the promise of a toffee apple, but then two girls saw him and tried to persuade him to join them. It was just the diversion Mabel was hoping for and she readily agreed that he could go.

“It’s a lovely sight, isn't it, seeing the children so happy and playing together?” Willem startled her and she found herself blushing again as she looked at him. He was so handsome.

“Yes, Father Willem. Sadly we have not had much opportunity for him to experience these things, but he seems to be fitting in very well.”

“How old is he now?” Willem asked.

“He’s just 10. I’m so proud of him. He really seems to be a happy child. I’m very lucky.”

"No doubt thanks to you. A good mother's influence is everything." Mabel blushed again.

"I think you're being too kind. He has a loving nanny and a governess, both good influences on him, and of course his father. The pair walked around the fair and continued talking.

"What are you going to do for his next stage of education?" Willem enquired.

"I'm not really sure. I'm happy with the governess, but seeing him here today, I think he needs more interaction with children his own age." Mabel added.

"Well, you know we're opening a school here later in September. God willing, all the building work will be complete by the end of next week. Maybe he could join us? We have 12 other children of a similar age, some from Sunday school whom he may already know, so he can make friends as well as get a good grounding in education. I'll be teaching there myself. It would be good if he could come."

"I will have to speak with his father, but I will let you know. That sounds like a very good idea." She smiled at him and felt herself go red again.

"Father Willem. How are you?" The tall man Mabel recognised from the gallery approached them.

"Mr. Leiger. How are you? How are things at the gallery? I've been busy at the church and with the new school, but I'll get there again soon. I was just telling Mrs Dottin that I hope we can entice little Florian to join us at school." Willem was charming as well as handsome, "Have you met Mrs Dottin?" Mr Leiger took Mabel's hand and kissed it.

"Why yes, in fact I have. She stopped by the gallery and purchased some pastels, but she did not tell me that she is a fine artist, just that she painted cameos. I understand that you painted the lovely landscape they are auctioning? That's marvellous."

Mabel, blushing again, nodded in agreement.

"Mrs. Dottin, seeing you now just saves me the postage. I would like to invite you to exhibit one or two of your landscapes in the gallery. People will love seeing local scenes, so beautifully rendered. Do you suppose you could allow me to view a couple? I'll put them up right away."

Mabel was dumbstruck.

"Are you sure? I mean, yes. Yes, I'd like that very much. I'll have my man bring a few early next week Say, Monday?" Mr Legier nodded in agreement as he bit into a sugary treat.

"Delighted to make your official acquaintance, Mrs Dottin, I look forward to working with you."

As he walked away, Willem turned to Mabel. “He’s done very well for himself. From what I have seen through the window of his gallery, he has some stunning works in there and he wants to put yours with them. When he puts yours up, that will give me an excuse to pay the gallery another visit.”

Mabel was suddenly overwhelmed. It had been a long time since she’d had any attention from Johan and now here she was, having so much from men she hardly knew.

“Mamma, Mamma”, Florian interrupted, running towards Mabel and threw his arms around her.

“Florian, this is Father Willem, he is a missionary but now he’s going to be a teacher at the new school.

“How do you do?” Florian asked.

“I’m very well. And you, young man? ”They shook hands. “Are you having fun? Florian nodded, jumping up and down in excitement. He was desperate for his mother’s attention and did not want to appear rude.

“Yes, Pastor Willem. I’m having so much fun today.” Florian smiled, wide eyed. “Mamma, please can I have some apple juice?” Mabel dug into her purse and pulled out a coin for Florian and off he ran to the stall and back to both girls he had earlier befriended.

“Yoo hoo!” It was Rayne.

"Mabel, sorry not to have greeted you before. It's very busy and I hope everyone's having a good time. Are you? Hello Willem. Are you taking good care of my friend Mabel?" She asked with that famous twinkle in her eye.

Mabel left for home the next morning with a true sense of accomplishment. The fair and her decorations were a triumph. Her son finally had friends he could play with. He had a school he could attend and thrive in with his peers. Her art was being recognised as truly professional and not just a hobby. But maybe most of all she did not feel lonely. Johan's indifference and neglect since the baby died left her parched for camaraderie and support. Now she felt whole again.

Chapter 6

The sound of galloping horses woke Mabel. She went to the window to see what was going on. A buggy pulled by two horses was speeding towards the house and the rider? Mabel could barely see in the dark but then recognised it was Johan's silhouette, furiously whipping the steeds to speed them up. Her heart began to race. Only one thing made Johan so keen to get back home, and she would welcome the attention. He'd been so distant for such a long time. She looked at the clock on the mantelpiece. The moon casting light across its face showed it was two thirty in the morning. She slipped on her gown and mules and headed downstairs to meet him.

He swung open the door with such force the stained glass transom window it contained shattered and Johan staggered into the hallway. He was shaking and angry. He picked up the carver chair underneath the mirror and threw it at the very door through which he came.

"Damn him! He will live to regret this." He threw the floral vase at the wall and it shattered, the water and flowers cascading down the wall; petals scattering like confetti.

"Johan! Johan, what's wrong? Please, calm down, Darling, whatever is the matter?" She ran down the stairs to try and calm him. "You'll wake the household!" Johan looked at Mabel as guilt set in. It brought him to his knees.

"I am ruined!" He cried. "I am so very sorry. He's ruined me. He's ruined us." Job and Flossie, both jolted from their sleep, rushed in at the racket.

"Can I help, Mr Johan?" Job asked. Flossie, seeing the debris on the floor, went to get a broom to sweep up the glass. Mabel shook her head and pulled Johan up, almost like she would a child in a tantrum, and moved him to the drawing room, for privacy. She closed the double doors and looked at him, crumpled on the chaise. She had never seen him in such a state.

Mabel managed to calm Johan down and watched him draw jagged breaths as she studied his ruddy face, red from fury and alcohol. Calmly she asked, "Johan, what's going on? Why are you so upset?" He shook his head and looked at the floor.

"Mabel, I'm very sorry. We have to leave."

"Leave why? Johan, are you drunk? Why do we need to leave? What on earth are you talking about? You're not making sense!" Mabel had never seen Johan so apoplectic and was very confused. "Johan. What is the matter? What has happened?" Her voice became more anxious with Johan's utterances.

“Here! Mabel, we need to leave this house.”

“Why on earth do we need to leave this house, it’s our home for God’s sake. Johan!” Mabel tried to understand his ranting. “You’re not making sense! Please! What’s going on?” Johan sat on the corner of the chaise, almost as if he were ready to make a bolt for the door.

“I lost. I lost everything, I lost the house in a game of cards this evening, to Henri! He cheated. He cheated me. I am convinced he cheated, but I have no way to prove it. I’ve lost the house!”

Johan stood up and walked around in circles, repeating himself also in disbelief. “I’m sorry, Mabel, but I have lost the house, in a game of cards, and before you ask, yes, I was drinking but I did not have so much that I lost lucidity. He cheated me. He cheated me out of the property.” Silence. Mable, shaking at the news, stared at him. She could smell the alcohol on his breath.

“You have done what? Lost the house doing what? I don’t understand. You’re delirious and scaring me Johan” Mabel uttered a nervous laugh.

Johan had no other words. “Mabel, I have lost the house in a card game. I was cheated. I lost our beautiful, God forsaken home.” His voice broke in anger and regret. Suddenly his words registered as facts. She sank into a chair.

“What?’ The words were beginning to sink in. ”Where? Where are we going to live? What do you propose we do, Johan? How preposterous you are." Mabel was suddenly alert and focused but also floundering for a life raft.

"I'm sorry, my love." Johan knelt before Mabel and held both her hands in his, trying to demonstrate his sincerity. "We will move to the West Indies. Remember I invested in Conquerabia there?" Mabel stood, unable to stay seated as reality began to sink in.

"If this gets out that I was cheated out of house and home in a card game, I will be a laughing stock and will be summarily fired from the bank, then who will employ me? I am ruined, Mabel. We are ruined!"

"Oh, dear God Johan, what have you done? You gambled our lives away? You have brought shame on us. All of us." She spoke calmly and firmly, not wanting to share her situation with Flossie and Job. "I can never show my face again in church. My parents, what will they think? Oh, Lord! Imagine the ignominy we will receive if this gets out." Mabel paused as the severity of what happened gradually sunk in. "Johan, you have damn well ruined us. You gambled away everything! Everything!" Mabel emphasised the word. The devastation of the news and all that it implied, now hitting hard. "And now you tell me we have to live in that God forsaken, backward island with the savages! Please tell me this is all a dream." She paced, trying to think.

Johan rose to try and comfort his wife, "Mabel I am so very sorry. I cannot say it enough. It was just one of those things that got out of hand" Johan realised he was sounding pathetic as his hands dropped to his side. "And the plantation is doing very well and it will be cheaper for us to live there." He tried in vain to rationalise. "No one needs to know about this. It will work out if we can stick to a plan. I can make this right!" Johan, realising he was making excuses, reached his hand out to rest on her shoulder in reassurance, but Mabel swiped it away in anger. She thought hard, she needed to be smart. She was not her mother.

Mabel stood up, squared her shoulders, looked directly at Johan and it withered him, making him back away, feeling for the chair behind him. He did not recognise this woman before him.

"Never, ever did I imagine my name being dirt, being ruined in such a disgraceful manner." She was shaking with anger. "Do you realise we are going to have to live amongst those s-s-s-savages?" The words barely squeezed through her tightened lips. "Uncultured, uncivilised animals!" Mabel walked across the floor and slapped Johan across the face so hard her hand smarted. "How could you do this to us?"

Johan walked towards the window, holding his cheek, surprised that his wife would strike him but almost glad she did. Almost. Silence.

"I deserved that, but please sit down and let's discuss this rationally." Johan led Mabel to the table where they sat opposite each other. It felt like a game of chess. Johan moved first. "Henri assured me he will not disclose what happened last night but we have to vacate this property by the end of the month or he will go public." Mabel listened to each word he uttered, but they echoed in her ears as if he was a long way off.

"That's three weeks away Johan. What about Florian? My poor child? He is just about to start at the new school with all his new friends? Her words were measured.

"Henri suggested we place him in a boarding school in England. It's one of the best. He'll get the best education."

"You've thought it all through, haven't you Johan, without even consulting me. How dare you! If we have to leave Peutie, my son will come with me!" Suddenly she realised Johan was still gambling, only now he was waging she'd be a good wife and dutifully absolve him and go along with his social coverup.

"Forgive me, Mabel, but there is no decent school to speak of in the Spanish Antilles. If we send him to London he will have a better education and he can take over the business when he's of age. "Johan's voice softened. "Mabel, you have to trust me that I can make this work. I realise what I've done is reprehensible. I cannot undo a very grave mistake. If I could, I would find every way to do so, but …" Johan choked up, a repentant child. He struggled to compose himself.

He took Mabel's hands and held them to his heart, his eyes searching hers for a glimpse of forgiveness but also something else?

What were his eyes revealing? She pulled her hands away, Mabel saw abject contrition in his eyes such that she had never seen before, nor had she seen him so tearful or weakened by failure, and yet still he was making plans for all of them, still certain he was in charge. He was certain she would go along.

And she realised he was right. She had no other route to go. To return to her parents would not only bring shame on her and Florian but them too. She instinctively knew she had to trust Johan as there was no place in this world for a divorced woman such as herself without independent means.

"Johan, I have no option but to believe what you say and go along with all of this. Whatever I decide to do I am dishonoured and without recourse. I am aware that society has no place for me without you. I can adjust to anything, but I will be damned if I'm going to give up everything I've worked towards and also lose Florian, the one I love above all else." Her words cut through Johan and he was, for once, speechless.

Mabel knew they were in the endgame of this chess match. Thinking as quickly as she could, she planned her next and most crucial move. Because she was a woman she knew that Johan had the advantage but she stood up, straightened her back and, looking down at Johan, still seated, she went for the unexpected draw.

"That you have been spending time gambling with our future should not completely surprise me. I know that you have been cheating the bank and the Spanish government in the Antilles by using my Catholicism as a beard." Suddenly Johan stopped his snivelling and turned his head to see who was speaking to him this way. How could she possibly know? He visibly shrank before her, again.

"Yes, I know. I read about the Royal Cedula. I know you had to swear when you signed the Velum Book of Population that you profess the Catholic faith and are in service to both the Pope and the King or you would not have been able to own Conquerabia, would you?" Mabel stared at him enjoying her moment of power. "You must also have used my name and named the church that your son was baptised there as proof that I exist because…and this may be the worst because you are cheating me…. I also know that all the land that they are giving away there can go to both men and women! As settlers we are equally granted four fanegas and two-sevenths of land that increases with the number of slaves you can support on your land. You have been using me to acquire more land in my name as a Catholic settler without telling me, thinking that I would assume that property laws banning women from owning property in their own names would be the same as here where I can't even have money in my own name. I was happy to allow this, as you are my husband and I assumed you were doing what was best for our family, but now I..."

Johan interrupted her, "My darling, how did you, I mean, my dear, I, I, never would..."

Mabel stopped him. "Yes, Johan, you would and you did. You gambled our home away and now I need to secure things for Florian and me." Mabel, still square shouldered and resolute, added: "These are my terms. I will have my own money. 100 kronenthaler per month, cash or local currency equivalent, without fail or further negotiation and without asking or you acting like it is a gift. I know I can't have my own bank account but you owe me this now. The portion of Conquerabia you acquired in my name is mine and you will treat it as such and make legal provisions that if anything happens to you the plantation comes to me through whatever conservatorship makes it binding until Florian is of age to inherit it outright, with a stipulation that I live out my days there in the manner to which I am accustomed, unless we can return to our homeland, free of shame."

Johan was flabbergasted. He could only listen and try to understand the stunning reversals now happening, first at the gambling table and now in his wife!

Mabel continued, "I know that our bank accounts are in your name, as per the laws, but from now on we have de facto joint ownership of the bank accounts you currently hold and nothing goes out of it without my knowledge or consent. I will know everything about how you handle the accounts from now on. I will never again be subject to your base whims. I will never again be put in a situation where I have no recourse to safeguard my security and that of my son. Never again, so you hear me. It may not be the law of the land but I insist you understand that I share equal status with all our assets from now on."

Johan sat in the chair, looking at his feet, letting Mabel's demands and admonishments sink in. He was astonished by her demands but knew it would be unfair to deny her. Everything he had built in Peutie was now gone, including his job from which he would have to resign. He knew he also needed Mabel by his side as a status symbol, if he were to make a success of the Conquerabia Plantation. He sat up, and took her right hand in his.

"My dear, you will have it all. I guarantee it. I will contact the solicitor tomorrow to start the proceedings. I know this is pointless to repeat, but Mabel, you have my word. I am deeply sorry for what I have done. I will not disappoint you or Florian ever again. I will endeavour to make sure you will never want for anything else in life." Mabel looked at him and pulled her hand away. Her heart was heavy but she had to believe what Johan said. She had to, for Florian's sake. Her poor child. She ached for everything he would not be able to understand.

"Tomorrow you hand in your resignation and I will issue a notice to inform my dear friends and family that we have chosen to emigrate to warmer climes for the benefit of your health. They should understand recalling the time you returned with such horrendous ague. I will tell the gallery that they can donate any money from the sale of my landscapes to the church. I will also notify Fr. Willem that Florian will not be enrolling in school after all. It would also be appropriate for you to join me in church, for the next three Sundays, so that we quell any possible rumours, if you are sure Henri will keep his word. I am sure you can appreciate that Henri, under the influence of alcohol, may well be compelled to speak after he sobered up and wanted to gloat. You need to guarantee that he will keep quiet at least until we have left". Mabel found the next part hardest to figure out, so she hesitated, briefly.

"And tomorrow, we both speak with Florian and tell him of our decision to emigrate and we will tell him it is a happy adventure we are about to embark on. He has new friends at Sunday School, and I'm sure he will speak freely of our exciting plans, don't you think Johan?" She looked at Johan with unmistakable anger and there was sarcasm in that last comment. She knew it would be difficult to explain it to Florian. He was finally settling into their new home with his new friends and this would be a wrench. "Florian needs to understand that this is a decision we have taken jointly. We'll explain to him that opportunities have opened up in the West Indies, we are hoping to make a new and exciting life" She looked at Johan as her words sunk in.

During the silence which ended her monologue, Johan turned away from her, emasculated. He had never seen her this strong before and he did not like being made to feel inadequate in her presence nor to be ordered around, though he knew he was in no position to argue. Johan took to his knee and once again held both Mabel's hands in his.

"You are right. This is the best way to go about telling Florian, then when he speaks with his friends it will be believable, even if he tells them he doesn't like the plan. I know you will never forgive me for putting you through this nightmare and I understand why you now speak to me in such harsh tones. I deserve it. And I'm scared, too. I have been to the Spanish Antilles, but never to live, only as an invested tourist. Now that's all about to change." He began to weep.

"Please don't make a scene Johan, it doesn't become you. I don't like such public displays of weakness. The staff can hear you." He stood up to embrace her, whispering 'of course my dear' in her ear. She repelled his embrace and stared towards the door, unemotional. Johan left the drawing room.

When he was gone Mabel exhaled at length. Her life was in shambles, she was suddenly thrown into chaos and uncertainty, she had no idea what was to come, and yet she had found her courage. Somehow, in the midst of disaster, in the throes of panic and fear, she also felt proud of herself, proud of how she took control, proud of how she suddenly saw Johan clearly and how she stepped into the lead. Her heart was pounding in her chest, as though she had escaped a predator. She didn't want to cry, though her training suggested she should.

She looked around. This house in Peutie, once decrepit and now beautiful, changed as Mabel changed. This house became liveable as Mabel found the will to live, moving out of her deep grief. It assuaged her pain and it felt her love. Now she had to leave it behind. Another loss for her to bear.

For a moment she questioned God's incomprehensible judgement against her. Then a sense of guilt overwhelmed her and she went to her room, knelt down at her dresser holding her bible and sought His forgiveness and, Dear Lord, his guidance. Mabel's sheltered upbringing, amongst polite society, did not prepare her for life on a slave plantation. She had understood from the newspapers that negroes were a violent breed of animals. Images of male slaves she saw in the papers, shackled and untamed brutes, terrified her. She made a mental note to send Flossie shopping to buy two small knives, small enough to hide in her purse or about her clothing. She needed to be prepared.

Chapter 7

The grandfather clock chimed four times. The last trunk was carefully packed in the wagon. Florian was left to sleep for as long as possible. There was no need to wake him and his excitability would inadvertently be a reminder to Mabel of her loss.

A lot of large items were sent ahead, such as furniture and some clothing. Just the necessities for the journey were all that were in the wagon. What else they needed for the journey and a few things for the tropical weather could be purchased in London, where they would have to spend a few days. Everything else they would get once they arrived, since Johan said that the tailors on the island were very good.

Three weeks had not been enough for Mabel to adjust to the idea of a new life, but she was determined to make the departure as swift and as clean as possible, for Florian's sake and hers. To family and friends they were moving to the Spanish Antilles for Johan's health and to oversee their profitable plantation. She hated the deceit but it was a believable half truth and she prayed each night for forgiveness.

Rayne, broken-hearted at losing her new friend, gave her a gold crucifix necklace, a family heirloom, as a travel blessing. It was beautiful in its simplicity, even more so because of the sentiment. Her generosity embarrassed Mabel. She wore it constantly and every so often would hold the pendant in prayer.

Flossie brought a sleepy Florian downstairs. As soon as Mabel saw him it brought tears to her eyes. He was a victim of this situation and did not deserve for his life to be disrupted in such a manner.

"Mamma." He said sleepily, and reached out for her. Turning her head to deftly wipe a tear away, she hugged him down the last few stairs and swung him around.

"We've got an exciting journey ahead of us. We're going to have a great adventure!" He may have heard her voice falter but he was too sleepy to enquire. He just wanted the reassurance of her hugs.

Flossie was going with them. It was her choice and wished to continue her employment with the Dottins. and it would be a blessing, as her presence would help Florian feel less upheaval. Most important of all was her loyal discretion. She and Mabel took their seats in the wagon as Johan closed up. Florian immediately rested his head on Flossie, the coach's movement, rocking him back off to sleep in the early hours. His blond hair flopping over his closed eyes. He looked angelic.

Mabel looked out the window to see Johan hand a small amount of money and the keys to Job. Leaving Job behind was heartbreaking for everyone. He had served the family and now his life, too, was upended through no fault of his own. He undid the reins for the horses for Johan the last time and the family rode off into Peutie where they would catch a stage coach for the next part of their voyage.

Johan's heart was more than heavy. He couldn't bear looking back as they left the estate. Mabel, on the other hand, watched until it was out of sight, knowing she would never see her beautiful home again. The sound of the horses hooves on the dirt track was the drumroll of the end of this life as she knew it.

It was to be a long journey, endless from Mabel's perspective, but Johan was accustomed to it. He looked at it like a business journey, which alleviated the anxiety of leaving his home behind. On the morning of each day he would buy the day's paper and read on the journey. Mabel had taken to her bible and then she read Johan's discarded newspapers.

Each night they stopped off at local inns, exhausted, with only time to dine, wash and sleep. Early mornings they had a quick breakfast and commenced on the next leg of the trip.

Florian was excited to be on the water as they departed France for England. He would hang on to the railings to watch, under the protection of Mabel. He studied the sea gulls vying for food. He was fascinated by the workings of the crew on the ship and the ever changing nature of the water. He made friends with other children and Mabel with other mothers. Johan would discuss the affairs of the day with fellow male travellers. It all helped make the journey pass more quickly.

After what felt like an interminable amount of days they finally reached London. With only four days in the city Mabel was determined that her time with Florian will be filled with joy, before taking him to boarding school.

They marvelled at the city, travelling with their hired Hansom cab being rocked to and fro across the busy cobbled streets. It was too fast paced for them to enjoy their time sightseeing, shopping for the much needed uniform and other essential items the school recommended for its students. Florian found it exciting, trying on his hat and shoes. Mable treasured his laughter and smiles.

Sat in the 'cab on yet another journey to find a different part of his school necessities, Mabel sat pondering the frenetic energy of being in London, a buzz she had never experienced before. Growing up in Antwerp, in a sheltered family environment, then marrying Johan and moving to a country house in Peutie, protected her from city life. Mabel wondered why she had not been more curious about all these bustling places Johan saw all the time? Why hadn't he shared them with her, allowed herself to experience all this with him? And now he was denying it to her forever.

With all Florian's school and civilian necessities purchased they ventured to walk around the Hyde Park Pleasure Gardens filled with people, couples with one or two children strolling along. Elegant women with their parasols up to shade themselves from the late afternoon sun's rays. Clowns, jugglers and musicians, vying for an audience and the few pennies thrown into a hat. Florian delighted at the swans gliding on the Serpentine lake. Mabel was in both heaven and hell.

The next day Florian was shown to his house at Harrow. Despite how heavily she and Johan had been singing the praises of the school and the fun he would have with all the students he'd meet and the opportunities he would have, Mabel was surprised at the way in which he instantly took to the school. He met fellow boys with whom he formed instant friendships and together they explored the school and its environs. She was hurt that Florian would rather go with the other children than spend these precious last moments with her, but in some respects it made saying farewell to him easier, with only Mabel feeling what a wrench it was to have to leave him there.

She cried all the way back to the Ruben Hotel. She could not be consoled. Flossie was also heartsick to bid Florian farewell but she, too, was relieved that he was not fretful. She feared he would cling to her. They had formed a bond since the day she was hired when he was still a baby. In grief, at the thought of losing him, she hugged herself in the coach and missed him already. Florian was as close to her as if he was her own. Unbeknownst to Mabel, Flossie had kept as a keepsake one of his monogrammed handkerchiefs. Both women, sitting in silence in the 'cab, wondered when they would see him again.

This final day they were staying in the Ruben's Hotel in Victoria. Mabel feigned a headache and Johan took Flossie off to collect the final few sundries they needed. In truth she needed some time to herself. Mabel wanted to indulge herself one last moment in civilisation in a gentile way. She dressed for an evening out and wandered downstairs to the elegant foyer and took a seat in the lounge where she could observe those checking in, going out, and those meeting friends before dinner in the hotel.

A little girl saw Mabel and decided to play peek-a-boo and Mabel obliged, hiding her face behind her hands before her parents whisked her off. Then something caught Mabel's eye. A few feet away, what was that? It looked to be a small person, 13 or 14, a young boy, but black as ebony and dressed so strangely. A red pillbox held on his head by a red band under his chin, smart black breeches, black shoes and red jacket with a red tie over a white ruffled shirt. Mabel thought the image too bizarre for words.

He came towards her without looking at her. It was his job to collect all the dirty crockery; the used cups, saucers and glasses. He was aware of Mabel's eyes on him as he approached her table. She stared at him shamelessly when he came close to collect the dishes from a nearby table.

His face was remarkable. His nose is wide and flat at the same time. His cheeks smooth unblemished, his coarse hair, shorter than half the length of her little fingernail, was parted in the centre. In many senses he looked like the mini man he was intended to represent. She couldn't help herself. She reached out and touched his hand. Then she brought her hand up, looking at the point where she touched him, to see if his colour had rubbed off on her dainty white glove. There was nothing there. "Sorry miss." He respectfully bowed his apology to her again without making eye contact.

'What a peculiar thing!" Mabel said under her breath, rubbing the perceived dirt from her gloved hand. As she stood up, she took off her gloves and gently placed them in the umbrella bin, as a shiver ran up her back. Johan arrived, ready to take her out to dinner.

Another few days on the road before they reached Falmouth and boarded the packet to the West Indies. This leg of the journey was as hectic as the trip to London. Anger returned to Mabel as she recalled the predicament she found herself forced into. She longed for Florian, for her familiar home, for the life she was accustomed to. She resented being separated from her friends, again, she was furious about having to abandon her paintings at the gallery just when her work achieved some serious recognition, and she was terrified about what was coming next. Sadly, Johan thought the house was all they lost. It was so much more.

As soon as the Stagecoach reached Falmouth, she saw too many vessels to count. Small boats nimbly darting about and large ships with their billowing sails distracted her from her malaise. Tomorrow they set sail for the Spanish Antilles. Despite her anger and sorrow, her sense of adventure returned.

Through Johan's experience of previous voyages, he had booked them a cabin to share. It would be small, only one of two. Flossie would have to sleep in a hammock below where there was very little privacy. What light seeped in came through the floorboards above or the gun apertures.

The Packet was small, known for its speed and within hours of settling into their cabin, Mabel joined Johan on deck to look back towards the shore, the calm sea gently rocking the vessel. It was reassuring and comforting to Mabel. The sea air fresh to her lungs cleared her mind.

Unsullied by his secret disgrace, Johan's status ensured that he was part of the elite and was introduced to Captain Wiggins, Chaplain Lettouche and the ship's surgeon Dr. Knight. They enjoyed meals with the Captain, his lieutenants, and the surgeon and his wife. There were few other women onboard and Mabel enjoyed chatting with them, but she especially liked that the ship's close confines afforded her more opportunities to listen in on the conversations the men were having. As angry as she was with him, she still admired Johan's ability to speak on affairs of the day, politics and other topics.

One evening, having enjoyed a rare, lavish dinner, Sebastian Lettouche, the chaplain, asked, "So how many slaves do you own, Mr. Dottin?"

"Oh, twenty odd, or thereabouts" Johan always gave offhand answers to this sort of question. He wanted to change the subject since abolitionists could be so sanctimonious.

"Well, Sir, how do you feel about the abolitionist movement? Could put you out of business, especially as you said before, you've taken over an existing plantation. Gave up banking? Surely, you'd be safer in the financial area?" Johan felt uncomfortable at the questions raised, as did Mabel, concerned about how her husband would respond.

"Mr. Lettouche, at this point in my life I would rather take advantage of this fine weather than weighing which of my career choices is better, especially now that I have clearly irretrievably decided." Everyone laughed. "But you do raise an interesting point. I think we have to use imported labour to advance the financial and personal circumstances for everyone. Imported labour trade enables schools and universities to be built, the cotton in your shirts, the coffee in your cup and the sugar in your coffee. Imported labour benefits, too, by bringing them out of the Godless jungle, so I think we are winning all around."

"How does owning many people who were taken from their homes by force, packed into slaver ships where many died en route, then worked so hard they have little rest and are often flogged for the coin, benefit the poor buggers, sir? Because you give them catechism on Sunday?" Mabel cringed.

"Mr Lettouche! I happen to know that the slaves in the Antilles are treated better than on other islands because slave owners are bound to follow Governor Chacon's mandate of The Code Noir, not to abuse them. He made it illegal to damage them. You may be right, but I don't think I can answer any more questions until I see things for myself. This will be my first job since leaving the bank for health reasons, and as a business man I feel that I can take advantage of this trade to contribute something to society. I'm sure my manager at the plantation does work them hard, but without hard work, what are we all to do? Sit idle? These slaves, as you call them, were brought over to be improved; to be taught Christianity and work. It is rather like being an apprentice, only they are kept on because they are little more than children. Just think how much better their lives are than living in the jungle."

Mabel winced at Johan's lie. Of course he had seen his plantation on his last trip. Why would he lie?

The conversation attracted the attention of the doctor onboard. "So you have not actually seen your manager manage your slaves, Mr Dottin? As it happens, surgeons are in demand in San Domingue, where I'm headed, due to the ill treatment of those poor people. I'd be surprised if the Spanish Antilles is any better. And you think they are better off in the Antilles than being in the jungle, where they are free, do you?" He huffed a breath with his last words, for emphasis.

"No, I have not, Doctor, and you may be right. All I know is what I have read in the papers that imported plantation labour is important to the development of the islands, they are brought into Catholic homes and that they recite catechism and receive communion. Their souls are saved. I look forward to seeing first hand how the slaves on the plantation are treated and if I find anything untoward, I shall rectify it"

"Mrs. Dottin, how do you feel about being the wife of a plantation owner? About having to leave your beautiful home and yanked away from your family? How about owning people forced to go even further from theirs, taken by sea to a faraway land, never to see their family again?" Mabel felt sick, recalling that day Johan uprooted her life, but she couldn't let this blowhard compare their situation to that of mere slaves! If she saw any abuse of her imported labour, she would stop it herself.

"Sir, I know my husband is a man who will try to do the right thing. I have every faith in him and his actions. Please excuse me, it's late," Mabel smiled at Johan, a very public act of support. "Good night all!" She went below, sick to her stomach for so many reasons.

-o0o-

Flossie started feeling ill about 10 days into the voyage. At first they thought it might be seasickness because the ocean had been roiling. Other passengers were also ailing. But after the waves died down and she was still unable to eat without retching and still in terrible pain, she was taken to see the surgeon. He tried the remedies at his disposal, but within days she passed. Her body and organs then examined by the surgeon uncovered a burst cecum.

A sea burial was hastily organised. Mr Lettouche, the chaplain, blessed the body. Johan and Mabel made the Trinitarian sign of the cross over her. Wrapped in sheets weighed down with two cannon balls, the moonlight illuminated the white fabric as it slid into the sea, down to the ocean's floor.

Flossie's loss fell heavy on Mabel. It was as if she lost another member of her immediate family. She retired to the cabin for the next few days. Johan brought her water and food but she ate very little, so painful was her grief. She felt she had killed the poor girl, dragging her into the mess of her life.

Some days later Mabel could no longer tolerate the blankets over her. The ship had become a floating kiln. She was increasingly disoriented and had lost track of time. She came up to the deck in need of fresh air.

There she passed the Captain, who nodded a 'good day' to her and she nodded in return. "Good to see you Mrs Dottin, I hope you're feeling better and my condolences for your loss." Her loss. Mabel thought, it's just my latest loss.

"Thank you, that's very kind, Captain. She was dear to us and will be missed terribly." He stood there unable to say more, concerned that his presence was more uncomfortable for her than him.

"Do let me know if there is anything we can do for you." Mabel nodded her appreciation; she had no words.

When land appeared on the horizon all the travellers took to the deck to see the outline of what would be for many their new home. To the left the three peaks in the distance and to the right, some distance away the island, The Spanish Antilles. The women took hold of whatever could pass for hand fans, the fathers lifted little children to see over the barrier in excitement they were finally near their destination.

Mabel's grief overshadowed any anticipation about the new world they were approaching. Johan kept his emotions in check by avoiding Mabel's grief and spending his time with the captain and senior members of the crew. Distraction worked for Johan, and since he swore off gambling, discussions about world affairs kept him occupied. But today, with their destination in sight, he felt he should make another attempt to communicate with his wife. He went down to see Mabel.

"My dear, how are you feeling?" She smiled politely at him. He could see that she was still pained by the loss but she no longer looked grey with grief, just pale.

"Would you care to come back on deck to see the view? Only a couple more days to go before we disembark." Mabel managed a smile of appreciation at the thought and, rolled off the bed, slid her feet into her shoes and took Johan's outstretched hand. He helped her over the raised threshold of the cabin after he followed her through the open hatch to the deck, he took her arm in his and walked to the side of the ship where land could be viewed. She stood, holding the wooden barrier enjoying the warm sun on her face and closed her eyes. Johan watched her enjoying the sun's rays. There was true relief in her eyes, due to a combination of sun, sea, air and the knowledge that the journey was soon to end.

"How beautiful you look, my dear." At this moment they were at peace with each other. Both realised how dependent on each other they were now, despite the general chill between them since Johan's fall from grace.

"Ah, Mrs Dottin. So good to see you again." Captain Wiggins kissed the back of her hand. "We are almost there. It's a relief to see land at long last, isn't it?"

"Captain Wiggins. I shall be relieved when we land." She replied, smiling at the Captain and then turning to Johan, smiling.

"Well, not much longer. Another day and they'll send out the shore boats to collect everyone. I hope you will enjoy what will be your new home."

Yes, I hope so too, she thought. "Thank you, Captain, we will." Captain Wiggins nodded to Johan and continued on to greet other passengers who were also excited at the sight of land and the end of their voyage. Johan took Mabel's hand and gently squeezed it. It was a reassuring gesture Mabel appreciated.

-o0o-

Mabel, Johan, and four other passengers were on the first shore boat to Portes des Espana. It was a bright, sunny morning and the islands Mabel had seen last evening were now in actual focus. The voyage was almost at an end and the relief was palpable. The travel book called them the Bocas Islands, and they were majestic.

It was already warm, despite the early hour. The wooden plank was raised onto the boat to help passengers walk down to the shore. The port was already very busy with people going about their errands. As Johan alighted and reached for Mabel's hand, he found her rigid, staring out into the distance.

"What is it my dear? You've gone as white as a bed sheet." Johan was momentarily puzzled at such behaviour. Mabel was frozen. As she stood transfixed, staring at the populace of the port, a level of fear overtook her. She had never observed so many negroes, and of so many different shades. This quantity of negroes, more than she had expected to see in her lifetime, now appeared to be freely walking about.

"My dear … ?" Johan gently pulled her hand.

"Oh! Oh Johan. I'm terribly sorry." Mabel felt foolish trying to explain her thoughts. She felt for her purse. It had the two small knives she'd asked Flossie to purchase before their departure. At least she felt she could protect herself from any attempt on her person. She composed herself, held Johan's arm, pulled the purse tighter to her side and she walked into her future.

Johan instinctively understood what the problem was. He recognised Mabel's surprise at what she saw. It took him some time getting used to it, too, when he first arrived in the Spanish Antilles. All the brown and black faces!

Their first night was spent at the Inn and Mabel was grateful for a firm, steady bed on which to sleep. Above it was a mosquito net which the maid dutifully set up for them. She was eager to wash the dust and dirt off her face. The heat was unbearable but as night was closing in, she rejoiced in a cooler temperature.

Johan had excused himself, giving Mabel time to adjust to her new surroundings. She only wanted a light snack so requested the innkeeper's wife to prepare a plate for her to enjoy in her room. Although Johan invited Mabel to join him for a lavish meal, she declined and Johan headed off to his favourite tavern for familiar fare. When he arrived back several hours later Mabel was fast asleep.

Having slept well, Mabel awoke disorientated. It took a while for the realisation she was no longer in her familiar home. Sitting up, looking around and feeling the heat of the early morning, there was no sense in crying. How would that help? She had to get on with it, it was a fait accompli. Today she and Johan would be setting off for their new home.

The landau was waiting outside for them, their luggage was loaded in and Johan hired a driver to take them both to Conquerabia. He explained that it would take a couple of hours for them to get there and he would act as tour guide if she wished, or they could ride in silence. She opted for silence so she could take in her new environment on her terms.

Like Johan when he first arrived she was taken by the array of colourful plants and foliage and watched in awe the variety of people going about their day. Freed coloureds, mulatto men, women and children. Women carrying their wares on their head or children on their backs secured with cloth wraps. Mostly men on the highways selling roasted corn, coconut water or fruit and vegetables. It felt so alien to her. They passed other varieties of carriages drawn by black men - slaves mostly. She feared encountering them and shielded further into her own carriage away from them.

For effect Johan asked the driver to stop so Mabel could take in the sights of the plantation as he was amazed by seeing it for the first time. Mabel asked if she could get out to see for herself.

Flies danced around her and she swished them away with her fan, they were irritating insects. A gentle breeze crossed causing her bonnet to dance and as Mabel stood taking in the ironwork archway and the magnificent sight of the plantation house she felt a moment of excitement. It was picturesque, reminiscent of images of other plantations she's seen in the newspaper. This was her new home.

A dog ran across in the distance chasing a chicken and then she became aware of the hubbub of sound coming from the plantation. She walked through the arch and saw people working on the land, around the house. Negroes working the horse and cart full of cut cane. Off in the distance men working the boiler house and then the sweet smell of sugar hit her.

Johan encouraged her to continue walking so that she could take it in her stride. She walked over to the cotton field. It was vast as was the land with sugar cane growing on it and the tall maize crop in the adjacent field There were many negro men and women, bent over, with holders on their backs in which they placed the picked cotton, they appeared to be selectively picking those balls of cotton they knew were ripe and leaving those that were not. It was a busy process and Diego was in the distance ensuring they were working hard. When Diego saw them, he ran to welcome them.

Mabel stared out at the negroes, looking at their unusual faces. So many black faces she struggled to decipher some of the men from the women. She felt threatened even though they were all at work and not taking too much notice of the plantation's new owners. A black child ran out in play, in front of her, chasing one of the dogs, sucking on a piece of sugar cane. It stopped and looked up at her. It was wearing a dress so Mabel surmised it must be a little girl. A strange looking little girl with short hair and large black eyes, no more than three or four years old. Called by her mother she ran away in fear that she had done something wrong. The girl was lighter in colour than many of the adult men and women slaves. How could that be, she thought to herself?

Diego called to an older black woman, who was at work in the house and introduced her as Tante to both Johan and Mabel. She recognised Johan and greeted her new mistress, taking Mabel's hat and purse from her and showed her to a table on the verandah and the refreshments it contained, laid out by the young domestic slave Johan remembered fondly. Mabel noticed the look Johan gave her. It made her momentarily uncomfortable and she knew not why. She dismissed the notion, eager to participate in the food on display.

Johan joined her. "Is this all our land and slaves?" She asked.

"Yes, my dear. As far as the eye can see. It all belongs to us. I know it can feel overwhelming at first, but you'll get used to it. You'll have more help in and around the house than before and all these negroes are making us rich!" He paused for effect. "I know I can't make up for what we lost in Peutie but I think we made the right decision to move here." He intended to sound reassuring.

Mabel was feeling anxious. She wanted to burst into tears and hold her son in her arms. She wanted the familiarity of Peutie and her home. Here, she had nothing to call her own. Her paints, her brushes, her favourite landscapes and her favourite furniture. It all had to be left behind. Suddenly she felt alone and vulnerable. She held onto her crucifix and said a prayer.

Chapter 8

Two years passed since they disembarked the packet ship. Time helped both Johan and Mabel settle into a routine and relax into Antilian life, including the unimaginable heat. Like Johan, Mabel divested herself of many European forms of dress in favour of lighter, cooler garments, most notably gone were all of the tight, restricting undergarments. And like most Europeans on the island, both she and Johan adopted two new forms of conduct, informal and less formal. The climate dictated. Days began earlier and then everything came to a stop in the early afternoon when the sun was at its hottest.

Not a day went by when Mabel did not think of her son Florian. Having to leave him behind in London almost broke her. She looked at the portrait she did of him in the gallery in Peutie every day. But Johan was right, there was no suitable schooling for a young boy of a higher social status on this island.

Occasionally she recalled that fateful day back in Peutie when Johan confessed his crimes. Thank God she followed her instincts and insisted Johan make the financial provisions she dictated. If she had meekly responded as women like her mother would have and just submitted to her husband's whims she would have no power. Now, with her shared oversight of their money and thus curtailing Johan's ability to gamble their home away. She felt more secure.

Even though he escaped public scrutiny in Antwerp under cover of his having property in the Antilles, Johan knew that he had forever fallen in Mabel's eyes. He thought of her slapping him, the look on her face when she told him she had read the business papers without his knowledge and that she knew he was keeping her land ownership a secret from her. And then she kept her knowledge a secret from him to lord over him in the future? What woman was this who cared to be so involved in a man's world of managing human chattel labour?

Johan knew he had made a huge mistake gambling at such high stakes but the turn of events after that was more shocking still. He was nothing but contrite in that moment and afterward because of the speed they had to leave made complete cooperation imperative, but since they arrived he had a lot of time to think about things. For a while he even felt antipathy for Mabel for upending the terms of their relationship. Over time, though, as they both adjusted to a world where so many of the mores they were used to did not apply, their trauma, fraught relationship finally became more accommodating and friendly.

Still, looking back, Johan could not comprehend why Mabel didn't immediately run to comfort him, as a wife should have done, but instead was compelled to strike him, to speak to him as harshly as she did, raising her voice, demanding property and money.

It was unseemly for a woman to behave so, even if her husband did err. He felt humiliated enough for losing that card game without her behaving so far out of turn. It was the subservient, agreeable, dependent Mabel he missed. This Mabel? For Johan, ever minding the accounting, this Mabel was an unknown quantity.

On paper they jointly owned the business, but there was a lot of it she had no interest in, had no practical understanding of, and further she preferred having no understanding of at all.

For example, she had no interest in managing the slaves or worrying about their propagation. In fact, that part of plantation life troubled her. Back in Antwerp, Johan said they reproduce on their own, but when they arrived she was shocked at the various colours of the slaves on Conquerabia. Clearly there was white blood in many of them. She also noted how many light coloured children were about four years old or younger. Interesting that there were few much older than this. Clearly the previous owner or other area white men had been sinning with the female slaves. No, she'll leave managing that aspect of plantation life to Johan to clean up. The previous owner was gone, so Johan just had to ferret out what white workers or outsiders were impregnating their female workers and discipline them. Best leave the slave to increase natural propagation among themselves.

Mabel understood that after she stood up to Johan, even though his gambling had forced her hand, he felt differently about her. She felt different about herself. Despite her devastation at learning of Johan's ruination of their lives, she also recalled the heady sense of disruption she had experienced that day by her responses. She would never have brought up her knowledge of his banking treachery if he hadn't lost their home, but since he did... It was a new feeling for her, personal strength independent of her marriage, and she held onto it and over Johan. She wanted to keep a close eye on the books. She no longer trusted Johan to keep to his word. She wanted to know exactly how much money they had, in which bank and how much allowance was allocated to Florian. She insisted Johan teach her about the books and also that once a month she and Johan go through the books together. It made him uncomfortable.

There was a lot for Mabel to learn about the Conquerabia ledgers. She was new to examining books. She could easily follow the basic idea: nothing going in or out that wasn't easily accounted for. But the books of such a large plantation were complicated. Money went out and came in at irregular times depending on shipping and demand, and there were regular recurring charges and income but also sometimes losses. Also much of the import and export business was speculation. And there were the employees and the imported labour and their costs to consider.

Johan complied with her unladylike demands and her unseemly desire to meddle in plantation business. He indulged her questions about accounting practices and he tried not to chuckle at her scribbling notes as he explained different entries and gave her general lists of the various expenses and the expected vagaries. They were newly emigrated, both were adjusting to the place, and frankly Johan expected that Mabel would gradually forget about the troubles of the past, take up her past interests of decorating and painting, and revert back to her more natural state of submission. She knew nothing about the workings of a plantation and even less about the human relations aspect of banking and accounting for a business as complicated as a plantation with shipping and importing and exporting concerns and human capital, too. And much of the marketing of their crops was speculative and done through relationships and hand greasing. She knew nothing about business expediency or that deal making often depended on the occasional blind eye to small details when your eye is set on a larger view. Accounting was much more flexible than Mabel understood.

But Mabel didn't tire of the bookkeeping side of the business and, to Johan's ire, Mabel remained interested in the ledgers, becoming adept at finding discrepancies that Johan hoped would remain unnoticed. Once she spotted a long overlooked discrepancy with sales of sugar loaves and a payment that was oddly missed and long overdue. Evidently Johan had given extended credit terms to a customer in Belgium and for whatever reason he was reluctant to chase it up. He couldn't even explain why he missed that specific payable and not others. Odd. Mabel took it upon herself to write to the customer informing him that the next shipment was on hold until payment was made.

Johan remained silent as she composed the letter. He knew the debt was a quid pro quo for a personal favour. The merchant had handled an obligation for Johan off the official books. Mabel hounding this obliging enterprise would be seen as harassment, but what could he do? Johan missed his financial privacy and the speculative elbow space it gave him. Mabel had a command of the language, too, which he hadn't appreciated before. Mabel was forceful but polite. Johan would have to find another way of finessing money.

The accounts auditing session ended with Johan agreeing that the correspondence should be sent and placed the letter on the pile for collection. Satisfied, Mabel decided she wanted to stretch her legs and walk through the plantation. When he was sure she was some distance away from the house, Johan removed the letter, placing it in his jacket pocket. It will buy him another few months of silence.

Mabel was thriving as the lady of the plantation and being involved in the business of domestic plantation life she was relishing each decision she made, especially when she could see the riches pouring in and the improvements succeeding. She loved having more responsibility, and best of all? Not having to go to Johan for money. This was liberating in more ways than just spending money. She found a true sense of owning herself through being able to access the vast profits from their business. She resented losing her beautiful life in Peutie, she resented being separated from Florian, but she had to admit that leaving Belgium and the restraints of that culture had some benefits. Looking out at the bustle of the brown bodies, having servants at her beck and call? Recalling her mother's broken body and spirit acting as a scullery and lackey serving father's cruel whims? Yes, there were things about this unwanted move that turned out to be rewarding.

As she walked through the gardens she redesigned, she derived enjoyment through the various plant colourings. The vibrant reds and purples of the hibiscus flower, the deep veined colours of the croton and variety of flowers which attracted the butterflies. It was a calming process to walk through the gardens and sit, at times, in the shade. She missed her painting and having instructed Tante to purchase items for her; easel, paints, canvas and more, she gently began trusting herself to paint scenes from in and around the plantation.

One afternoon, when she and Johan finished with the books, Mabel contemplated how much she missed Johan's attention now they were more wealthy than they could ever be back home. Money no longer proved to be his aphrodisiac and once, when Mabel questioned this Johan blamed the doctor's comments that she was too fragile to have another child and he could not bring himself to harm her. To himself, even he had to admit this sounded pathetic but Mabel bought it, reluctantly.

The negroes were overly deferential, even obsequious, to her. She was their master's wife. She had seen it before. People bowed and scraped before her sister after she married her rich and powerful local dignitary back in Antwerp. Her sister revelled in her unearned veneration. At the time it appalled Mabel. It seemed so degrading to the people doing it. Now, Mabel admitted, she liked the sense of advantage not experienced before. At times it made her uncomfortable, but she could live with it.

Mabel painted from the verandah where the light was most beautiful earlier and later in the day. Due to their nearness to the equator these times of day drew long shadows that would have delighted her in Peutie, but Mabel didn't only paint distant landscapes anymore. On their plantation there were so many other interesting things to paint, all visible sheltered from the sun on the veranda. Across the yard in front, Negro children too young to work ran noisily at play. On the right the boiler house and carpentry buildings and to the left and beyond were neat rows of indigo, tall rustling acres of cane, and the other crops they cultivated. Not seen but adding to her inspiration was the familiar smell of processed sugar, dancing in the air.

This morning, while she was painting, a number of negro men pulling carts stacked high with freshly chopped cane came into view. They were moving it to the boiler house where they unload it, pound it, and move it to the boilers. Later it will be cooled in copper bowls and syphoned into large clay pots for crystallisation and storage. The work was systematic and routine, the men efficient, but what Mabel was noticing, what she frequently noticed, was their muscular bodies, glistening with sweat.

The young men on the plantation had become a study in physical form for Mabel, the artist. She was intrigued by the variations of colour among the negroes and had become interested by one of the men in particular.

Cornelius had a physical form and presence she had not encountered before and right now she was transfixed by him. There were no more than twenty-five years on him. He was tall, more than six feet. His distinctive face and warm blue eyes, made him at once warm but also inscrutable and, what was it? A sort of natural manliness? He certainly was an attractive specimen. She imagined he would produce a great many healthy children. How odd to notice this in a negro male, a slave? Usually she only ever thought about the fertility of female slaves.

But Cornelius stood out among the slaves in other ways, too. He was clearly well liked by his fellow workers and the young boys looked up to him. He had a way of making them laugh even doing the most arduous work. He could quell any unrest between them by his mere presence.

Mabel, sheltered as she had been, had never been able to unabashedly stare at men and observe their forms in motion, had not noticed the natural way some men rose to leadership and power. It secretly stirred her.

She recalled how the young missionary Willem made her blush back in Peutie and the way Mr Leiger impressed her, and, God help her, there was something just as intriguing about Cornelius. He was self contained. He listened before he spoke and his words were measured and, most of all, he was not afraid to make eye contact. Those eyes.

Mabel was compelled to draw that picture, Cornelius in motion, a timber over his right shoulder. She reached for her pastels and began to outline his body on the paper. She took in every detail of his form, blending in shadows to emphasise the chevron shaped muscles around his navel, shading the hair just above the belt to his trousers, the curve of the defined tendons on his legs and the high arch of his bare feet. Mabel wanted to draw him so that a viewer would almost be able to feel his taut flesh. She added a little white shading to emphasise the sweat on his body and face, the glistening skin.

With a jolt, startled at her interest in him and horrified he might perceive it. she averted her gaze. But she could not deny it, her heart raced as she traced his body with her finger on the paper, blending the outline of his pectoral muscles and lower. God forgive her, in that moment she felt an overwhelming desire for Cornelius. The image she had produced was scandalous in its explicitness. She tore it up in a fury.

Mabel put the pastels and easel away and spent the twilight reading her bible on the porch until Johan arrived to join her for dinner. Tante, the house slave, cleared up the shreds of paper, in order to prepare dinner for the couple. Curious about why Miss Mabel hated this one so much, Tante collected the fragments, smoothed out the wrinkles and recomposed the image and there he was, Cornelius. Mmmm, mmmm, mmmm. Miss Mabel was a Christian woman, but she was no saint. Tante chuckled to herself. She knew Mabel's secret.

Throughout the meal Mabel could not help but compare Johan's features with those of Cornelius; Johan's rotund stomach and aging face, and Cornelius' handsome face and sinuous, muscular body. Mabel needed to seek forgiveness more urgently, She could not deny it. She hadn't felt desire like that in a very long time. May God forgive her.

Chapter 9

A gentle breeze crossed the plantation, quiet but for the usual machine sounds in the distance and the occasional dog barking. Mabel went quickly down the veranda steps and away from the house. Feeling the letter she had received in the day's mail in her pocket, she felt a sense of trepidation and excitement as she walked, swinging her skirt. The postmark was from Holland and she recognised Eloise's handwriting. She looked forward to news of her former homeland and updates on her family.

She picked a ripe Gros Michel from the tree and continued on her way until she sat down in the grass near the lake once she was out of sight of the house and the constant prying eyes. It was a place she often went for solitude. She reached into her pocket retrieving the letter. It had been over a year since she had heard from her sister. Her mother and father never wrote. Not even once. There were about eight pages so the postage was almost three shillings.

Eloise started with news about Mabel's niece and nephew, Lily the elder, now eleven and George at eight, three years younger. They were all doing well. Pietr had a couple of health scares but was recovering well and they were due to move into a larger house of 12 bedrooms. The number had been emphasised for Mabel's benefit.

Reading this now did not make Mable jealous at all, though it would have before. She would never trade what she now had for a large, cold mansion back home. How odd she could finally admit this. She had grown to love Conquerabia and the lifestyle it provided. Mabel was pleased that her sister was doing well and sounding happy. The letter also contained a lot of society information, Eloise being Eloise. Mabel could recall most of the names from living in Antwerp. It now felt such a long time ago.

Eloise tucked the hard news in the middle of the letter. She was sorry to report their father had passed earlier in the year from a lung condition, consumption, that made him bed-ridden for most of the illness. Greetje had cared for him as best she could. It was advised that Henck be sent to the coast, should the sea air aid his rehabilitation, but it was at the coast he died, too weak to even get out of bed.

Eloise continued with her news, saying that their mother became frail and could no longer walk without a stick. After their father died she moved in with them so she could be near her grand-children. Mabel thought that finally Greetje was able to live without constantly serving her husband's whims and demands and was able to enjoy some rest, and particularly she enjoyed her grand-children. Greetje made it to Lily's confirmation and the party afterward and peacefully passed away that night. Eloise expressed her feeling that Greetje's passing, after having been part of their special day, meant that their mother died happy.

Although the news of her mother passing upset Mabel, she was not distraught. She had long understood her parent's relationship was not based on love. She had wanted to speak to Greetje about how she had been able to gain more equality in her marriage but that would have been to betray the reason they moved to the Spanish Antilles. If that came out, the scandal on all members of the family, and by extension Pietr, would have been abhorrent. Mabel was comfortable with having kept their secret, and thus protecting those close to her. She contemplated returning to Holland to visit, but the voyage of many weeks there and back was enough to persuade her otherwise. She was sorry that Eloise had to deal with their parent's loss without her. At least she had Pietr around for comfort.

A cloud descended upon Mabel and she felt inclined to walk back to the house. Both her parents gone, her life in Holland now truly gone, and her life here? Certainly things were good, but there was always a sense of something missing. Florian? Of course, but this couldn't be all there was to her feelings of ennui, could it? As she came up the few steps up from where she had been reclining she saw a man in the doorway of the carpentry building, wiping his brow, fanning his face, and was he watching her?

Suddenly she recognised him, Cornelius, the head carpenter. looking in her direction. When he realised Mabel had seen him, he lowered his eyes, as he should, but she did not feel outraged by his impertinent gaze. No, she felt .... could it be that she felt flattered? Her first instinct was to hurry inside and deny it all, as she did when she ripped up her drawing, startled at her attraction. But this time she went over to speak with him.

"Cornelius, is everything all right?" You look troubled."

"I'm sorry ma'am, I was just enjoying the view - not you". He stammered, feeling awkward because he had, in fact, been staring at her, "but the view across the lake. It looks so pretty today. I'm sorry ma'am." In truth, Mabel reclining, her white legs exposed as she dangled her feet in the lake, were beautiful. like Mabel was beautiful. Rumour was that her husband no longer shared her bed and he wondered why, since they were so cordial. How could a man resist her?

Mabel couldn't help noticing the muscles in his arms, glistening with perspiration. He was handsome, for a negro, she thought to herself. He had rather fine features. His face was round, perhaps more oval shaped, she considered. His eyes, that odd smokey blue, were framed with long, gently curled eyelashes. His nose was only slightly wide and it didn't detract from his good looks. Certainly he had European blood.

Cornelius took the cloth he was using to fan himself and wiped the sweat from his chest and neck. To Mable it was as if she was watching him in slow motion. She felt slightly uncomfortable seeing a man, who is not her husband, in a state of undress, but why should she feel anything untoward observing the well formed torso of a young man? He was her young man. after all. Still, the only other naked male torso she had ever seen this close was Johan's, always pasty and pudgy, and even that image was from such a long while ago. Johan's skin was so dry and dull in comparison to Cornelius' firm glistening black skin. And just below, his thin loose trousers. Startling herself, Mable shook her head and straightened her back.

"Yes, Cornelius. I agree, it is a lovely view and just dangling my feet in the lake was a real treat for me." Looking over through the building's entrance Mabel saw an item on the bench. "Is this the bureau for Johan?" Mabel crossed into the workshop, sensing that frisson of excitement between her and Cornelius. Marvelling at the bureau, Mabel ran her fingers over the smooth ebony wood.

"It is ma'am. Do you like it?" Cornelius put down the cloth he was holding and went to where he had been planing one of the bureau drawers', picking it up and extending his arm to show her. Mabel noted the muscles more than the drawer, the marks on his arms where he had cut himself, his large hand. He became aware of Mabel's gaze, he felt her eyes on him, he felt…did he?

"Tell me, Cornelius, how long did it take you to make the bureau? It's stunning." Mabel ran her fingers over its smooth facade and marquetry again.

Cornelius put the drawer down, surprised at the question and her attention. Then he dismissed whatever he thought he felt. His mistress was just interested in what he was doing. It thrilled him to think she approved but also made him uncomfortable. "Ma'am, I've been working on this for six long weeks now." He wondered about her sudden interest in his work. He picked up his plane and resumed smoothing the drawer. Mabel stayed, watching him. She noted the smooth movements of the muscles in his chest and arms, the grip of his fingers on the piece. With each forward motion he tensed and flexed. Unconsciously Mabel started breathing with his rhythm. She allowed herself to be lost in the moment. There was something arousing about Cornelius using the cloth to wipe away sweat, about him standing up tall to stretch his back at intervals and then looking at her for just a moment before returning to his rhythmic planing. He soon lost his self consciousness and simply continued working, aware of her there, silently observing, even enjoying her presence, until she abruptly left.

Back at the house she asked Tante to draw her a warm bath, slipped in and allowed herself to think about the unthinkable. The soap slid along every part of her body, her fingers slipped between her legs. A moment of shame came over her but it seemed only to arouse her more. She will, of course, repent. But she can never unfeel what she knew at her core. Tante stopped in her tracks hearing something odd, What was it? Was that her mistress or a bird?

Chapter 10

Florian graduated Cambridge with a first in mathematics and went on to pursue his dream to serve in the Royal Navy by training at the Royal Naval Academy in Portsmouth, where he was in his second year. The sea air exhilarated him. He was a natural on the water and was well liked by his superiors and peers. He was one of forty looking forward to their assignments.

It had been a particularly long day practising drills on deck under an overcast sky that finally let loose a deluge, sending them scrambling. They thought they might wait it out but no luck. It was relentless. Florian headed back to his lodgings drenched through, tired and eager to eat.

He walked up the hill to his residence. It was nicer than his former residence in Cambridge, one he had grown to love, but this 'home' was more comfortable. Florian's room was at the top of the house. It was spacious, despite the eaves which meant he had to duck walking around them but with windows at the front and back, he was virtually surrounded with views of the orchard behind and the town, looking across the rooftops at the front. His bed was in the centre of the room so he could stand by it without restriction. It was also cheaper to rent than his last place and he was entitled to breakfast and dinner for the price. He was spoiled by his landlady who adored her handsome tenant. He was clearly her favourite and would demonstrate so by the addition of extra meat or vegetables or a top up of ale at mealtimes.

Unusually, tonight the house was empty. He was one of three men lodging there. All of them in the academy, like him, but they didn't seem to be about, and there was no sign of his landlady. She must be out shopping or maybe doing something at the church? She was devout, he thought to himself.

When he got to his room he could see his landlady had been in. On the desk was a tray with a plate of food covered with a silver cloche. Florian lifted it to see boiled chicken, cabbage and mashed potato. It was still warm. There was an additional small tray which contained a letter. The handwriting was familiar as was the seal. He shucked his wet clothes and donning his robe, he sat in the wooden carver. It was the only chair in the sparsely furnished room that was not adorned with scattered clothes. He dragged it across the wooden floor to be closer to the fire.

He ran the letter sheets through his fingers, imagining, as he had done since he was a child. There was always a childlike excitement, receiving a letter from his mother, and he always imagined that she was there speaking with him in person. He expected the usual newsy froth:

My dearest seun, Florian,

I hope this letter finds you well and you are continuing to enjoy life at the Naval Academy. You must be nearing the end of your two year sea training. Your father and I are eager to hear of your activities since your last letter, and of course to find out where they will be sending you. There is always so much to catch up on. We are so very proud of you.

Conquerabia is thriving! Your father has been acquiring more land and we have expanded significantly. Our labour has been healthy and increasing apace accordingly. Your father and his longtime manager, Diego Manancala, are as busy as always, which is why I am writing to you now. Though both your father and Diego are well and act as though time doesn't apply to them, and this is a trait I hope that you inherit from your dear Papa, I can't help thinking about their ages. I know I worry too much, and Johan would be angry for my saying so, but your father is starting to slow down, although he refuses to admit it.

Please do not misunderstand what I am going to say and please do not think I am asking you to forgo your Naval aspirations, but I am concerned about your father.

As you know the plantation is yours to inherit. Johan fondly speaks about the idea of the two of you working side by side but we both understand your Naval career is paramount. However I can see it is taking its toll on him. I know Johan would never ask you to give up your first calling, but I hope you will consider coming as soon as your second year is over?

None of us is getting any younger. Diego is still managing the plantation and overseeing the mechanical parts of the estate alongside his 17 year old son. Diego isn't ready to retire, and I suspect your father isn't either, but the truth about the future is clear. He is going to need you.

Furthermore we are concerned about potential uprisings, as other islands have experienced, as the abolitionists movement gains momentum. News does get around. So far things are peaceful here, as the Spanish Governor understands the special circumstances on this island and maintains generous freedoms for the imported labour. Your father has a very good relationship with his labourers. Still the rumblings we're hearing about Saint Domingue is a concerning complication that adds to the managing an enterprise like our beautiful Conquerabia.

I am exceedingly proud of you, and I love reading about your successes and grand plans while you are serving in the Navy, but please remember that Conquerabia is here waiting for you in your future.

You have much to learn about this place, your heritage, and your loving parents are longing to see and teach you about life in the Spanish Antilles, eventually the home for you and your own family.

Godspeed, dear one,

Mama

Conquerabia

Caroni

Spanish Antilles

20th March 1797

Florian stared into the distance with a mixture of sorrow and disbelief as he absorbed the seriousness of his mother's letter.

There was a knock on the door. Consumed with the letter, he forgot he'd made an appointment with a frequent lady companion, Ellie. He let her in as he didn't want to attract unwanted attention from the landlady or housemates, but he barely acknowledged her entrance. Florian sat and stared into the distance. The letter in his left hand, dangling towards the floor.

Ellie moved to the bed and as she passed Florian she ran her fingers gently through his hair and smiled at him playfully. He looked up at her, angered.

“Florian, what's wrong? Is it bad news? She undressed, figuring he'd want her attention sooner or later.

“Mainly”. He got up, pacing across the floor rubbing his head and talking out loud. “Where do my loyalties lie?” Ellie wasn’t usually privy to anything more than his amorous attentions and did not know how to respond. Florian turned and looked at her, or rather through her. “My mother has written .... my father ...” The realisation sinking in.

“Florian, I'm so sorry.” Ellie felt awkward, not knowing if she should stay or leave him. “Come, sit here.” She added seductively.

“I have been trying to follow what’s been going on in the Spanish Antilles.” Still pacing up and down, he reasoned to himself. “My parents moved there many years ago for reasons I have never understood and they made a life for themselves there, but they left me here. I was raised here. They have prospered under Spanish rule, but I feel I owe a lot to England for the life I have enjoyed here. I signed up to the Royal Navy, a boyhood dream of longing to belong.” He looked in Ellie’s direction. She didn’t matter to him right now.

“I, I don’t understand … .“ Ellie’s voice trailed off.

“I’m Belgian by birth. Florian shouted at her. “but have lived here most of my life. I feel my loyalties are being tested. I owe England more than I could give it, but I also owe my parents as much. I am torn … .”

“Don’t be daft. You need to go where the money is.” Ellie had priorities.

"How dare you?" He repeated, raising the letter at her, took some coins from his coat pocket flung over the chair and tossed them on the bed. "Get your things and go. Now!"

Ellie climbed off the bed and wrapped the sheet around her. She stood up tall, the sheet draped around her making her look statuesque. In that moment Florian was struck by her beauty, but more pressing things were on his mind and he turned to stare at the flames in the fireplace, resting his elbow on the mantelpiece. He looked deeper into the dancing flames.

"Will I see you again Florian? He did not respond; too engrossed in his own thoughts.

As Ellie wrapped her coat around her, she picked up the coins and threw them into her purse. Florian did not move when she walked over and kissed his cheek... He watched her leave his room. He was filled with a sense of determination but he needed guidance. He picked up a folder, sat back down and devoured his food. It was now cold but he did not care. He read through the pages and made copious notes.

Florian rose with the sun and the birds. He saw the letter on the desk where he placed it the night before, thought about the commitment he made to himself, and dressed. As he read it, he reassured himself the message in his mother's letter was clear, he was going to have a lot to learn about before he would be ready to take over Conquerabia. His father and his manager Diego were getting older. He had to see what could be done as a matter of urgency, even if he had to pay his way out of service.

He left his room with the folder and letter. He walked out of the house and he did not hear his landlady call out about breakfast or see her usual smiling face. He went directly to the Academy, knocked on his tutor's door, and he closed the door behind him as he entered

The community of the Royal Naval Academy is a small one, the reach of the British Navy is vast, and empire building countries like Great Britain, Belgium and Spain map their conquests on information provided by the banks, who run the world. Florian Dottin was about to become the embodiment of this convergence.

The Admiralty in London was in need of qualified and capable men to protect Britain's interests in the West Indies. His tutor at the Academy grew up with the now Captain Strong who occupied a position of procurement and knew where materials were being moved. The two dined after Florian's visit to his tutor and Captain Strong recommended a letter of introduction be despatched swiftly to Captain Woodriff, Transport Agent in Southampton, who knew everyone.

Less than two months later Florian was summoned to his tutor's office and was handed a letter which contained instructions. Florian was appointed a midshipman bound for Britain's latest empire foray, to eventually arrive at the very island where his parents had gone so many years earlier. He had around ten days to get his affairs together and report to the Transport Agent, but first he had to go to Captain Strong's tailor to have his uniform fitted.

The garments came together in an efficient Naval manner. His cutaway coat with its stand collar adorned with white tabs, over his white shirt and trousers with its button cuffs transformed him. As he stood in front of the mirror admiring his reflection, he was filled with pride. He also longed for his mother to see him, if only for her to feel proud of her only son. He knew in his heart, he made both his parents proud. Above all, he felt proud to be English by education! His boyhood dream was coming true.

-o0o-

Florian arrived at Southampton to a yard throbbing with activity. It was a scene reminiscent of the images he had seen in books and newspapers. His romantic notion of service at sea, born from his exciting childhood seaboard passage to England, stirred him still.

Florian lived most of his life far away from his parents, who thought it best he should not visit due to the long voyages, which would take more than half the year there and back, and his education was their priority, so Florian spent holidays with legal guardians in England or summers with his grandparents and aunt in Belgium. He knew his mother mostly through her letters. It is she who kept the line of communication going and it is she who wrote of Johan, who was a distant memory.

Florian felt a sense of unease at the prospect of meeting his parents in person again after so long. How should he greet them upon first meeting? Should it be a formal handshake or a full on embrace?

These thoughts and more occupied his mind as he stepped out of the carriage that was dropping him off to his destiny. The sea air hit him, he breathed in deeply, squared himself, and started looking for signs to the Transport Agent's office. When he arrived there were two men ahead of him and he did not have to queue for long.

"I'm here to report to Captain Woodriff." The surly older man at the desk signalled for him to sit on the bench.

"He'll be back. On errand," was his brusque reply. Florian nodded at the two men already sitting there. They nodded back. They sat in silence, Florian took out the local paper he just purchased and scrolled down the list of departures. One of the other men shuffled his feet with apparent unease.

Before long a man rushed in, his uniform rustling, his coat tails flapping behind him. It was Captain Woodriff. He picked up some papers from the table and without looking up he called out their names.

"Midshipman Florian Dottin. Cadet Rogers, Cadet Boston?" All three men stood. "You are booked in at the Partridge Inn, where you will be given your papers for your respective ships. Cadets Rogers, Boston can you read?" It was not patronising but the mark of a man who was all too familiar with the low level of literacy with many of the cadets.

“Yes Captain.” Rogers replied. Boston nodded.

“Then, if you have questions, please ask me now. Once I send you away to your lodgings for the night, you are under the charge of the ship's captain. Understand?” Again, the same responses from the cadets. “Then, you are dismissed. Midshipman Dottin, please wait.”

Florian watched the two men head off with their sacks over their shoulders. The younger lad appeared tearful but was encouraged to be strong by Cadet Rogers.

“Midshipman Dottin. Welcome to Southampton. Trained in Portsmouth, did you? So you are familiar with the area.”

“Thank you, Captain Woodriff. I’m not as familiar as I hoped. I had to ask to find you.”

Woodriff was chatty. “You will be sailing with Rear Admiral Henry Harvey and the fleet in a few days, then. Good man. Lucky to serve with him. Will teach you all you need to know about the Navy. And it seems you’ll join Lieutenant General Ralph Abercromby in the West Indies as well. Hmmm. Such a stellar company. That’s a lot of battle experience the King is sending off. It gives one pause. No matter. You’re to report directly to your ship, The Prince of Wales. It’s out to the harbour so someone will have to ferry you over. It’s that one there.” He pointed in the direction of a group of 18 ships of varying sizes, all looking majestic. "I gather you're going to be responsible for several of the cadets too." This was news to Florian. "That'll keep you busy. Aside from your immediate superiors, who knows what sort of motley crew you'll be with, considering His Majesty's recruitment policies these days!" Woodriff, shaking his head, handed over the paperwork for Florian to read through.

Florian understood Woodriff's reference. The Royal Navy, the largest employer in the world, was in need of manpower. Men had been lost at sea due to battles, disasters, and then there were the inevitable deserters. His Majesty's Navy had taken to using press gangs as part of its recruitment strategy. This method drew plenty of unsavoury characters in addition to impoverished young boys and rag tag volunteers. Some of the younger boys cried, not wanting to be separated from their families, others were excited by the thought of the adventures they may have, and some were criminals escaping the law.

But now, papers in hand, Florian had just enough time to buy himself one last drink on land before joining his ship, and he wanted to savour every last moment of civilian life, and life as he knew it.

He set off to the same Inn Woodriff directed the cadets and ordered a Scottish Malt whiskey. He put his portmanteau under the table and spread the papers out. He would board his ship the following day and then depart for the West Indies three days later once all the victuals and other goods necessary for the journey were supplied. Then reality hit him. He may be leaving England for the final time. He looked around him, at the inn, his fellow drinkers. This may be his last night on English soil. He raised a toast to his homeland.

After he finished his drink he decided to walk back down to the dock to look at his ship. Other ships were being loaded with horses, military equipment and victuals. Each also carries the destinies of all aboard. He found the shore boat that would transport him away, turned and looked back at the harbour. A wealth of emotions went through him and he blew a kiss to the land that informed and made him. A new era was beckoning and he was eager for the exciting new experience.

-o0o-

It was the 15th November 1797 and the first few weeks sailing across the ocean went smoothly. The weather was relatively calm for a couple of days, but nothing threatening the ship and its crew, and when they reached Grenada Florian joined his new commission.

The Prince of Wales was a gun ship of the line, a war ship, the type favoured by admirals needing a vessel useful for both battles and naval tactics. The three gun decks had an assortment of armament including various sized powder guns and cannons. When Florian saw the colours flying proudly on the quarter deck behind the main mast his patriotic heart swelled with pride and broke with grief.

Rear Admiral Henry Harvey was a veteran of many battles for territory, and a blasted debacle in the former American colonies. Experience made him stern and efficient in his work and he expected the same efficiency from all of his crew. He was joined by Commander Ralph Abercromby, in charge of the vessel along with 10,000 troops scattered among 18 other ships, ready for deployment.

On occasion when duty and weather allowed, the ship's surgeon, the lieutenants, and privileged midshipmen, like Florian, were invited to dine with the upper-crust, French educated Harvey, and the Scotsman Abercromby, often held court. Abercromby told ribald tales that had the men roaring with laughter, especially when granted the odd whiskey or rum. On other occasions, Florian would join the other midshipmen and young cadets in the mess hall for meals of meat, beer and ship's biscuits or 'negroes heads', a term he disliked.

On rare occasions libation loosened the more reserved Harvey's tongue, he could also be rather indiscreet talking about members of the Admiralty and certain politician's of the time, sometimes even divulging insider stories. These occasions allowed Florian to gather important knowledge about British colonial aspirations. Most of his higher level shipmates were to the manor born, that they were born to Army and Navy families and he was somewhat intimidated, but his Cambridge education provided Florian with a near level playing field, and as time went on he became more comfortable in their company. He did not, however, allow himself to become as drunk as his colleagues. He did not particularly like feeling out of control and his restraint provided him with useful knowledge and he observed discretion.

Since his behaviour was exemplary, he was respected and often became party to key information, since his superiors felt he could be trusted. Florian was shown how to study the maps, which interested him greatly and became the unofficial deputy to the captain.

Florian was busy and anxious. With this much fire power and these many troops, Florian knew this was no casual manoeuvre, but during his time off he had so much else to think about. Mabel often featured in his thoughts. It had been so many years since they last saw each other that he couldn't clearly remember her face. He was concerned for her well-being and his fathers' but he did not know either of them, really. Her letters were whom he knew, a page or two at a time, until this last one asking him to come. Who would she be in person?

He thought of Johan's legacy that he would one day be expected to protect and expand - Conquerabia. Would he make his father proud as he learned by his side? Would life on the plantation fulfil him? His obligations to his parents weighed heavily on him. And how would he find them as people? His memories of Johan and Mabel from his childhood were now faded, though pleasant, and the occasional letters were of the success they were making there. There was nothing personal. Still his feelings about his parents were warm.

Suddenly Florian's musings were broken by shouting from above. He went on deck to find out what the commotion was about.

Chapter 11

Presiding over a small dinner party and a few drinks into the evening, Governor Don José María Chacón was feeling proud of the state of his island. Previous governors failed because they attempted to impose order using hubris and force. For this to work required cultural and racial homogeneity and an unquestioning adherence to entrenched class roles, all distinctly absent in the Antilles.

Chacon saw this would never work on an island with so many cultural backgrounds, so many mixed races, and so many levels of personal freedom. You could never put free black or mulatto slave owners on a different class level than white slave owners. It would be a fool's errand to attempt to restrict their rights on account of race since there were so many race mixes here. There were free men who came from free men. This was not Spain. Try to govern them using the European model and they would look at you askance, say, "¡Y tú quién te crees?" Who do you think you are? Then sabotage your crops, drive you off and trip you as you run away.

He chuckled to himself, proud of his cleverness. His skill at negotiating the special situation of the Spanish Antilles' disparate inhabitants included reimagining regulations about the treatment of slaves. Compared to the Draco Code laws about the treatment of enslaved persons in other places, where sadism ruled, Chacon adopted rules about slavery that were positively enlightened, by comparison, and the colony prospered under his governorship. The spectacular success and profitability here since his instalment as Governor in 1783 proved his instincts true. While nearby islands had slave revolts, things were peaceful here in the Spanish Antilles. He felt confident about the internal political stability on his island.

And as for any outside military threats? Chacon looked across the table, well satisfied that he had this covered as well. His dinner guest, Rear Admiral Don Sebastián Ruiz de Apodoca, had recently arrived with his fleet of 12 vessels: the San Vincent, the Gallardo and the 74 gun Arrogante and the 36 gun San Tomaso anchored in the Gulf of Paria. Chacon felt secure.

At the beginning of the desert service Chacon was presented with a message on a silver salver. He opened it, read it, blinked twice, composed himself, rose, and smiling said. "Admiral Apodoca we have some naval housekeeping to attend to, I have been informed that British vessels are situated in the Gulf, not far from the fleet." Apodaca stood as the severity of what he had heard sunk in.

"Querido Dios! We must get to the port immediately." Apodoca saluted the Governor and raced on horseback back to the port. Where he convened the officers Apodaca issued instructions for the British vessels to be engaged and sunk, taking no prisoners.

An officer on deck, Captain Gabriel Sororido, stood up, saluted his Admiral and requested to speak. "Admiral, I do not think we can over power them. A scouting patrol counted the British fleet at 17 or 18 armoured ships probably carrying many thousands of troops. We are no match for that level of artillery, nor can the army defend against that many invaders on shore. We will be little more than cannon fodder. With great respect. I urge you to rethink this strategy."

Admiral Apodoca knew Captain Sororido made sense and would have the support of the other captains. Trying to wage a defence under these circumstances made him feel at risk of mutiny. After a quick assessment of his options, the Admiral stood tall, drew in a deep breath, and walked back to the long table. With a turn of his wrist he bid them sit down and laid out his plan to the captains. They had no time to waste. It was going to be a long night.

-o0o-

Ralph Abercromby awoke to the knock on his cabin door. He tied his robe together and headed out onto the deck where he joined several of his men and Admiral Harvey watching the warm glow of fire in the distance. Standing on deck not far behind Captain Harvey were the midshipmen, including Florian Dottin, staring out at the orange glow in the distance.

"Who did this?" Abercromby asked Harvey.

"I don't believe it is any one of us. I gave no command to set fire to the fleet. You gave no command to attack. Did those Spanish bastards set their ships on fire themselves?" Harvey was incredulous.

Abercromby shook his head. “It’s a distraction. They’re up to something. It doesn’t make sense, destroying their own ships? Leaving the harbour defenceless? We need to act quickly and get to the mainland. We need to capture Trinidad. I’ll send a full complement.”

Looking at the conflagration in the harbour through his scope, Harvey scratched his head. “Be careful, it could be a trap.”

Fully loaded vessels set sail towards Gasparee and Portes des Espana. Thick smoke hung heavily in the warm early morning air, as explosions lit up the dark sky. Abercromby’s men were set for full scale war but when they arrived on Gasparee the only men there were civilians. Cautiously Abercromby redirected them to search for the marines and army on the mainland and they headed into Maraval. To their surprise their advance was not met with the confrontation they were expecting. They incurred only a single casualty. With an almost disappointing lack of fanfare, they claimed the island for the King.

-o0o-

“I, Ralph Abercromby, on behalf of His Majesty King George III, I have the honour of installing you, Thomas Picton, to the office of the Governor of the British crown colony, the Island of Trinidad, It is your responsibility to govern the island and its peoples and to represent His Highness in all areas. Exercise justice as your conscience dictates. God save the King.”

Picton saluted Abercromby, who returned the gesture. With that Thomas Picton, formerly a Lieutenant-General, became the first British Governor of Trinidad.

"Gentlemen," a beaming Abercromby turned to the assembled crowd, which included midshipman Florian Dottin, "May I present to you the Most Excellent Governor Thomas Picton!" Then Abercromby started clapping, quickly joined by the rest of those present, each of them aware of the enormity of what had taken place. First the effortless routing of the Spanish, then Abercromby's decisive action to install Picton as the island's governor. Florian and the rest knew they had witnessed an historical moment.

The ceremony was mercifully brief in the dunning heat, plus there was a lot at stake. The rapid change of regimes left no time for Abercromby or anyone in charge to fully plan a transition of power. As the group dispersed to enjoy a few refreshments and to loosen their too warm clothing, Abercromby, speaking solely to Picton, returned to the business at hand.

"I leave with you the Articles of Capitulation, Governor Picton." Picton enjoyed how the emphasis on his title made him feel. "I have appointed John Nihell Chief Judge and I've asked several local patriots experienced in the laws of the land to aid you in understanding the status quo around here. Until then it's impossible to know how best to make this island serve the Crown."

Both Abercromby and Picton knew that the Spanish capitulation was stunningly quick. To avoid confusion and unrest among this unknown population, Trinidad, though now under the British flag, would need to retain Spanish laws for the foreseeable future, allowing Picton time to decide on what new rules and transitions his version of government would take.

"I look forward to learning of your plans, once you have had a chance to determine what needs to be done. Harvey will leave enough armed vessels to help deter the French but the rest of us must soon set sail for Martinique, once our victuals and supplies are restocked."

Another salute was exchanged and Abercromby left the Governor's house in San Jose with his men, each on horseback. Their hooves kicked up the dust as they drummed away on the dirt path.

It was now entirely up to Picton to strategise. As methodical as he was, and as ambitious as he was, this was not exactly the career path he planned. His was a life devoted to service in the Royal Navy, a role at which he excelled and one he imagined he would continue fulfilling, until now. He may have vaguely toyed with entering the political arenas one day, true enough, but in England, not this godforsaken furnace in the ocean.

Nonetheless, he liked the sound of Most Excellent Governor Picton, He repeated it several times in his mind. When Picton heard the horses' hooves trail off in the distance, he sat down in the chair nearest to him, put his booted foot on the stool, undid his collar and shirt buttons, and started to assess the momentous changes in his life and those he would make in this island kiln.

The unexpectedly swift capitulation of the Spanish made getting a leave of absence easier than Florian anticipated. As soon as he got free he planned to travel to the plantation he had never seen and the mother and father he barely remembered. The long voyage, the historic military success he has been a part of, and the historical statesmanship resulting in the expansion of the British Empire paled compared to the dramatic reunion he was about to have. He felt as excited as a boy. How would they react towards him? How should he behave towards them? Should they embrace? But they were virtually strangers. Nonetheless, at this moment his heart felt a longing for a mother's embrace.

He headed to a nearby livery to hire a carriage. The driver asked where he wanted to go. "The plantation Conquerabia in Caroni. I have business there. Do you know it?"

"Everyone knows Conquerabia. I'll be happy to make that journey for you," The carriage rode off at a gentle pace allowing Florian to take in his surroundings.

"Sir. I've been wondering about how things are at the grand old place. Things are so unsettled there…." He trailed off.

"Yes, well the change of flags certainly has been abrupt, but I wouldn't worry about too many changes for the plantations. I don't believe things will change too much. Your new Governor Picton is a Royal Navy man. He will want things to be stable." Florian thought the driver needed reassurance.

The driver shook his head. "It's not about the Governor, Sir. People have been speculating about what's going to happen now that old Master Dottin passed on, I hear of apoplexy. Sad Mrs. Lady there alone now with that whole place and the people…" He trailed off again.

In shock, Florian barely noticed the verdant land which rolled out ahead of him. His father, dead? Dead? His ears were ringing so loud he couldn't hear another thing the driver was saying. He sucked in air then forgot to breathe for a moment. It was hard to make sense of things now. He sank into an emotional quagmire. He was hoping for a family reunion and then years of learning about the plantation. He sat in stunned silence.

Then he remembered that his poor mother was there, alone, and she had expressed concerns about the uprisings on other islands. Her fears may well be founded in fact. Several bloody slave revolts had occurred on neighbouring islands.

But Florian also knew that slave laws were different here. His parents were keen on telling him in letters that Conquerabia was nothing like the cruel plantations he may have heard about and that he shouldn't believe the stories. The Antilles was different. Their laws forbid slave abuse and in fact some Negroes and coloured people even owned slaves themselves!

But now all he could think about was that he was going to Conquerabia without knowing what he'd find, save that his father was gone and he would certainly be expected to take over a completely unknown business without a scintilla of experience. And was there something ominous in his driver's comment about things being unsettled there? What did he say? "Sad Mrs. Lady there alone now with that whole place and the people…" What did that mean?

After uncounted hours of riding in the tropical swelter, Florian finally saw an impressive house rise on the horizon. A high arch with the plantation's name was the gateway to a different world, one without his father forever and one with a widowed mother he hardly knew. Conquerabia. It had been nothing but a name before. He asked his driver to stop some distance away so that he could take it all in and compose himself. It was larger than he envisaged from his mothers letters. He saw a building with smoke billowing out of the chimney and a sweet smell hung in the air. He could hear men's voices calling to each other and the laughter of children playing.

He alighted from the carriage so he could walk under the arch, studying its ironwork, and to absorb all that he could in that special moment. A gentle breeze danced through the trees. When he got to the verandah he saw a woman, dressed in black, rocking in a chair.

He stepped up the stairs, a board creaked, and the lady sat up, startled. Her expression was initially of fear. She did not know this tall stranger. Then Florian said, simply, "Mother" and she stood up to greet her son, slowly and awkwardly for a moment but then rushing to embrace him, holding him tight in disbelief as tears ran down her face. Her only son was home. Finally,

Chapter 12

Those heady first days of capitulation soon melted into weeks and then months of Picton learning about this place. His governorship was a possible sure line to getting a knighthood, or so he thought. He had little knowledge of the island or its people. All he knew was the way in which Britain was organised and adopted some of those rules to help run his government.

He soon became friends with the French planter John Nihall, appointed to his office by Ralph Abercromby. Saint Hilaire Bergorrat, a French creole immigrant who was also a prominent planter, would join him. Bergorrat was an educated man and republican whom Picton admired, especially since he discovered Bergorrat's deep hatred for freed coloureds, and with his ear to the top, Bergorrat warned Picton about the agitation and bloody nature of the maroons in nearby Saint Domingue and Jamaica. A quick promotion followed and Picton appointed him as Registrar to the Cabilda becoming part of Picton's inner circle. He would later entrust the revision of the Code Noir to this ally.

It did not take long for Thomas Picton's dictatorial nature and volatile temper to emerge. The islanders, used to the relative leniency of their Spanish Governor, didn't like Picton's stern approach nor were they accepting of the military style rule he imposed. In this land with free coloured people and indigenous folks who had intermingled with white sailors for hundreds of years, his decidedly draconian views of proper treatment of slaves and coloured folk, free and native, seemed misguided. Many islanders expected Picton would soon adopt the island ways like all of the other overly formal European settlers did. It was too hot to do otherwise.

But to Picton there was not now, and never would be, anything appealing about the loose decorum and utter lack of deference of the coloured people toward the white people here, regardless of whether the coloured people were owned or free. In fact, that there were free darkies made him even more uneasy. He distrusted them all.

And he wasn't sure about most of the white settlers here either, with good reason. He could tell they didn't like him. Used to more relaxed island rhythms, many bristled at Picton's rigidity. But Picton wasn't just an iron rule lover. He was an iron ruler. He knew change was rarely welcome and force was the most efficient way to make it happen.

It was a lesson he learned early in his career. As a new Captain he was required to inform the Seventy-Fifth Regiment he was disbanding their divisions. Instead of respecting his new authority Picton was met with internal rebellion. He clamped down, identified the ringleaders and ended what could have been a mutiny. The perpetrators were dealt with decisively and without mercy. It was the only way to prevent anyone having the idea of trying to question his command or his resolve ever again.

And it didn't matter whether they liked it or not. With Bergorrat he was informed of the growing number of slave uprisings against the French overlords in nearby Saint Domingue and other colonised islands. He suspected they all tried to govern under something like the overly permissive Code Noir, which Picton's passive predecessor Chacon enacted Surely it was the lack of respectful fear which emboldened darkies in Saint Domingue. Those damned French were entirely too lenient with dissent and look what's happening there! Dear God, the monarchs are in the hands of the rabble.

Swift preemptive action was required. He spent all day at his desk, barely touching the foreign foods offered, roasted sweetcorn and fried chicken. Corn! Food for pigs. The weak Spanish Code Noir, with all its slave mollycoddling, was thoroughly revised. Once enacted, plantation owners could reclaim the right to exert whatever necessary beatings on their lazy negroes they felt appropriate. How else but through fear could the slaves be made to submit?

A few days later he assembled the Cabilda to outline his revisions. He was met with resistance to a number of laws he hoped to introduce, some fearing such radically severe changes to the current island "demasiado indulgente" were ill-considered. They feared the sort of revolt that seemed to be sweeping the nearby islands, indeed the whole world! Marie Antoinette was headless!

Abolitionist thought had been cultivating for decades. Had Picton not heard the news?

The meeting went on for several hours. He needed more support for his orders and eventually his frustration got the better of him. Picton flew into a rage, throwing over the table and its contents to a stunned silence. He ordered everyone to leave. His head throbbed, his back ached, the infernal heat made his clothing damp and uncomfortable and more than anything, he was alone.

Picton needed some air and walked to the verandah. Fanning himself, he placed his foot up onto the verandah's wall, resting his elbow on his knee. What was wrong with these God damned people? Didn't they realise that the mixed and classless natives were too comfortable. They no longer respected the sovereigns and the rights of the ruling class. They had all been infected by this island's apathy. Can't they read the writing on the walls of rebellion? Can't they see that without more authority they will lose every advantage the King's Navy shed blood to achieve?

He huffed with satisfaction at his new power over civilian life, something he never had before. Things were surely going to change around here. Things needed to change.

Then something caught his eye, a young woman, barely more than a girl, carrying pails of water with the aid of a milkmaid's yoke, walking back towards the nearby barn.

Tall and lithe, Rosetta Smith, humming softly to herself, was unaware she was being watched as she laboured under the weight of the sloshing buckets. Picton noticed the tendons of her slender neck bulging from the strain of carrying the water as she walked, keeping her balance and trying not to spill. There was a gracefulness about her gait even now, so encumbered. With her arms up over the yolk, he could see the outline of her high firm breasts, so taut still that they barely moved as she stepped. He absently wondered if she was still pure.

He felt a familiar awakening and was shocked that his lust was stirred. No, of course not, he thought about both his desire being aroused by a coloured girl and then the ridiculous possibility of her being still untouched. With that thought, he adjusted the crotch of his trousers and went back into the office to finish up for the day.

He made a note to finalise the new order that required citizens to swear allegiance to King George III of Britain and its Governor, Thomas Picton. Soon, the first laws would change and then more amendments would be made to the Spanish laws to make them fully British. Everything would be focused on behalf of the interests of the crown and legislated by Picton, further enhancing his influence. He was relishing such power.

Such was the appeal of Trinidad that by 1789, the population of the island had grown to more than 9,012. Sugar cane crops were abundant, as were cotton, indigo, molasses and rum. Trade between the islands, Spain and Europe was profitable.

Picton stretched. He had a strong drink and changed into his civilian attire. Before he arrived he had not been able to understand the local men's predilection for mulattos, but now he was able to see how these island seductresses lured decent men to their beds. He decided to go into town to that tavern near the harbour. What was the name of that place? Mirian's was it? Perhaps he would seek out some pleasure.

Chapter 13

Central in the lives of the slaves on Conquerabia was the longhouse, a combination of dormitory for the single slaves and a general meeting space for all workers. It was a communal building, split into three sections, built upon a stone foundation with brick columns, sturdier than most buildings to withstand the frequent storms. It was used for all manner of things, like the weekly Catholic masses the Spanish required they attend. The space was open so that breezes could flow through but the doorways could be reinforced and boarded up against strong winds.

The men's sleeping area was divided off by a wooden wall, more of a functional divider than reinforcement. In spite of the wattle and daub used to fill it in, it had minor holes where the younger children picked at it or had knocked it with stick toys. Next to that, in the centre, which also formed the main entrance, was a spacious communal area.

It was in this area that Evalina gave her weekly lessons to the younger children. She told the keepers she was giving Bible lessons and she did it to help keep them distracted so their parents could work more. In truth, she could not bear keeping the children in the ignorant and submissive state that some of the white plantation owners wanted to keep them all in. The Bible study was a ruse she used to be able to share her book knowledge when they weren't being observed.

Evalina didn't feel right keeping her privilege to herself. On Conquerabia, for some reason, she and a few other slaves, mainly lighter skinned house slaves, had been given lessons and been taught to read, but they were discouraged from sharing their knowledge with other "lesser" slaves. Some trotted the educated slaves out for guests and had them demonstrate their intelligence by having them recite poetry or read Bible passages, like trained circus animals.

Evalina understood more and more why the plantation owners would want to keep their slaves ignorant. The papers were filled with reports of far away peasant revolts and nearer slave rebellions. She understood the unhappiness and frustration of the poor and downtrodden. Her life on Conquerabia was relatively unchanged but the new Governor, Picton, was hated universally on the island for the draconian new laws he enacted and the cruelty of the enforcements. Gossip had it that he was brutal to everyone, not only the natives and slaves, but that he was especially vicious to coloured female slaves.

Today in the common area of the longhouse, about 20 brown skinned children were sitting cross legged on the floor, restless. Half of the room was already boarded up ahead of the storm they knew was coming because they had seen animals moving inland, away from the shore. The natives knew this indicated a storm was on its way.

Partly due to fear and the excitement of experiencing a severe storm and partly because they loved school, their eyes were bright and their attention was trained on their young teacher, the heavily pregnant Evalina.

"Trinidad was originally populated by various tribes like the Aracuas, Chaymas, Tamagagos, Cumanangotes and Nepuyos, who were mostly peaceful people. Some of these people might even be your ancestors. Can you imagine?" The children were interested in this. The children who were of native descent knew of tribal ancestors. Children whose ancestors were African had heard their family members speak about family far away or long gone. All were somehow aware that though their families may have come from different places originally, they were considered the same here — slaves.

"In some ways their lives were not so different from ours. For instance, their food was mainly cassava and cascadura from the rivers and chip chip from the coastline, just like we enjoy today." Some of the children uttered 'Umm" and made delicious sounds with their mouths. They all enjoyed eating the familiar fish and the tasty root vegetables.

"What happened to them?" A voice from the back piped up.

This was a difficult question for Evelina to answer. The oral history of the island told a terrible story. How do you explain an invasion and social domination to people so young? How do you explain being violently ripped from your homeland and shipped into slavery? How do you speak honestly about slavery to slave children? Certainly they notice that white children have better lives. And if you tell the truth, how long before you are punished and have to stop teaching them? Today she stuck to the script. They would learn the truth soon enough.

"A long time ago, in 1498, a man from Spain named Christopher Columbus came in a big ship all the way across the ocean in search of great riches and he found our island. He was looking for someplace else, a place called the Orient, but he found us first. After he came a lot of other people from across the ocean came. We don't know exactly what happened but we know that most of the people who were already here died.

Questions came from every corner. How did they die? Were they war ships like the ones that burned in the harbour? If they all died, where did we come from? Children are smart. They knew Evelina was holding back something. Evelina chose her words.

"No. They were exploring ships. He was the captain of three magnificent tall ships called the Vaquenos, the El Correo and the Santa Maria. All three set sail across the Atlantic, which is the sea surrounding our island. Can you imagine how long it took him to reach here?" Evelina pauses for effect. "It took about 70 days or so. Imagine that?"

"But Miss Evie," the same boy put his hand up. "Columbus doesn't sound like a Spanish name. Was he Spanish?"

"Well observed, Oscar. No, Christopher Columbus was from Genoa, in Italy. A country not too far from Spain. He gave the island the name "La Yslas De la Trinidad". What year are we in now, do you know Oscar? Does anybody know?" The children shook their heads and looked at each other, hoping one of them knew. Evelina arched her aching back as she sat on the bench and continued.

"We are in 1798. That means how many years ago did Columbus discover this island?" Another young boy of about 13 put his hand up and shook it in excitement.

"Me, Miss Evie. I know. I know."

"What is the figure, Joseph?" He proudly stood up, finished his mental calculation on his fingers and said without hesitation: "Miss Evie, it was three hundred years ago!" Joseph bowed his head confidently and sat down once again.

"Well done. You are right Joseph. Can you imagine what it would have looked like over three hundred years ago? This plantation certainly would not be here. There would have been more trees, shrubs and flowers. Now, remember the tribes I mentioned before, well they were attacked by the Caribs who arrived here from other islands. They were fierce people, they were cannibals.

"Miss what does "can-i-buls" mean?" Gabriella asked.

"It means they ate other people, not of their tribe." Some of the children pulled faces in disgust. Evelina continued.

"They lived in ajoupas, huts made out of palm leaves and wood, a bit like some of ours. They were circular in style with a round, pointed roof which they covered in palm leaves to protect against the elements. Some of us inhabitants of Trinidad may be direct descendants of them. Most of us, I understand, are of African descent due to our dark skins and tight curly hair. As you know, the Spanish bring people from Africa to work here. The Spanish have straighter black long and wavy hair, at least some of the ladies do. Most of us here speak Spanish. The language of our nation as the island belonged to Spain until two years ago when the island became British. Can any of you tell me what the name Trinidad means in Spanish?"

Once again she was met with silence and the children looked at each other. Outside the sky was darkening ominously and the wind was picking up. The lesson was no longer on their minds.

At the back of the room, Evelina looked up to see her sister Camila had arrived, along with a number of mothers. They all noticed the change in the weather, too, and they wanted to collect their children. Who knew what the winds portended? Camila could see the weariness in her sister's eyes but none of the children noticed. Undaunted, Evalina was determined to finish the lesson, regardless of what the winds were blowing in.

"La Trinita means 'the Trinity'. Columbus named the island after God, the Father and the Holy Spirit. You recall this from mass, don't you children? From Sunday School?"

"It is said that Columbus sailed up the Boca de la Sierpe, through the Gulf of Paria and along the Boca de Drago. As he approached the land in one of the three vessels, he saw the three mountains - the Trinity from which we get our country's name. Can anyone tell me what the original capital of Trinidad was called?" Evalina looked around at the children puzzled by the question. Joseph put his hand up about half way, then changed his mind, reluctant to put his hand up again, as he feared teasing by the other kids who thought him a know-it-all.

"Would anyone like to try? Anyone?" Evelina looked around, there was silence.

"Go on then Joseph, I think you may know the answer."

"Miss Evie. The original capital of Trinidad was San Jose. In 1757 Conquerabia, an Arawak name, meaning 'the place of the silk cotton trees', became the capital, which we used to refer to as Puerto des España, Miss". Evalina looked at Joseph with immense pride.

"How do you know this Joseph? You certainly are a font of information, aren't you"?

"Yes Miss. I read anything that I can get. Mr Elders lets me read the newspapers Master Dottin has finished with and some tracts that come to the plantation. He says he thinks that I am interested in history, Miss."

"I think he may well be right." As he sat back down, two of his friends slapped him on the back by way of congratulations and Evalina could see how thrilled he was to be correct with his knowledge, but she would have to talk to him about not letting the wrong people know he could read so well. Joseph was not a light coloured slave. His knowledge could be seen as a threat to the status quo. But she loved Joseph's intelligence and drive.

She rubbed her hand along her belly and wondered if her own child would grow to be as bright as Joseph. In that moment she felt it kick, almost in confirmation that she was right.

A branch of a nearby banana tree smashed against the boarded up window, jolting Evalina, back to reality. The wind whipped the building hard, and the roof rattled. The wind whistled through the gaps in the walls and a number of the younger children covered their ears in fear, and cried.

Evalina looked back at her sister and the women who were growing anxious about the weather. Their concern was to get the children out of harm's way.

"Well children, I will have to leave it there for the time being. We can pick this up next time. The children ran to their mothers or out the door, home. Though storms were common enough this time of year, somehow this one seemed different.

Evalina and Camila went to the doorway, looked and listened. Already some of the floor was wet where the rain was coming in. The single men came back to wait out the storm on their side of the longhouse but they began boarding up the centre before any more water from the deluge came in. Evalina and Camila sloshed through the puddles pooling on the floor to the women's side.

Once in their quarters, after they nailed boards behind the front shutters to make them stay closed against the wind, they moved to the windowless back room and Camila caught her sister up on the latest instructions. "We've been told to stay inside for the duration. Seems like they think it is going to be a bad storm. How are you feeling Evie?" Evalina was rubbing her swollen belly.

"I felt the child kick just now." She responded. "I think it may be as anxious as I am. Only a few more days to go. The child may be picking up on my fear, Camila. This is the worst weather I can recall and I pray God will help us get through it safely."

Camila looked at her older sister and saw how she had blossomed with impending motherhood. She offered her sister a banana leaf with cassava bread, chicken and okra. Evalina declined but Camila was hungry and ate.

"You need to keep your strength up. We don't know how long we're going to be here. I say until daybreak, easy. I have made up your cot for you to lie down when you're ready." Camila added.

"Oh, Camila, the bread looks good, but I just don't have any appetite for it. However, the cot does sound like something I can use, storm or not." Neither thought they would be able to sleep much through such a storm but at least they would be together.

-o0o-

The school day was not the only thing disrupted by the impending storm. Florian had to hurry about, securing as much as he could. He began by instructing the livery men to send the horses inland then he told the other workers to get to cover and stay there. He knew he had to get back to the house where his mother was waiting. She would be scared of the storm. By the time he reached the house, it had started to rain heavily, and the low cloud cover brought further darkness across the land. Tante, his housekeeper, arrived with a hurricane lamp for him.

"Mother? I'm here." He called out.

"Florian! I'm here in the front room." Mabel's voice sounded stronger than he thought it would. He imagined her to be shaking each time the door or windows rattled, in fear of the worst. Florian entered the room and sat in the armchair next to her and took her hand.

"It will pass, Mother, don't worry. We should be safe here. You can stop fretting. I'll be with you."

It was intended to be reassuring, and of course she was afraid during these storms. They were terrifying. However it came across as impatient and arrogant. And Mabel knew Florian had never experienced a tropical storm while she had lived through several. He had no idea.

In fact, he truly didn't know anything about the island or the underlying workings of the place or even why they were there! She hadn't told him about the arrangement between her and Johan, wanting to preserve his kind thoughts about his father, but she was sometimes tempted, especially as he had already become impatient with her over little things. It stung. She worked hard to be a full partner in Conquerabia before Johan died.

Florian saw he was too cross and bit his lip. He was tired from attending to the plantation; shoring up windows, doors, loose animals, and his negroes, but Mabel would not appreciate the work he did to keep her in the manner to which she was long accustomed. Oddly, the place was running more smoothly than he expected when he arrived, and Mabel was more acquainted with the ledgers and business side than he expected.

Florian brought a paper to distract himself while the house was being battered. He expected to find Mabel clutching a Bible but instead she had a rosary nestling on her lap and a copy of some odd book called A Vindication of the Rights of Women, by a Mary Wollstonecraft. He shook his head. What on earth could it be about, rights of women? Nonsense.

Then, with a crack of thunder and a flash of lightning their small individual grievances instantly disappeared, refocused by the immediate danger of the storm. Holding hands, by the light of the oil lamp, mother and son, finally reunited, silently prayed, trying to ignore the crashing thunder and the ominous banshee winds screaming around them. Roofing from nearby huts blew off and rocketed across space, crashing into the side of the house, along with branches and other debris thrown by the wind. Then there was a loud crash outside followed by vibrations that shook the house and jolted Florian and Mabel. Immediately they heard men shouting in the distance. Florian ran to look between the slats across the window, trying to see what was going on.

The pelting rain and the random leaves and debris blowing made it hard to see but it looked like the roof of the boiler and curing house had been blown in. The walls appeared to still be standing but he was concerned the roof collapse had damaged some of the sugar pots or boilers. He could not venture out to check. The winds were howling and demonic and the rain was like bullets, a weapon against anything in its way.

“I think the boiler and curing house have been hit.” No more explanation required. They both knew there was nothing anyone could do until the storm passed. He squeezed Mabel's hand and she was grateful for the reassurance. This time she knew it was genuine. Florian was beginning to understand the violence of these storms and that she wasn't being a silly woman. She was thankful for him being there with her.

Back in the longhouse, Camila was gently rubbing Evalina's back. Even without the fury of the storm outside Evalina was too far along and too uncomfortable to sleep and the storm made it terrifying, too. Camila could not sleep either. Perhaps this is an omen, Camilla thought to herself. She offered up a prayer and closed her eyes but was disturbed by the sound of the crash, nearby. Someone on the men's side yelled "The roof of the boiler is down!"

"I hope no one's hurt." Evalina, sitting on the end of the cot, looked at her sister anxiously. Camilla, took her hand and smiled her bravest smile. "You've got to rest up for both of you. Please, this is just nature being angry at the moment. It will pass."

Evalina shook her weary head and closed her eyes to pray, trying to find stillness within. Camila pulled across the nearby cot and lay down next to her sister. There was nothing else she could do. It was the fear of the unknown, but Camila had to be stronger for Evie's sake. The women held hands and waited.

The first cockerel's call woke a battered Conquerabia. The winds had calmed down and the rain stopped. It was already quite humid and soon, given a chance, the sun would dry the land. Camila peaked through the wooden plank across the window and saw the light from the sun, emerging through the clouds. Around it was a full circular rainbow. Camilla felt it was a good omen. Evalina's baby would be strong enough to live through all life's storms.

Florian awoke with a start and checked on Mabel as soon as his thoughts became lucid and he recalled what happened. She was asleep in the chair, where she sat all night. He got up and stretched and tiptoed out the door to allow his mother to continue her slumber. She stirred, but only to draw in a long deep breath and her chin sank to her chest.

Tante had been up for some time. The kitchen took a direct hit and flooded, so Florian found her tidying up and sweeping water out of the kitchen. Elders was out with the menfolk, clearing up outside. The land was unrecognisable as he looked across the horizon. The banana trees looked very sad as the tips of the heavy leaves were bent into the mud in the ground. The ripe Gros Michel's bananas were scattered all around, already covered with flies, and the indigo field over to his right was flattened, the purple flowers mashed into the mud. Some of the men in the distance were shouting to each other as a line had grown to discard the remnants of the boiler house. It was quick and efficient.

Elders realised he had to get back to what he was doing and took the brush and swept up the debris from the front of the house and its path. He had already swept the verandah and sweat dripped rapidly down his brow. There was too much to do to be that bothered by the sweat. He and everyone else that was able, had to do their part to return order and get back to normal.

The smell of petrichor permeated the area, enhanced by the tropical heat. Apart from that, all was still and quiet, a gentle breeze danced in the tops of the nearby trees. Florian went to investigate and he saw the destruction. The boiler and curing house were roofless and the ground was strewn with debris and detritus. The longhouse and dormitory withstood the impact better, however some of the wooden ajoupas had been destroyed. All that remained for some of them were the wooden poles which supported the makeshift walls and conical roofing. He could only hope that those that had sought refuge in the mission nearby were safe. He feared for the well-being of anyone else. He realised he knew nothing of the storms of this place, and maybe nothing of so much more about the place itself.

Florian was bereft. He'd never been through anything as violent as the storm or even feared for his life, or his mothers', to that extent. Confused and shaken, Florian headed through the destruction to the plantation's cemetery, to his father's grave. The stone was covered with debris. As he cleared the matted leaves, grass and mud off the stone, he spoke aloud.

"Father, today more than ever, I wish I had gotten here in time to learn about this place from you. And now I wish even more you were here to help me figure out how to put this place back together.

"How arrogant I was! On the ship here I thought it would be relatively easy. With so much labour available and such profitable crops, I foolishly thought I would be able to simply walk in, take a few lessons at your side and I'd be able to take the helm. I was so wrong. This storm has ruined the crops and destroyed the boiler house and so much more I can't calculate yet. I can only pray that no one is killed. I don't even know where to start righting the place. But I promise you this— I will not let you down. I will rebuild this place to its former glory, in memory of you. I promise I will take care of mother and all your people."

Florian stood back and assessed the grave. At least some semblance of order around his father's grave was restored. He brushed the dirt from his hands, made a sign of the cross, and looked back at the flattened plantation.

Then, resolute, Florian headed off to his manager's office. There, to his surprise, he found the elderly Diego, actually humming a happy folk tune, busily gathering up wet papers and debris from the floor. The place was in complete disarray. Some of the documents were now illegible as the ink had run. The ink pot had been thrown and ink was spattered against everything. The cup that held the quills, gone, its contents scattered on the table and what was left, on the floor. The other furniture was splintered, Why was Diego singing like a half wit?

At Florian's puzzled look Diego said, "After the storms life begins again, Mr Florian. Your father used to say, "Don't worry about a bad hand. Fortune will return if you stay at the betting table long enough." These storms come from time to time so we just clean up and start again."

Florian felt a strange tingle down the back of his head and neck, he could almost hear his father speak those words, the expression wasn't unfamiliar to him. There and then he was determined to honour his father's memory.

Camila arose to the hustle and bustle. She peeked through the planks of wood over the window to see many of the men at work. She looked back at her sister fast asleep, after a restless night, and she tried to be quiet and not disturb her sleep. She had to go and see what needed to be done, maybe help the other women who would be preparing food for the men and children. She wanted to get something for Evie to eat when she woke too.

Some women were back in the fields trying to correct the flattened plants in the hope they would be resilient enough to survive. Some were collecting debris and dragging it to carts or to piles for burning later. Some were gathering the fallen bananas, guava and more corn and shatine was already on the boil. Others were making flatbread over iron stones. Leftover chicken, fish and goat meat, stored away, were being checked and if suitable, prepared as part of what will be the first meal of the day. The women took the trestle tables from the dorm house and placed three of them outside. There would be an eating rotation. All three tables could accommodate 10 persons at a time.

The low thrum of men hard at their cleanup activities could be heard through the plantation, punctuated by occasional shouts to each other. The ground was drying out, making it easier to navigate wagons and debris laden skids. Some of the younger children were able to play outside once again. It was good to hear their laughter.

Diego and Florian organised a list of repairs according to what urgently needed attention first and a schedule for work shifts. They would have to work night and day for the next few days, to get production up and running.

Camila kept popping in to see Evalina. This time she came and found her standing in the doorway of the dorm, fanning herself, her stomach full with child. She smiled at Camila.

"I needed to get up and stretch my legs. I'd been lying down for too long. I don't think I've seen the men so busy at one time." Camila handed her a cup of hibiscus water. It was sweet to taste, thanks to the honey she added. "Umh! That's good. Thank you Camila."

"Why don't you come and sit in the shade. Can I get you some food?" Her sister asked.

"No, I'm good with this hibiscus water for the moment. Despite my back aching so much, I don't think I can sit down. It feels good to stand." She waved at little Joseph walking towards them with the eggs he had in a basket. Evie admired his happy disposition. She loved him as if he were her own and wondered what her own child would be like at his age. Camila saw him too and waved.

"He's such a bright boy, that one. I hope one day he can go on to teach. He looks like he has it in him."

"I think so too." Camila agreed.

"Oh my! This child is restless." Evie rubbed her hand over her stomach to calm the baby. "Put your hand here. You'll feel how strong he can kick!" Camila did as she was told and waited.

"You think it's a boy, do you? I hope you're right." The child kicked. "You're really looking forward to being a mother, aren't you? You're going to make a great mother too. Your child will have such a wonderful future. It will be beautiful, bright and charming and will make you so proud."

Evie took her sister's hand and looked into her eyes.

"Don't forget you're his kin too. With both of us watching out for him, he will never believe that he is less than any other man. And he will read about the world and know he is a part of all of it." Both had a strong connection with this wish for the future and with each other and they embraced. Suddenly Evie leaned forward in pain. Camilla worried she had hugged too hard, and jumped back.

"Oh, that was something!" Evalina rubbed her belly.

Camila took her by the hand and led her to the nearby bench at one of the trestle tables. Evelina was winded. She felt as if the whole of her stomach tightened. It left her breathless until it disappeared. "I think maybe the baby's coming. But maybe it's nothing yet. Bring me some peas, perhaps I can shell them to help take my mind off this, the child will come when it comes."

"It will be sometime soon. I was in labour for 2 days with Maria. I will pass you the peas, only if you're sure. You don't want me to call the 'mother'?" Camila was anxious.

"My waters are still intact. It's not ready to come and I'd rather be useful if I can. There are so many mouths to feed. It's not time." Evalina was surprisingly calm as she nodded reassurance to her sister, who went to get vegetables to peel and shell.

Two more days went by and the plantation was considerably more organised but they were still unable to get the boiler and curing house up and running. Florian was not too disappointed as it could have been far worse. All the other plantations in the area experienced damage, some much more than Conquerabia. Many people had died in the storm. Florian was not alone in the suffering and at least he had not lost any of his people.

Mabel made herself useful by helping to sew potato sacks together so they could be used to help transport waste and detritus which would be placed on the back of a wagon for use elsewhere or burned, if not required. She was waiting to find out the tally of their losses, but there wasn't much else she could do to help. There were so many others who could do the physical labour better.

Florian remained ignorant of Mabel's rightful outright ownership of half of Conquerabia or how she had been keeping the books for all the years before he arrived. When he got there he assumed it was Diego who knew the ins and outs of running the plantation, not his mother, and he turned to him to learn the ropes of the business. Mabel felt a self righteous annoyance that her expertise and experience were discounted but she was silent about Florian's deferment to Diego when he arrived. It upset her but to disclose her true role would be to betray his father's flaws and foibles and that would pose too many questions. She did not want to revisit the pain of those days nor did she want to tarnish her son's memory of his father.

But now she was bored, and, truth be told, a bit resentful by her curtailed involvement and authority. Why shouldn't she be able to be in charge of her own property? Why shouldn't her contributions be seen as equal to Johan's, who may have lost it all again by gambling or other ill pursuits, or simply through sloppy bookkeeping, if she hadn't insisted on taking over more? Mabel followed the usual submissive women's role for appearance's sake, but having been able to do so much more, she chafed at her diminished position. That Wollstonecraft woman gave words to what Mabel had been feeling about the absurdity of being thought of like a child when she was a grown woman. She too wished that men would simply respect women's abilities, as Wollstonecraft said, "instead of flattering their fascinating graces, and viewing them as if they were in a state of perpetual childhood, unable to stand alone."

When the mood struck she still painted; but lately she longed for her old familiar homeland and friends in Belgium. As she looked into the distance, towards the Caroni River, she was lost in her memories, only to have them shattered by the cries of one of the farm hands, calling for Florian. Mabel went to the verandah to see who it was.

"What is it boy?" Mabel asked.

"Is Master Florian there Miss Mabel?" The young boy looked serious.. "I have an urgent message for him please."

"He is not here. He will be back later this afternoon. Can I take the message?"

"No disrespect Miss Mabel. I am instructed to give the message to him and only him or I will be punished and I don't want that, Miss Mabel." He stood before her with his straw hat in his hands. He was afraid of her. She liked the fear she sensed in him, but not that something was being kept from her. She hated secrets ever since she found out about Johan's gambling and all of the other lies. It all came flooding back. She tried to be rational and remind herself that Florian wasn't his father.

"Very well. What is your name, boy and I'll tell him to come and find you?"

"I am Santiago, Miss Mabel. Santiago. I work with the cooper, Miss Mabel. Thank you Miss Mabel." Santiago bowed his head at Mabel, turned and replaced his hat and ran back to find Diego.

As Mabel turned to enter the house, she caught sight of Tante who nodded acknowledgement, a gesture of politeness. There was no love lost between the two women. Tante thought she knew why the boy came, put down the cloth she was using to dry the utensils and went to see Evalina, should her birthing skills be needed.

The birthing hut was situated as far away from the Conquerabia main house as possible so the screams of women delivering babies could not be heard clearly. Today it was Evalina's turn. On a timber cot, covered with sacks, hay and fabric remnants, Hagan and Tante were assisting.

Hagan and Tante Solomon were the plantation midwives in addition to their other duties. Hagan was just 20 years of age, Tante was in her 40s. Hagan had two boys of her own, Tante had lost all five of her children, not one living more than five months after birth. Camila knelt on the floor beside Evalina, holding her hand and offering words of encouragement.

Tante and Hagan were both concerned with the time that Evie had been in labour. They could see her energy waning. Something was not right. Hagan suggested to Camila that the baby may now be breech. Tante felt the tummy and discerned the baby's bottom. She had to help manipulate the baby to turn it around.

"Can you stoop?" Tante asked, having manoeuvred the baby into a better position. "We will support you. I can feel the baby turning but we need you to help birth the child." Tante asked Evie who nodded in agreement. Hagan and Camila gently raised Evie and helped her to the end of the cot, where she squatted.

Evelina gave one more loud, long scream as she bore down, pushing hard as Tante gently caught the child. Hagan was right. The baby was born breech. When the child was clear of its mother, she removed the umbilical cord from its neck and waited for the placenta to follow. She did not have to wait long, and once out, Hagan and Camila lay Evie back on the cot where Tante placed the new born girl on her stomach.

Evalina laughed in relief as she cuddled and kissed her daughter. At long last her child was here. The child instinctively sought out her mother's left breast and began to suckle.

"I name her … Adisa." She whispered, eyes closed in exhausted contentment, feeling the warm bundle on her tummy. She had lost a lot of blood. In a moment she took hold of Camila's arm, looked up at her sister and smiled weakly. Camila clasped her hand and nodded back in acknowledgement, both grateful for this quiet moment.

Tante collected the dirty bedding, in which the afterbirth was folded, and took it to the rear of the hut to be buried.

As the child fed in secure peace, Evie began to wander in and out of consciousness as Camila mopped her brow. She looked at her sister and realised that something was seriously wrong. Evalina had begun haemorrhaging.

Tante! Hagan!" Camilla shouted for help. The women rushed back but there was little they could do. Camilla was still holding Evalina's hand when Evelina closed her eyes and gave herself up to God. Tante took the child, wrapped up in a torn sheet, and walked towards the House. Florian was standing on the verandah watching her walk up with a child in her arms. She stopped just in front of him and the pair looked at each other.

"A girl." She said,

Not another word was exchanged. Florian nodded at Tante. Mabel looked on at the child, noticing how light its skin was, and the look between Tante and her son.

"Did her mother give her a name?" Florian asked.

Tante, facing him squarely, answered. "Yes. Adisa. She is Adisa." She repeated. "It means 'one who is clear'. She is a special child, Sir."

"Thank you Tante." Florian turned and started walking away.

"Sir." Tante said, louder and more accusingly than would ordinarily be allowed. "Her mother died in childbirth." Florian showed no reaction save for looking at the floor for a beat too long. When he looked up, their eyes met and then, infant in her arms, Tante walked away. She waited until her back was to him before she started to cry.

Florian turned away for a moment and walked toward the rail of the verandah, looking out toward the yard, still littered from the storm. He would have to arrange for a wet nurse and a guardian to care for the child's needs, but before he could do anything…

"Florian, you are a disgrace. You have brought shame on us. I thought that you, at least, would be able to control yourself." Mabel thought about how the number of mulatto children didn't seem to go down even after they moved to Conquerabia and after Johan promised to put a stop to it.

To Florian, Mabel was far too opinionated for her only son's liking. She was welcome to think whatever she'd like, but a woman should know her place, even if she is his mother.

"Mother, you are in my house now and I ask you politely to keep your words to yourself!" Flustered by his impudence, Mabel fanned her face. It was already hot as the bell rang to announce lunch was served.

Mabel was unable to dampen down her long bubbling sense of resentment about all the "fatherless" light skinned slaves they had.

"That 'thing'." Mabel seethed, "will never call me grandmother." She stressed every syllable, "do you understand?"

Florian could feel his temper rising. He did not need her comments or judgement. A man has needs and furthermore it is no concern of hers. There is no need to speak like that to him. Certainly the child was without fault, whoever's child she is. He dramatically stood aside to let her go to the table, clearly indicating that he was dismissing her outrage. "Mother, after you!" Florian bowed with insincere respect.

Mabel bridled at his insolence and walked along the verandah, to the dining table where lunch was served. The young house maid poured both a cup of tea and served them cold meats, fried plantain and cassava bread. Florian took the newspaper from the salver and engrossed himself in the business pages. They ate in frosty silence.

Hagan stayed by Evalina's still body, comforting a weeping Camila. Soon other women would be there to wrap Evalina's body for burial.

"I'll call Elders to dig a grave. She never deserved any of this. He's a bad, bad man. One day he'll pay for this!" said Hagan.

At hearing her say that Camila stopped her weeping. "That child is cursed. No one can know she is the master's daughter. It's not safe for her and with no mother to care for and protect her, it may fall to us to bring her up. Don't you dare do anything or say anything to anyone", Camila begged. "We know the white women hate the innocent mixed children because they are evidence of their men's dalliances in the slave quarters. This child could be evidence of the master's power over the captive women and evidence that the captive black men can't protect their women. That information goes into the grave with my sister. We don't know for sure she's Master Florian's and I don't wish to cast my sister in such a sorry manner. I know for sure she didn't give herself up for this." Hagan nodded and left the hut in search of Elders.

Later Elders and two other men removed Evalina's wrapped body from the hut, followed by a small procession of mourners who had been granted time off for the internment. As Elders shovelled the dirt back into the grave, Camila threw flowers and in turn, Tante and the others each made the sign of the cross and stood by in prayer. A Catholic priest blessed her body and committed her to the earth. It was an unusually brief ceremony. Indeed, those present felt lucky to be able to get this time off to mourn. Diego was clear it must be brief when he allowed the funeral. There was so much work to be done that personal heartbreaks couldn't be attended to like they would be during normal times. The storm clean up took precedence.

Florian felt a secret pride at having fathered a child. It was a shame about her mother. He would make sure the child was cared for and given a place as a house slave as she grew older. And then Florian refocused. There was plantation work to attend to.

Sometimes in these days after the hurricane, despite the heat and extra chores, in the evening, after the main part of the work day, some of the slave women sang folks songs while resting under the eaves. They were singing to free their souls, their voices floating on the gentle breeze, traveling throughout Conquerabia and into the house where they inadvertently serenaded those inside.

It was on such an occasion, while dining with Florian, that their sweet harmonies drifted in. Usually this was a welcome gift but tonight they sang a love song. She looked over at Florian, smiling and nodding his head with their rhythm, and it triggered Mabel. They suddenly sounded like the Sirens and reminded her of when she learned how treacherous and seductive coloured women could be. Dear Lord, he is just like his weak father Johan. Look at him sitting there, like he's done nothing wrong, utterly self satisfied and feeling as if merely getting back to business means all his sins and vices are minor technicalities since he got away with them. It reminded her of her worst days with Johan, but at least Johan had some sense of propriety and he kept his indiscretions away from home.

She thought back to how disgusted and hurt she felt when Johan lost their home in Peutie, and how they had to leave to avoid facing the shame he brought upon them. And then again, the next time, when they couldn't leave their shame behind …

It was common knowledge that the men on the island, the profiteers, military men, seamen and plantation owners, all had undue advantage over the exotic free coloured women and the slave women on the island, and they took it. The island atmosphere seemed to enhance their carnal natures and, despite the Catholic requirements for their presence, few seemed afraid of incurring God's wrath.

When they first got there and Mabel saw the number of mixed race slaves on the plantation it shocked and disgusted her. Mabel blamed the previous owner and his men. She even thought that was why he died so young. It was God's retribution.

Right then she told Johan in clear terms that he was to ferret out and put an end to the immoral breeding of slave women by white plantation workers, delivery men and anyone else with access to them. She reminded Johan that he said they would increase on their own, and he agreed to her terms. And technically he did, in that equivocal way that Johan conducted most business. Mabel's stomach still churned at the memory of it, all those years ago.

They were serving luncheon to Mario Triccoce, the captain from one of the ships they frequently used to transport crops away and bring the things Johan and Mabel imported from Europe. Johan and Mabel entertained him every time he returned to the Spanish

Antilles. They both enjoyed his company. He was especially humorous when imbibing his favourite Puerto Rican rum.

On this occasion, halfway into one of his ribald stories, Captain Triccoce commented on the derrière of the woman in his story, and he winked at Johan and compared hers to "that wench Mirian who sashays her prodigious posterior around her cafe down near the harbour."

That comment hit Mabel like a thunder clap! The name was familiar from looking over the ledgers. She noticed the regular money going to the Mirian account and she questioned Johan about it. It seemed like a lot of money to a non specific plantation expense, unlike all the rest of the annotated outgoing expenses. Johan waved it off. He said the business he called "Mirian" handled the "care and feeding of Conquerabia workers" who loaded and uploaded the ships for Conquerabia. He said "they" organised the loading of victuals for the vessel's return trip taking Conquerabian goods to market. He even reminded her that he told her about the place, Mirian's, and that he visited it and ate there often when he had business in Portes Des Espana. His nonchalance kept her from investigating further. What a fool she was.

Johan didn't seem to notice that slip of the Captain's tongue, since he had been drinking too. They certainly seemed to think the Captain's story about some woman's backside was hilarious, but Mabel seethed inside and, even though she smiled and laughed along with them, she vowed to find out the truth about who and what Mirian really was.

While the men were still drinking and the Captain was still regaling Johan with stories of his exploits, Mabel excused herself and went to find Tante. She knew if anyone could it would be Tante who could tell her about Mirian or Mirian's place or what or who Mirian is.

As nonchalantly as she could, Mabel said, "Tante, the gentlemen were talking about someone or a place in town but I couldn't quite follow. They were talking so fast, you know how men do…" Mabel didn't want to sound too anxious. "I thought I heard them say Mirian, but it could be something else, maybe something close. Or perhaps I misheard them?"

Tante knew, of course, but she didn't let on immediately. Slaves always had to calculate what the whites would do with news they don't want to hear. She didn't want to be punished for telling Mabel what everyone already knew, but she also didn't want some other less trusted slave to have to be the bearer of bad news either. Tante, knowing her position to be secure, decided to tell her as obliquely as possible.

"Mrs. Dottin, Ma'am, I have heard some talk about a free coloured woman who runs a tavern in town whose name might be something like Marie, or Margaret, Minnie or perhaps Mirian. I have no knowledge of anything other than there is a woman like that."

"Thank you, Tante. I was just curious." Mabel knew all she needed to know. Every emotion possible swept through her. Anger, at all the lies, every broken promise. And embarrassment. Surely people knew of this. He was carrying on with a woman in town. People would certainly be talking. And then jealousy hit her. Johan was giving the affection he should have been giving to her to another woman… A coloured woman!

Mabel knew she had to leave the house lest she make a scene. She had to collect herself. She found herself heading back toward the location by the river she hadn't been back to since she was there reading her sister's letter. She had to pass the carpenter's building and the door was open…

Cornelius didn't hear her arrive. He was too engrossed, sawing the timber. Mabel watched his muscular body moving up and down. When the blade stopped, she knocked on the door frame. Turning and seeing her, down in a slave workshop but dressed for company, he could tell that something was different. He was going to speak but she motioned him to be silent.

He watched her eyes taking him in, so he stood motionless, wondering what to do, then Mabel walked towards him. She got up close in front of him, hesitated a moment, and then she reached out and touched his bare chest with her fingers, gently feeling his soft hair.

Cornelius looked down at her tapered fingertips slowly moving across his dark skin, tentatively at first, then he felt her opening them so her warm palms could apply more pressure as they smoothed over him. Cornelius was caught off guard trying to negotiate the wrongness and danger with the pull of the moment.

“Ma’am?” He could see her pulse beating hard in her neck as she stroked him.

“Ma’am” He tentatively grabbed her wrists to stop her. He knew that touching her could get him killed.

“Miss Mabel,” he said her name, his voice low and trailing off. They looked at each other. “Maybe you want to sit down for a moment?’

She slipped her wrists from his hands, and removed the pins from her hair, letting it fall in sun bleached auburn curls over her shoulders. She then ran her hands up and down his muscular arms. He could smell her perfume. He caught her wrists, this time more firmly to emphasise the importance of what he was going to say. “Maybe you want to think about this?” Mabel reached down and undid the leather belt and the loose breeches fell to the floor. Her hands moved to the thick triangular carpet of soft tightly curled black hair that ran from his chest down and she stroked him there. He took in a deep breath. This was dangerous territory for him. It was dangerous territory for both of them.

Some time later, Cornelius got up, quickly dressed, and left. He knew his life was suddenly precarious. He wanted to let her save whatever sense of propriety she might need to recover. White people need to feel in control.

Mabel knew his departure from the building was to protect her modesty, and was thankful for the time to compose herself. She ached and it felt wonderful. It had been years since Johan touched her in that way, and she missed it but could do nothing. She could not demand it. Today was on her terms and she relished in her power.

"Mother! Mother!" Florian clapped his hands and laughed at Mabel's trance. Florian's sharp tones snapped her back to the present.

"Oh, my! I'm so sorry. I was lost in a memory, Dear. I was just thinking about your father. You remind me so much of him sometimes."

-o0o-

Florian developed a deep love of Conquerabia - his father's legacy, and the lifestyle it provided. Those dark days of British winters were now far behind him, as was the cold weather. Here he was guaranteed good weather most of the time and the outdoor lifestyle was idyllic.

Florian could not understand the notion of shame over having a child with a slave woman. In Trinidad, it was tacitly understood that white plantation owners would pick a black or mulatto girl from time to time as it would add to the workforce when the children were born; no need to purchase slaves. Florian also thought it added a sense of relatedness, and loyalty, too. After all, some were actually kin.

Regardless, that was a very small part of the way he benefited the plantation. When not working in his office on the plantations' books and projections, he was often out in the fields surveying his property. Florian had expanded the plantation, by investing in land, slaves and crops. Conquerabia now owned more than twenty-five hectares with over 200 negroes. They were a formidable workforce and they made Conquerabia profitable. The handful of older females taught the younger ones the various women's jobs and the older male negroes attended to and taught the younger ones the lay of the land, or repairing the machinery which often needed mending. Florian hated to spend money on new tools. He hated spending money on anything unnecessarily. His frugality was paying off. So what if he loved his rum and the young female negroes and the occasional card game a little more than he should?

Chapter 14

The Church bells rang out in the distance waking Picton from slumber. He rubbed his head. It was sore. A smile crept across his mouth as he recalled the previous night's drinking with members of the Cabilda. Governor Thomas Picton had little time to wash as he was running late for Church.

Another bell chimed in the distance and the sound of hooves on the dirt track outside the small house in Port of Spain reminded him to sober up quickly. He was unsteady on his feet as he headed towards his landau. His behaviour spooked the horses and Picton was caught by the wooden vehicle as it moved, and he fell to the ground. He swore under his breath.

"Are you alright señor?" A young lady who had seen the commotion came to his aid. He felt humiliated and brushed her hand away, as she offered it to help him up.

"I'm fine! Stupid horse. He could have killed me." Picton stood up and dusted his jacket and trousers down. By now there was a small crowd tittering among themselves at the commotion. Picton looked at the people around and decided that he needed to compose himself. He looked at the handsome lady in front of him.

"I'm sorry. Thank you señora. I am sorry if I offended you with my language. You were more than kind to try and help me up." Maria smelled the stale alcohol on his breath and stepped back, politely.

Picton looked at the woman. She had wavy black hair and friendly dark eyes. He smiled and she smiled back. "I best get going now or I will be late for church." He bowed . "Thomas Picton, señora!" She lifted her hand and he kissed the back of it.

"Maria, Señor. Maria Calderon. Good day to you." Maria thought he was a rather fine looking man, in his uniform. She hoped he would be able to remove the remaining dust from his clothing before he entered the church. Maria rejoined her daughters and headed off to church too.

As he left on his horse, Picton glanced around to see Maria and her two daughters walking in the shade of her parasol.

As time went on, the island profoundly changed Florian, as did most emigres. More and more he bristled at Mabel's increasingly fussy, outdated ideas. Mainly he ignored them. When she reprimanded him over the birth of Adisa or the time he spent in the slave quarters, or criticised the child mercilessly, he did not allow her to see how much it irritated him. As her only child, he felt it necessary to accommodate and indulge her.

Tante could see Florian working more and more and using his work as a device to keep clear of Mabel. He also depended on Tante to manage the house and to manage Mabel. He knew Tante could stand up to Mabel in ways he could not, especially about Mabel's harsh treatment of Adisa. Mabel always liked to feel that she could control slaves with threats of punishment, but she never threatened Tante. They both knew that Mabel could not lose Tante, the only woman capable of looking after her in her dotage. Tante, alone, could challenge Mabel on her behaviour toward Adisa, or any other slave.

Besides, Florian truly had a lot to manage on Conquerabia. There were always books to reconcile, politics near and abroad to keep abreast of, animals, slaves and workers to oversee, and shipments to manage. Plus there was always general maintenance.

The Boiling and Curing houses were in constant need of repair. Larger boiling coppers were needed to help increase production but Florian was loath to buy new ones when the old ones could still be patched up.

He felt the same way about some personnel, too. His father's trusted longtime manager of the plantation, Diego Manancala, was still on the job. Diego, who had taught Florian everything when he first arrived, was suffering with his joints and unable to keep up with the needs of the plantation, but Diego insisted he was still able so Florian allowed him to remain in his position. An emergency forced Florian into making the final decision.

Their head boiler caught his arm in some malfunctioning machinery. Diego tried to rush for help but his bad legs slowed him so much that by the time help arrived the poor man's arm was mangled beyond repair and the only chance to save him would be to take his arm. He begged Diego not to do it. The look of fear in his eyes at the thought of losing his arm was near hysterical but with one brutal hack the arm was severed and the man's body fell to the ground as the blood pumped out of what remained of his upper arm. But even this was too late. He went into shock and bled to death, there on the mill floor, the tourniquets too late to staunch the flow.

As soon as Florian arrived and saw Diego and the dead worker, he recognised the need to retire him. He asked Diego's son, Manuel, who had learned from his father, to take over. It was Florian's plantation now. It was up to him to manage his personnel.

-o0o-

The next few years passed according to the usual rhythms at Conquerabia. The rainy seasons were followed by glorious weather and cloudless skies. Ships came in and ships went out. Old people died and children were born. There was unrest among the slaves on some of the other islands, but Florian felt those were due to the mistreatment of the workers, and there was none of that on Conquerabia.

Mabel's health slowly started deteriorating and she spent more time in the garden room of Conquerabia where she could see out of the double doors which lead into the flower garden and beyond. She struggled to breathe in the heat and most exertion became an effort. The 13 year-old Adisa was instructed by Florian to take care of her, which infuriated the old lady, who had long shown antipathy for the young maid, and it baffled Adisa.

Despite her best attempts to attend to her mistress's needs, Mabel was relentlessly critical of her. Adisa could do no right. Cold jugs of lemonade were either too sweet, too sour or not cool enough. Cups of tea were either too strong or too weak. When Adisa was not looking, Mabel would knock glasses off tables or spill food to make more work for the child.

Adisa was also blamed for spilling food on the bed covers, and was often on the receiving end of anything the old woman could use to strike the girl. Adisa kept quiet, knowing that responding with anything other than "I'm sorry" would cause further aggravation. She learned quickly and did not give Mabel the satisfaction of seeing her upset.

Tante, who cared for the child since that fateful day she was brought into the world, loved her like one of her own. Tante knew the extent of the wickedness the old woman meted out but was in a difficult position. She both wanted to protect her and encourage her to grow, but Tante also needed Adisa to conform to some rules and expectations for her own good. Tante wanted Adisa to be able to maintain her house slave status. It was the best possible position for a female slave.

But it was more than that. Tante knew, everybody knew, that Adisa was charmed. Tante and her husband Elders taught the child the Bible to shape her soul, but they also valued more formal education. They let her read books and papers they could take from the house when the Dottins were through with them. She was bright, she absorbed everything, and because she was precocious it all fuelled her interest and stoked a desire to explore more of the world.

Besides work and lessons for a few, there was a lot for children to do in Conquerabia. The plantation, when harvested, became the children's playground. The smell of the cooking sugar cane was delicious, and during cooking times some of the men folk would cut up cane for the kids to suck. Some of the kids would weave the cane leaves to use as hats or trays on which to eat food, if no banana leaves were available.

In an adjoining field, sweetcorn was grown and what had fallen, was often taken by the negroes to eat. A Sunday afternoon lunch was always a treat. After church, held in a small outbuilding, the women changed back into work dress to prepare the goat and vegetables. Adisa looked forward to the sweetcorn. It was her favourite. When the ears were roasted they became sweeter and more delicious.

Tante loved Adisa above all, but Tante was a motherly figure for everyone on the plantation. Her family was gone and she craved familial attachments. She and her brothers were snatched from their home and brought to Trinidad on a slave ship. The brothers were taken when they arrived on the island some thirty years before. She knew not where there were rumours they were on Tobago or one of the islands in the Gulf of Paria.

Tante was a strict Christian and lived her life according to the Bible. She was appalled by the way Mabel treated her Adisa, even worse than other slaves who were not her kin. Other slaves criticised Tante for not hating Mabel, and for not doing little nasty things behind her back, like spitting in her food. But to prayerful Tante that would not be Christ-like. Tante was a believer and was convinced that goodness will prevail eventually, if one had faith.

-o0o-

From her bed, Mabel could hear the children laughing and singing as some of the negroes performed on makeshift instruments, fiddles, drums, and accordions. More and more the happiness of others seemed to exasperate her. Tonight, distracted by the singing, trying and failing to read her book or the newspaper Florian brought in, Mabel was irritated and restless. She couldn't settle.

It was hot outside. The fan in the ceiling was gently rocked by a young man outside her room, and despite it and the gentle breeze through the window, Mabel could not cool down and this irritated her further. She rang her bell to call Adisa.

"I need water. More water now!" She barked.

"Yes m'm", Adisa obliged. "Can I get you anything else?"

"No. Go now." Mabel said wearily. While waiting, the laughter and music died down and Mabel dozed off to restless sleep. Adisa arrived with the cool water and saw Mabel in slumber. She gently put the glass down on the bed side table and filled it. Placing the jug at its side. She tiptoed out. Within 30 minutes the familiar bell rang and Adisa was summoned back to Mabel's room.

"I need the commode." Adisa drew up the wheeled furniture and a privacy screen, helping the old woman onto it, leaving to save Mabel's dignity. When Mabel was done Adisa wheeled the chair outside the room removing the basin and discarding its contents in the external toilet. Adisa noted it was the only time Mabel was more courteous and it was the time she realised the old woman's frailty in so many respects, Adisa saw her for the frightened, frail, lonely old lady that she had become. The bell rang again as Adisa returned to the room to replace the commode and find out what else Mabel needed.

"Ma'am, would you like to sip some water?". The old lady nodded and Adisa handed her the glass of cool water. It was refreshing and Mabel was grateful for it. Outside the jollity began again and Mabel tut-tutted, as Adisa plumped up her pillows and made sure her mistress was comfortable once again.

"Ma'am, you good now?" Adisa checked. Mabel nodded and wearily motioned her to leave. Another cool breeze entered the room, billowing the net curtain in the process.

That evening, Adisa and Tante sat on the rear verandah reading and writing. Using a framed slate and chalk for her practice, Elders dictated short sentences for Adisa to write out. He checked her spelling. Over the years Elders gave her basic sums to do, and she did the equations and showed how she got the totals. She was quick to learn and loved these moments when only she was the centre of attention and she did not have to attend to the awful old woman or her other chores.

The cicadas sang out hailing the night. The rest of the negroes went about their own chores readying for the following day, too. Sounds of busy people getting as much done as possible in the cool of the evening was much different from the sounds during the light of day. The full moon shone brightly and there were no clouds in the night sky.

Later Tante tucked Adisa into her wooden bed, kissing the sleepy girl on her forehead. Her final chore was to check in on Mabel. All was well and calm. It was not long later that Tante found sleep next to Elders

Chapter 15

In Saint Domingue, Azacca or Zac, as he was known, was out celebrating his freedom with friends and compatriots Damerae and Agwe. They were with several others who had won their freedom from France as the abolition movement swept across Europe and finally was being applied in the West Indies, voluntary or otherwise. They went along to the nearest liquor stand and drank rum in celebration.

Saint Domingue was the most profitable of the islands in sugar cane, cotton, coffee and other commodities. Under French rule, the island's governors were aware of the tensions taking place among the negroes. There had already been rumours of slave revolt and even small outbreaks over recent years. And tensions were tangible. France was experiencing its own social revolution and in 1789, it led to the freeing of some negroes, predominantly those of mixed race.

Uniquely, Saint Domingue was already more profitable than the British island colonies or the colonies in America and the taxes it raised improved France's fortunes, for a time. It had successfully conquered Tobago from Spain, greatly enhancing its status, strategic position and profitability. It was, on the whole, rich.

However, Saint Domingue was on edge. There were outbreaks of slave rebellion on many of the island colonies and even reports of slaves murdering their owners. The plantation owners assembled in their regions to raise concerns about the impact a major uprising could have on their wealth, their safety and that of their families. Despite missives being sent to France for guidance and support, response was slow and when it arrived it was to request more money to fund the homeland. There was unrest there too. Church leaders and plantation owners urged the local government to take action to increase the size of the military and provide more weapons and ammunition.

A group of insurgent freed negroes had gained power with certain sections of the military, which would provide arms for a price. At the port, Le Cap Francais, Zac and his friends continued their drinking. They and their families had already enjoyed the 'freedman's' Sunday lunch, following church and Zac wanted to enjoy what it really meant to be free, by walking the streets around the port.

The heat of the day was at its peak and Zac ran into the sea to cool off. His friends followed him immediately and they all splashed about in fun. They then decided to race each other to certain points along the coast and when finished, decided to dry off by lying on the beach, which was busy, but irritated by the young men's uncouth behaviour, some of the affluent and noble families were rushing to leave.

Zac and his friend did not have a care in the world. Agwe got up and walked over to the crate of prawns the local fishermen had caught and brought a shirt-full to share among his friends. They snapped the head and tails off and enjoyed the salty, juicy flesh.

They talked about securing their freedom and wanted the same for the rest of their family and friends. It brought a tear to Zac's eye, thinking about the injustice of what slavery had done to him and others.

Brodie Henderson, who owned the biggest cotton plantation in Saint Domingue, was a brutal man. He ruled by terror. His own wife was scared of him and when he discovered she called the doctor to attend to a desperately wounded slave without his permission, he gave her a black eye, fractured her left forearm and cracked a rib. She was too afraid to mention it to anyone. And it wouldn't have mattered if she did. It was his land, his wife, and his slaves and they were all his property. His superior taxable revenue and his huge personal profit were proof enough to the king and proof enough to himself that no one had the right to tell him how to run his business; private or domestic.

Brodie's overseer, Mr Grey, arrived at his office to announce The Rose had arrived from West Africa with a large cargo of slaves and an auction would be held in town on the Saturday.

"They're going to parade the new goods from mid-day tomorrow, if you want to go and see them. You're invited to attend from 11:30 am in a private viewing. The vendor said you need to come along as he has stock you may be interested in, Mr Henderson!"

"That's good. By the way, we are down on sugar production this month. I need you to get them working harder. I've ordered a new piano wire whip which you will have within the week. If you can't improve things with that, then we'll have to look at your situation again"

"Sir. I will do my best, sir. This talk of revolt is growing and despite me telling them it's nonsense, they doubt me. Sir! I will do my best." Mr Grey, an older man of wearisome years knew his job was at stake.

"You're not indispensable! You have fourteen days to improve things. Now go!"

Mr Grey left. Brodie was no longer interested in discussing things and found it boring. He had little patience for those who bored or even tired him. He heard talk of revolt and as a member of the Plantation Owners Association, knew the seriousness of its implications. All this anxiety was feeding his ruthlessness. He had a lot to lose and was not going to give up that easily.

The next time five young runners were recaptured, they were locked up in stocks, had their toes cut off and thrown on the ground in full view of the onlookers.

Chapter 16

Chef Doxey was an angry slave. Angry at the injustices he witnessed on a daily basis at the hands of the barbaric Brodie Henderson and his overseer Mr Grey. He had the measure of Brodie who was afraid of the rumours of uprising on the island of Saint Domingue where he owned one of the largest and most profitable plantations. He earned the moniker Chef due to his love of fried chicken, He was rarely without a drumstick or other piece of chicken. He was lean, strong and at 6', 4" he was statuesque. With skin as dark as the freshly boiled molasses his mere presence was imposing.

Trafficked from his beloved African homeland he was considered a prince, but on a day of celebrations on the coast in Senegal he had been kidnapped by a number of white men with weapons he had never seen before, weapons that were loud and killed instantly or maimed. Three of his brethrens he witnessed lost their lives in this violent manner, chaos ensued. Stunned by what he saw, he was chained along with five men and women, one a young boy Sam. Both witnessed a heavily pregnant woman shot dead, her unborn cut out of her belly did not survive and was left by her mother's body on the sandy beach as both their blood flowed deeper and darker into the earth.

On the ship, Chef tried to console the boy, only to find the lash on his own back prevented him from further attempts.

The ship was packed full of slaves. It made two more stops before the long voyage over to Saint Domingo where many who passed on the voyage were thrown into the sea. It was callous. Both were then sold to the owner of their new home.

Without the liberty of his former privileged life and witness to the continued brutal rule of his plantation owner, Chef felt compelled to fight the injustice meted out to him and his fellow men. He would often take himself to the farther reaches of the plantation where he could not be troubled and studied the martial arts of the East, he found on pages of the books he coveted.

Due to his build, Chef was put to work on the land subject to which crops needed harvesting. If working in the boiler house, any beam or joist became his place of exercise. He had more energy than most and soon became one of Brodie's valuable workers for yield. He witnessed the travesties that took place around him and it was all that he could do to contain himself, but in time, he often said to himself. All in good time.

Sam was put to work in the sugar mill working to help crush the freshly cut cane. It was a simple job but with the repetitive nature and weight of the cane, his sickly body struggled. Every now and then he would feel pain in his body. It was thought he was, like most other negroes, aching from the arduous work load. Fellow slaves tried to help him but Brodie's wicked manager Mr Grey's constant cracking of the whip aimed at Sam, was hard.

There were two older boys who were responsible for rotating the crusher that released the sticky sweet liquid. They began to work in time, picking up a rhythm and moving quickly through the cane. Their lives depended on exceeding the daily quota.

Sam grew more tired and he longed for the plains of Africa and the river where he and his friends swam. He missed his mother and often had nightmares having witnessed her death. Chef Doxey, who shared his dormitory, saw how the boy struggled to cope.

Sam quickly learned to trust Chef. When he found the going hard, all he needed to do was look up and Chef was there for him. When the manager and his deputy were out of sight he would go and help Sam lift the batches of cane. He felt sorry for Sam whose eyes were often a shade of yellow and red from crying.

Sam and Chef would often talk about their past and family and with Chef's guidance Sam began to teach himself to read and write. He soon learned that attending church was sometimes all the escape he needed. After a couple of years, he realised that this was now his family. He longed to see his sister JoJo, also taken with him. She had been sold to a different owner and the last time they saw each other was when they were sold. He longed to see her and hold her again and to reassure her that all would be well.

Sam was about to celebrate his 18th birthday. He thought about how he and his family would have honoured him - a village party with lots of food and dancing. He loved to dance.

The older members of the negroes organised a celebration for him after Church one Sunday. It was a surprise and was just what he needed. What they all needed. He was given a new pair of breeches, made from old bed sheets that were redeemable. They looked smart. He was also given a necklace made out of small shells taken from the beach. He did not want that Sunday to end. He was the happiest he could recall. Twilight heralded the end of celebrations and joy. He had enjoyed too much of the rum his master had permitted for the celebrations and Sam was happy.

Chef, also beginning to tire from the celebrations, sat on a barrel, tucked into more fried chicken and peas, and enjoyed a cooling glass of mauby. He sensibly avoided the rum, knowing full well his own limitations with alcohol. He wanted to be lucid and look out for Sam. He knew 18 was a dangerous age for a restless and lonely young man. From his seat on the barrel he looked over at his tipsy surrogate charge. He had witnessed how Sam had grown and developed and looked beyond their enslavement.

Sam came and sat near Chef. The low light was beautiful and they watched the happy people, laughing and dancing.

"One day my son, we will all be free. We will be free." Chef whispered. Sam was beginning to fall asleep so Chef walked him to the dormitory and his cot.

-o0o-

Four years had passed and Chef finally managed to buy his freedom. It has cost him $80. He had two more weeks to work and he was relieved that he was finally going to enjoy a new life. Once released, he had more access to newspapers and pamphlets about the revolts taking place on other island colonies. He sought out Dutty Boukman and began to attend his talks.

He befriended Boukman, but grew concerned when Boukman began to talk about using violence. Witnessing what he did before he was captured, Chef wasn't sure about this and began to lose respect for him. Chef tried to promote reason and knowledge but Boukman was determined that he and his followers take up arms.

Chef soon amassed a strong following of his own and tried to instil in them the power of the book - knowledge and strength of mind and body. He adopted the abolitionist stance and continued to fight for freedom, not just for him but for fellow negroes. He presented more public meetings and his followers increased.

Sam, not yet free, tried to attend as many of Chef's meetings as he could. However these became less and less. He could no longer justify his prolonged absence from the plantation and, threatened by punishment, chose to abide rather than suffer, his body constantly ached.

Each week, Chef delivered pamphlets to Sam so he could read the latest news about the anxiety the Government and owners had at the prospect of revolt; how money was no longer being sent to the homeland but used to buy weapons and train more men to join the militia and full time serving officers. The flyers promoted talks aimed at the nobles and landowners with instructions for self defence. Plantation owners and prospectors were living in fear. Once read, Sam would burn them so as not to be caught with them. Every detail recorded to memory and recalled when needed.

Soon, word began to spread about several marauders - Boukman and L'Overture, a third name was added, Doxey's. Governor General Blanchelande placed a bounty on their heads. Chef had to admit he needed to defend himself as the threat of attack was now a viable prospect and along with two henchmen gathered himself a small army and acquired blunderbusses, duelling guns, ammunition and other weapons.

Driven by fear, more negroes tried to flee the plantations but were returned, despicable horrors were meted out to them. Lynchings increased and unnecessary amputations were being inflicted, including on young children. The more Chef heard of these incidents the more his anger grew. As a result he began raids on those plantation owners most culpable. Under his direction some of his followers that now included Zac and Agwe started to set fire to crops and out buildings. Some even set fire to homesteads which Chef denounced. Damaging equipment and property was fair, not killing.

The military had found a number of covens in the mountains along with weapons and ammunition. Arrests had been made but the more arrests taking place, the more attacks on plantations. Finally Saint Domingue erupted in violence.

Brodie Henderson along with Mr Grey, fled for their lives to The Spanish Antilles. So did Chef and Sam.

-o0o-

Florian recalled his father writing about his experience with runaway slaves, and a bit about negroes damaging equipment. It was frustrating. His father, like most Trinidadian owners, used varying levels of brutality to control their labour. It was how it had always been done and if their successes were any proof, then these tactics worked well. And oddly, Johan and Diego found that most slaves simply followed the implicit rules without much resistance anyway. They did things the way they had always been done, too. Diego Manancala substantially tightened up the rules when Johan died, knowing that the whole operation would be under threat if anyone thought that there was no one in charge during the time between Johan's death and Florian's arrival, he exacted harsh remedies between ownership, reigning his tactics in when Florian took possession of the plantation.

Florian was no saint. Although he did not lift a finger to any slave, he turned an eye to Diego enforcing brutal ways to control the labour force. He too was concerned with rumours of potential uprisings and those immigrants not intent on positively contributing to Trinidadian life. There were headlines about rebellious marauders that were intent on wreaking havoc on the island. A major threat to the yield and profitability. Trinidad was not ready for full out warfare. Despite his attempts to ban access to tracts, pamphlets or newspaper on the plantation, slaves still talked to one another and rumours spread rapidly.

Diego warned him about Conquerabia being a target so he took measures into his own hands by instigating a curfew between dusk and dawn and riding through the plantation with his flintlock pistol, ordering two new pistols and four muskets. Mabel didn't like having such weapons around, they frightened her, but she understood safety was paramount. For her she recalled those fears when she first arrived on the island, and searched for the small knives Flossie purchased for her, for the voyage across the Atlantic.

Florian noted an unsettling atmosphere when Picton instigated his version of the Code Noir, but felt he knew his own slaves and he never adopted Picton's harsh reforms, believing they would definitely insight rioting.

A meeting of the local Plantation Owners Alliance was taking place. These plantation owners were scared, threatened by their own slaves turning on them and the influence migrants would have on their status quo and it took a while for the members to settle down. Florian began by proposing that since Trinidad was profitable, they should now start to consider paying wages to their workers.

"Respected Chairman and members, I urge you to consider this. If we increase our workers' pay by a minimum of 10c per month, we will still be in profit. Our workers will be in a position to save and invest in more land for themselves and their family, which we can sell or rent to them. Such independence will give them security, stability and …." He was interrupted.

"Mr Dottin, you sound like you're a nigger lover,," one member sneered. "We're protected by Picton's' latest revision of the Code Noir. If we allow the negroes to think they have a stake in our country, how can we ensure they get to work? Are you mad? Whose side are you on, sir?" The chairman asked.

"Mr Chairman, I object to your offensive remark! How dare you?" Florian was angered. "I agree the idea is rather shocking, but give it some consideration. Aren't you aware of the pace at which the Abolitionist movement is advancing? Very soon we may have no choice in the matter, so I suggest we try and take things in hand. Don't forget our workers outnumber us. Look at what's happening in Saint Domingue and Jamaica. This could so easily happen here and then where will we be?

“Mr Dottin, Florian if I may?”, said Mr Garnier. “Are you out of your bloody mind? These darkies are nothing more than pack hounds. To do the bulk of the labour. They have no more value to us than my horse. Legally they are considered 3/5th of a man. If he gets injured, I get another horse. I don’t placate him. He gets punished. So long as he is fed and watered, that’s all that matters, man!

“Here, here!” Added a number of other members. Florian was outraged.

“Mr Garnier. You take better care of your horse than your negroes.” Laugher ensured. “I don’t believe you’ve ever kicked your horse! Besides the Code Noir states you can’t draw blood. Do you wish to be fined for this? Even your horse gets weary of carrying you!” The room filled with laughter as Florian’s remark scored points on the obese Mr Garnier, and he smiled to himself at the response. Mr Garnier was outraged by such indignation and blustered in response.

“If we punish them, who are they going to run to, to tell?” They won’t tell the local Alguida’s as they too benefit financially from us; we have to pay taxes to them! And don’t think any negro will be taken seriously either. They know they’ll be punished if they try to speak out. It all works in our favour, Dottin! You don't know what you're talking about!" Came an arrogant reply from a fellow planter.

"My good men. Can't you understand the revolts taking place in Jamaica, St Kitts, Saint Domingue are spreading? If we don't manage this, we will be contributing directly to any potential uprising and therefore damage to our own livelihoods. These negroes could already be plotting to harm our crops and our homes. If you've got a better idea, Garnier, I'll be pleased to hear, but I suggest we act sooner rather than later!" The room went silent.

"Think about it! We need to listen and come up with ways in which we can respond without losing position. At least, don't you think, if we start to make improvements, we come from a position of strength? We provide wages, provide better accommodation and opportunities for them, which will go towards safeguarding what we value. That's not too much to ask to save our livelihood in the long term? When you think about it, Trinidad has, to this date, not seen such attempts at rebellion and I believe that is because we look after our negroes".

"Have you not heard what has happened to Mr Brodie Henderson? He owned the largest plantation on Saint Domingue and the most profitable. His negroes started to rebel. First, they refused to work, then when made to do so, when he metered out more severe punishment, the negroes began to destroy machinery and the property. It took several weeks for the sugar mill to regain momentum when their largest boiler was damaged. "Then, a Chef Doxey, one of the first freed negroes to lead a revolt, instructed his men to attack the whole plantation, and those in the surrounding area. Henderson lost his youngest son and wife, and has fled the island. Do you want this for yourselves? We have to start listening and changing our ways." Chairman Mr Carson looked at Florian and seethed.

"You are asking far too much of us. We are the owners, these negroes are our property and we treat them well enough! We owe them nothing more. If we try to give way, no matter how small, they will take advantage of us and who knows where this ends? I vote to remove Mr Florian Dottin from our company. I for one welcome him and his ideas no more.'' Mr Carson was joined with cheers and jeers. A vote was taken.

Two days later, Florian received the Caroni Digest and turned to read page three where he saw reports of the meeting recorded. Its headline read, 'Slave Sympathiser Evicted from Plantation Owners Alliance' with his likeness printed alongside.

As he read it, he saw that it reported how his ideas angered the local Alguida and proposed action towards him and his plantation to exclude him from distribution. Florian hid the paper from his mother. Adisa found it in the garbage and retrieved it.

Chapter 17

"Today, we need to prepare for Mr Florian's luncheon guests. There will be five guests, and even though three are children there is still a lot to do! Adisa, please ask Emmanuel to prepare two chickens for me to cook and collect a basket of corn ears and some cassava? I have to prepare the dessert and make the bread. So much to do! Quick Adisa, do as you're told." Tante was all business when preparing for guests.

Adisa set off to the herb and vegetable gardens, filled the basket, and headed off to tell the plantation's butcher to prepare the chickens. He said that he'd have his boy bring them straight to the kitchen. Relieved he didn't want her to wait, she set off. She did not like hearing the squawking of the chickens being caught or the sound of the axe when it severed their necks. It sent a shiver down her spine.

Adisa was already perspiring and it was not even 10am. She longed to dip her feet into the river, but if she did, she would meet Tante's ire, and on a day like today, with special guests expected, she would hate to upset her.

Tante had already started on the bread. The second loaf was in the kiln. Adisa was to lay the table using Mabel's finest Damask table cloth. She removed it from the cabinet drawer and threw it onto the verandah table.

The plates, a legacy of Mabel's life in Antwerp, contained the blue detailing that reflected their Dutch heritage. They looked pretty against the white tablecloth. Next the cutlery had to be cleaned properly and laid just so. Each setting had a side plate, with a smaller knife, and the main setting contained two forks, one smaller, as with the knives. To top off the setting a smaller spoon was laid with a matching fork. These, Adisa was told, were for dessert. Tante was to serve her best pumpkin pie.

Soon the table was laid with all the place settings, glasses for wine and water and a high-chair was positioned towards its head.

Tante inspected her work, noticing Adisa's dirty apron and demanded she go and change.

"Quick Adisa, they're coming!" Adisa rushed and returned with her smart, clean apron and fixed her hair in the mirror. She stood before Tante, who smiled in approval, then she instructed her to be ready to take out the tray with the lemon water. Adisa was back just in time. The guests had already been shown to the verandah.

Standing in the afternoon breeze where a man, a lovely pregnant woman holding the hand of a toddler, and other two children when Florian strode out.

"Quintin, how lovely to see you, and this must be Delia. I have heard so much about Quintin's better half. But he didn't say you are positively blossoming." Florian kissed Delia's hand.

"Mr Dottin, how lovely to meet you at long last. I've heard so much about you, too. Yes, I am blooming again. Have you met the twins? Peggy and Felix? And this is Myles, he's 18 months old now."

"How do you do Mr Dottin?" Felix shook hands with Florian and Peggy gave an awkward curtsey. "Pleased to meet you Mr. Dottin."

"Let me get you something to drink?" This was Adisa's cue. As she stepped out onto the verandah, she twisted her foot and fell. The clatter of the tray landing and the smashing of the glasses and jug caused such a noise that everyone looked in her direction.

Tante saw what had happened and became annoyed at her for causing such a scene. Quintin was nearer and offered his hand to help her up as Felix and Peggy began to laugh at her.

"How clumsy," offered Felix as he was bent double in laughter. "That has to be the funniest thing I've seen today."

"Be quiet you two, she could have hurt herself or more importantly you with the glass smashing!" Delia added.

"Are you hurt? Go and change, I'll get Samantha to help clear this up." Tante was stern but she knew it was an accident. Adisa shook her head and went to change. When she returned all that was left was the mark from the liquid, but it was swiftly evaporating.

"Quintin, how are things as the Alcalde De Barrio for Caroni? I understand you're fairly new in the role."

"Yes, Florian. It's an interesting post. We are responsible for the region and have to ensure the law and order of the land is obeyed. I'm enjoying the position and it's giving me an opportunity to stretch myself and put my language skills to test. It's good to meet so many people that live and work here and be responsible for the health and well being of those under this region."

"How do you feel about Governor Thomas Picton? I've been hearing some rather unsettling things about him." Florian asked.

"He's a very clever man, he impressed Ralph Abercromby and the British government although I'm concerned about certain things I'm hearing about him, too, such as all the Machiavellian changes he made in the Code Noir. But I'm happy to give him the benefit of the doubt. He might have to be strict with the wave of abolitionist thinking these days that has the labour riled up."

"Ah yes, and the poisonings and uprisings. People here are very nervous since Saint Domingue fell to the savages." Florian added.

"Indeed, the poisonings. Makes you want to keep a dog nearby to test all your food! And the bloody darkies don't care if they sometimes poison their own trying to get their masters! What else can Picton do but show them the whip and the cane? There are more of the darkies than there are of us. The French were too lenient and look what they lost! Not only their heads but Santo Domingue, too, and as I understand it was hugely profitable to the motherland. That loss might hurt worse than the guillotine!" Quintin chuckled.

Florian nodded. "It's not an easy job. And remember, he's having to manage all the different native cultures in addition to the international prospectors that were attracted to the Spanish Cedula all those years ago."

"Ah yes. He has to prove loyalty to the crown under whose sovereignty we are now, while pushing back the very influential Spanish laws, and with the increasing number of French settlers fleeing Saint Domingue for places with more favourable labour practices. We have an even more diverse and interesting population here. Abercrombie chose well."

"I concur about Ralph. I was actually a midshipman serving under him during the capitulation of Trinidad when it was the Spanish Antilles! In fact I left the Royal Navy immediately thereafter to take over running this plantation when my father died." Florian added.

"How very interesting, Florian. A Royal Navy man! You've gone up in my estimation! I saw in the local paper you were turfed out by my predecessor. I'm sorry about that. There are changes afoot and I think the Plantation Owner's Alliance was unjust to you. You have to understand that people are terrified for their lives as well as their crops."

"Indeed Quintin, I have to say it's good to have some new blood around these days, and thank you for your kind words. Yes, we are all concerned about our lives and livelihoods, understandably so and Picton has been, shall we say, interesting to observe. However I don't wholly agree with his direction."

"Yes, he's a very interesting man. The country is flourishing and we now have better trade deals with other parts of the world, no longer just with Spain and, God-willing, it grows year on year. But there are lingering problems from before he got here. I know in Port of Spain they are still having to deal with some of the French and Spanish demimonde who came here before the Cedula to make their fortune, illegitimately. The creoles. So yes, we have had our own issues in the region from them, too, but so far, not as much as elsewhere."

"It will be interesting to see where the country is, in a year or two and if Trinidad can weather the threat of potential riots and uprisings. I don't think it will survive what happened in Saint Domingue. Then, where will the likes of us be?" Tante took the chicken to the table and placed it in the centre as Adisa followed, carrying the smaller platters of vegetables.

"Stay out of her way! She's so clumsy. If you aren't careful she will trip again." Felix said, reaching out to poke her as she went by. Peggy giggled and elbowed him.

"Stop it you two!" Quintin chided, continuing the conversation with Florian. Adisa became self conscious and took great care to handle the dishes. She despised Felix for making fun of her.

"And the twins will be 11 by the time the new tutor arrives next month …" Adisa heard the remark.

They're the same age as me! Adisa thought to herself. Away from their gaze, she was determined not to let them see they were upsetting her. She hurried back to the kitchen.

"Are you all right Adisa?" Tante had observed the bratty boy interfering with her.

"Yes, I am." Adisa nodded even though she was not.

"Don't mind them, those two nasty devils. God is watching them. And that boy?? Probably learning that bad behaviour to girls, from his father. Thank goodness it won't be long and they'll be going home. I will save you a sweet treat for later."

"Why would Felix's father teach him that? And why in particular is he mean to me?"

"I would not give them a second thought. They are Mr Florian's friends and we only have to see them today. As I said, they'll be gone in a while and hopefully you will not have to see them in a hurry." Tante tried to reassure Adisa. "Don't let them see they have upset you. Now go on, you've got work to do. It won't be long." Adisa pursed her lips in annoyance but knew Tante was right. Felix and his sister would be gone shortly. She had a job to do and did not wish to be punished by Mr Florian or even Tante!

After all had dined, Adisa started gathering the dirty plates and cutlery from the table and each time she passed Felix, he attempted to trip her up again. He would stick his foot out or knock one of the cruets off the table and other subtle plausible little undermining actions that did not appear too obvious to the adults, engrossed in heavy conversation.

"We're concerned with a bout of smallpox in Toco and a number of people have died as a result. We need to prevent its spread. Some of the military men, too, have contracted the illness. Have you lost anyone from the disease Florian?" Quintin asked.

"Not as yet. But I know further down south it's a problem. I hope it can be contained." Florian added.

Peggy was busy playing with her doll's hair, and Miles was playing on the floor, now that the main dishes had been taken away, but Felix had other diversions on his mind. When Adisa came back out, carrying a tray of cups, saucers and a teapot full of fresh leaves and hot water, Felix pushed the now empty high chair into her path. It was too late for Adisa to avoid it and she stumbled trying to maintain her balance. The tray and its contents were jostled headed towards the child on the floor and Felix beside her. Adisa swiftly twisted in front of it and bumped the tilted tray up and away from them both, taking all the scalding water on her hand and side of her dress before the teapot, cups and saucers went all over the table and then a few breaking on the floor away from any one. It all happened in slow motion. Adisa's eyes watered from the hot water, fury and embarrassment.

Tante and some kitchen help rushed out to find out what had happened. They hurried to make sure none of the guests was hurt. Miles was quickly picked up away from any shards of broken glass and china. Despite her badly burned hand, Adisa was picking up sharp pieces and apologising for an accident she did not cause.

"That damn worthless darkie has caused enough scenes today. Thank God neither Miles nor Felix was scalded. She's a very clumsy slave, Florian, you must get rid of her. Put her to work out on the land where she can't harm anyone."

"But Ma …" Felix said.

"Are you OK my darling Felix? Did you get hurt by that ordeal?" Delia swiftly went to Felix and mollycoddled him. Myles was crying due to the commotion. Delia examined Felix for any of the water which may have landed on him or shards of porcelain or glass. He was unhurt.

"Ma! I'm fine." He wrested himself from her arms.

"Oh my baby, thank God you're alright." Delia continued smothering her older son.

Felix looked for Adisa, but he could not see her. Samantha brought a fresh pot of tea and a plate of sugared candies for the children. Peggy helped herself and gave one to Myles to pacify him.

"Quintin, I think we need to go home now!" He looked at Florian with apologetic eyes and Florian understood how he felt.

"Thank you so much for lunch Florian and your kind hospitality. I hope we can get together again soon."

"Come on Quintin, we can't stay here a moment longer. I wish to get my children home where I know they will be safe! Delia headed towards the landau and their footman and with Myles on her hip, Felix holding her right hand, Quintin took one of the candies for himself. "See you at the next meeting." The men shook hands and Florian waved the family off.

As the landau departed, Felix looked out the window in the direction of the house, eager for signs of Adisa.

Once the family was out of sight, Florian returned to the house. He was going to have to speak with Tante about Adisa. Once he neared the kitchen he overheard the animated sibilance of the women speaking. Good, he thought. Tante would reprimand the clumsy girl. He waited out of sight, just to hear. Adisa was crying. Her words were staccato because of her shuddered breathing.

"It's, it's, it's not fair. All afternoon he kept poking me. He pushed that chair into me! He saw me coming with the tray! Why didn't anyone stop him?" Adisa hugged Tante and cried a little more. Tante stroked her head and held a cool cloth on her burned hand.

"Why do I have to wait on them? Why don't I get to wear pretty clothes like her and get to do as I wish? Have a nice luncheon? I don't get the chance to go to other people's houses and be entertained. No, I have to wait on the likes of those stupid people. Why? Why?"

"Be quiet now, child. I saw that little devil. I know it wasn't your fault. But in this world we all have our place and this is yours. We all have to do things we don't like. I know it's hard, but you need to count your blessings. You have a roof over your head, food, a better life than those field workers. I guess you would rather trade places with someone the same age as you who works picking cotton or processing the sugar cane all day?"

Florian had been angered that his guests left so abruptly and he wanted to throttle Adisa, but now he just secretly listened.

"Listen chil'. I guess you have to learn this someday. Might as well be today. They think we are no better than dogs. We do their bidding because they think their skin colour is better than ours. There is no sense in letting the likes of them get to you. Your mother would be proud of you and what a smart, beautiful little brown girl you have become. As am I."

"But why Tante? I don't understand. Doesn't the Bible say we are all equal? Why am I not considered equal? Why didn't God make my skin white? They are supposed to be Christians too, but they did not behave that way? This is so wrong Tante. Why? Did you hear what his mother called me?"

"Adisa there is so much for you to learn about this life. We are what we are and for the moment that will not change. It will someday, but it will take time, more than my lifetime to change. Read your bible, stay on the right side. God sees your pain. People like that will have to answer at the Gates eventually." Adisa sobbed her frustrations out and Tante held her and comforted her, as she had done for all the other children when they suddenly realised their place in the world would be limited by unfair things outside their control.

Chapter 18

Adisa heard the bell, but she could tell it wasn't the old lady. It had an urgency about it. When she entered the room the priest was there.

"Yes, Ma'am, Father. What can I do for you?"

"Call Master Florian, please. His mother would like to speak with him. Urgently." Mabel's breathing was laboured. Adisa knew that her condition had been deteriorating. The doctor had been over many times, but this is not the doctor. This was the priest. He was about healing different things.

Normally she would have curtseyed to her mistress but the urgency meant that she had to run to find a young boy to summon Master Florian quickly. Then Adisa returned to her mistress' side.

"He's on his way ma'am. Can I get you anything?" Mabel nodded and indicated with her hand a familiar gesture which requested Adisa dip a cloth in the basin and gently wipe the old lady's face and arms. Mabel was feverish and the damp cloth had the desired effect with the gentle breeze through the window of cooling Mabel down.

"Where is he?" Mabel whispered. The priest began making motions in the air and praying the rosary.

Adisa grew frightened. She ran to the kitchen to call Tante, who would know what to do. As soon as Tante saw Mabel, she instructed Adisa to get lemon and more water. The priest was asked to leave the room, and the women stripped the covers off Mabel and with the cool water, washed Mabel down.

Florian knocked on the door. Tante and Adisa made Mabel decent and opened the door to Florian who stood in shock at the sight of his mother. She seemed so much better this morning.

"Florian, my son. Come." Mabel extended her frail hand to him. He pulled up a chair to sit by her side. "Florian, I have given my confession and I want my soul clean with you, too. I begged forgiveness. And you must too." Mabel's breathing was sparse. "You must do the right thing. You've got to put things right, sooner rather than later. It's too late for me." Tante asked Adisa to leave the room. She did not want the young girl to see Mabel in this state any more.

"My beautiful Florian! You will never know how like your father you are." A gentle smile crossed Mabel's lips in recollection. "You have his stubborn streak and his cleverness and his coldness, too." Mabel tried to sit up but was too weak. "I see Johan in you, my son." Mabel coughed repeatedly.

“I was wrong to punish that child for your sins. I was also punishing her for your father’s sins.” She trailed off again.

“Mother …?” Florian wasn’t sure what he’d heard. “I don’t understand.”

“She was innocent. I was wrong to punish her. It is too late for me. You must make it up to her. You must take care of her. You need to acknowledge that Adisa is your daughter.” Tante looked at both of them. I know what it is like to have had a cruel childhood. Adisa deserves more…” Mabel struggled to breathe.

“Mother?” Florian wasn’t sure what she was asking.

“I saw how much like Johan you were, when you first arrived. It was remarkable how similar. But I was hoping I was wrong.” Mable gave a wry smile. “And then you proved me right. You know you both brought shame on my own home? Your arrogance, just like your father’s...You brought shame on the family home and name and you both expected me to just accept it.” Mabel was increasingly breathless. Tante wanted to mop her brow with the cooling cloth but she stayed back.

“Mother, I’m not sure what you mean…” Florian’s words trailed off.

“You think I don’t know what goes on? My time is coming, but not before I let you know the truth of why we are here, what your father did. Back in Peutie he lost our house in a poker game which is why we had to put you in boarding school and move here. I was heartbroken to send my only son away, Those 16 or so years were torture. I pined for you. But I had to do what was right for you, not me. Now you too, must do what is right, God will provide for me. He will do the same for you. I want you to lead your life as a good Christian man. It is time for you to grow up, Florian. Grow up and do the right thing."

Mabel was becoming more agitated, coughing between phrases, but continued. "I have been no saint Florian, I beg God's forgiveness, but my lapses were momentary. I never courted sin the way you and your father did, not caring when you exposed me to it, never caring who else you left adrift in your wakes."

Florian tried to make sense of what she just told him. Father lost the house gambling? His father, the banker? He always wondered why he was sent to boarding school. He was home with a tutor, happy with new friends, then suddenly sent off to boarding school. Now he could understand why. His parents wanted to give him the best possible start in life. Conquerabia is no place for an upper class boy.

"Mamma, I did not realise. I never understood why you left me there. I missed you and Flossie and father so much. I couldn't understand why you didn't come back for me. Eventually I accepted you had sent me to boarding school like all the other wealthy boys who were with me. All of us were abandoned there. I never knew it was because of something my father did. I'm so, so sorry." His eyes welled up for the boy he was, so lonely for all those years, and for the son now about to lose his mother again.

"Florian, I have always loved you, I love you beyond words. I hope you will forgive me for not telling you sooner. You need forgiveness too. I forgive you for bringing the shame of an illegitimate, negro child you had with a slave on our house. And your father's betrayals to me and you, to our marriage? I pray that he made a confession before he died. I pray that he repented. Promise me you will make it right. Confess your sins, Florian."

Florian was shocked by his mother's words. It was the first time she had ever addressed him in this way and it made him feel as if he were five years old. Scolded.

Mabel fell back into a spate of coughing and wheezing, exhausted from speaking, Mabel's breathing became shallow. Florian knew there would be no more talking now. He would try to learn more later, his mother needed to rest.

Mabel lapsed into a state of fevered delirium. The doctor gave her tea made from the cinchona tree but it didn't help much. Muttering and fitful, she would sometimes be lucid enough to indicate thirst or wanting a cold cloth or more fanning. Johan tried to speak with her and she talked but he couldn't make sense of most of it. She said what sounded like your brothers and the name Mirian a few times, but there was no Mirian on Conquerabia. She also said the name Nancy. Again Florian did not know anyone by that name. He prayed that she would recover from the illness that had overtaken her. He couldn't bear to lose his mother. He felt remorse knowing that he had inadvertently embarrassed her. You'd think that after all her time here she would realise that no one cared about mixed race slave children, but she did. And what betrayals was she talking about from his father? As far as he learned, his father had not sired children with any Conquerabia slaves,

He had so many regrets and so many questions that he needed answered. Mabel languished a few more days and then succumbed.

After the funeral Florian ordered a bench to be made to be situated at Mabel's favourite spot, overlooking the water. Once it was installed he went down to view it. It was a beautiful bench. Cornelius truly outdid himself. The wood was planed and sanded so skilfully that when Florian ran his hand over it he couldn't feel even so much as a ripple of grain. The legs were turned with more attention to detail than Florian expected, Cornelius was known for his masterful carpentry. There was an engraved brass plaque with Mabel's name and year of her birth and death that glinted in the sunlight. Cornelius must have thought he would be punished if he didn't do a superlative job on the memorial bench for his Master's mother.

While he sat, Johan mulled over Mabel's words. He tried to understand the meaning of his lonely childhood at boarding school in a different way now that he knew a few things, about the circumstances. This really was no place to educate an upper class boy. By placing him in private education at Harrow, Florian's education had opened up the world and enabled him to have the best education available, then to pursue a life at sea and still inherit Conquerabia, beautiful Conquerabia. What privilege he had and didn't know it. Looking at the land, the crops dancing in the breeze, Florian thought how lucky he was, despite feeling abandoned all those years ago. He knew now that his life was one of riches, and not solely financial.

Chapter 19

Adisa was earning herself a reputation even among the field negroes. She was competent as a cook and household manager, thanks to watching Tante. She had also become educated through the care and teaching of Tante and Elders and the church. She was bright, alert and inquisitive. Of course with her thirst for knowledge came more questions about the world and why she was born a slave. In addition to the newspapers they were already secreting away as well as their constant quest for books for her to read. When old Miss Mabel died Elders collected a stash of books that she had ordered from time to time from Europe. Adisa absorbed all. She was both horrified but also understanding of newspapers stories about slaves poisoning their owners and slave revolts. People who have no recourse sometimes resort to behaviours they would not do under different circumstances.

She recalled several years ago there was a slave on Conquerabia who was so tired and in pain from an injury which caused him to lose his left arm below the elbow, that he refused to work and he got punished for it, severely. The manager felt the slave was shirking. Later that slave was caught sabotaging the boiler so that it would catch fire. His fellow slaves would also have been injured, not just the precious property of Mr. Dottin, but the slave didn't seem to care. He just wanted to do damage to the whole plantation. Adisa reasoned that the slave was so angry about his hard life and servitude that he wanted to destroy the entire place. Adisa was sure he wasn't alone, sometimes. She always pitied the field slaves. She knew their lives were much harder than hers.

But of all the things she read, her favourite book, the one that made her think the most was one that Miss Mabel left, called A Vindication of the Rights of Women. In it, the author, Mary Wollstencraft, a white woman, talked about the unfair treatment of women and slaves at the same time. She said, "Is sugar always to be produced by vital blood? Is one half of the human species, like the poor African slaves, to be subject to prejudices that brutalise them, when principles would be a surer guard, only to sweeten the cup of man? Is not this indirectly to deny women reason?"

Adisa knew that the author was talking about white women, but she also saw the plight of slaves on sugar plantations as equally unjust! What she said sounded exactly the way Adisa felt about being a slave, even more a slave than Miss Wollstencraft thought she was. As she read, she could see that almost everything the author wrote about the rights of women could be applied to the rights of slaves.

When Miss Wollstencraft wrote, "Would men but generously snap our chains, and be content with rational fellowship instead of slavish obedience, they would find us more observant daughters, more affectionate sisters, more faithful wives, more reasonable mothers - in a word, better citizens." Couldn't she just as easily have been talking about frustrated slaves? If slaves were freed from their actual chains, Adisa was sure they would be better workers and better men and women and better citizens. Adisa thought about a world where she could work like the free coloured people worked, just for themselves and their families. Free coloured women still washed and ironed clothes, but for money and with no threats of violence or unwanted sexual advances.

Adisa had heard talk and read about the revolts on other islands. Now Mr. Dottin and other plantation owners were worried about repercussions here. They all are worried about angry slaves turning on them. But isn't it interesting, she thought to herself, that they don't ever seem to ask why the slaves are revolting, only how they can use harsher treatment, more chains, more guarding and more restrictions to keep slaves in line? The owners talk about their slaves as children or savages, both incorrigible, never thinking that it is their servitude that renders them that way.

It reminded her of another thing, Miss Wollstencraft said about the treatment of white women that Adisa also could apply to herself and slaves. "They may be convenient slaves, but slavery will have its constant effect, degrading the master and the abject dependent. Make them free, and they will quickly become wise and virtuous, as men become more so; for the improvement must be mutual …"

To collect her feelings Adisa started writing in a journal about her experiences and observations of life on the plantation. She saw a lot of articles in the papers Elders and some others were able to collect about the arguments for and against slavery. She also saw a lot of articles about slave revolts and unrest, and even some about individual slaves causing harm to and even murdering their masters, but all of these were written from a white person's point of view. One day she decided to pen an article for the Trinidad Courant based on her life.

It took her several weeks to write, "The Tyranny of Privilege: A Mullato's Life As A Domestic Slave", before she was happy with it. She signed it 'A M'. When all was clear, she hid the letter amongst the pile of correspondence that was sent by the house boy to town.

-o0o-

It was a beautiful morning on the verandah of the main house on Conquerabia. Florian was having breakfast with his beautiful young bride, Ottilie. Usually only interested in the latest fashions, this morning she caught sight of an article said to be written by a slave!

"Can you imagine? Florian! Look at this. There is this piece in this paper written by a slave in this very island. A coloured slave girl! I'm not sure I can believe it. But Florian, it is so moving. I have never considered things from a slave's perspective, especially a girl's. The ones around here seem so happy and content." She handed it to him.

"Well!" said Florian, reading it through for himself, "I am not sure it was even written by a slave. It's simply too well written. Probably it is written by some abolitionists, but certainly not by a girl. If it is by a slave at all it is more likely written by an adult, a male writer under a pseudonym, but I must say, whoever wrote it, does have the ability to make one think!" He put the paper down and continued eating.

"But Florian, did you see the special notice at the end?" Ottilie was surprised he hadn't commented on the notice from the publisher.

Florian picked the paper back up and saw what she was referring to. "Well, I have never seen anything like this before."

In an outlined box beneath the essay by the author, titled A Special Invitation, the publisher of the The Trinidad Courant wrote:

To the writer of this piece, 'A.M.'.

We published A Tyranny of Privilege: A Mullato's Life As A Domestic Slave, because we felt that stories and observations from a young house slave's perspective might be of interest to our readers. Previously it has been our position to remain neutral on the subject of chattel slavery. Here on the island, the use of slave labour is the primary manual labour source without which the economy would suffer greatly on the plantations and all of the businesses connected to them. Hard hit too. particularly, would be shipping and the businesses that require the crops shipped from here should slavery be banned.

These are worldly concerns. We see now that we must also concern ourselves with our own eternal souls and also those of our enslaved brethren, the labourers toiling away on those plantations. Your persuasive words have caused us to reject our neutrality on the subject and declare ourselves in favour of the abolition of chattel slavery. To further elucidate our reasons, and to share them with our readers, we invite you to submit more of your observations, thoughts, and persuasive arguments. We will publish them herein in our support for the abolition of slavery."

Florian put the paper down and looked off into the yard at all the activity.

"I have never seen the Courant take a position like this on any topic. They will certainly incur the wrath of most of the plantation owners here. I was nearly run out of town for less, for merely suggesting we all find ways to reward slaves who remained faithful servants, to pay them a bit, to allow them the possibility of purchasing themselves."

Ottilie said, "This makes me concerned about the author. I know you don't think it was written by a slave girl, but Florian what if it was? Won't she be in danger? Won't they hunt her?"

"If it was a slave girl, rest assured she isn't one of ours. But yes, the writer should beware. Tensions are high because of the uprisings elsewhere. This writer could be accused of inciting unrest."

Adisa happened to have been answering nature's call and was on her way back to the kitchen when she overheard this exchange and was astonished. The paper read my work and is now abolitionist! They want more of my writing! Mr. Dottin thinks it could have been written by a white writer!

Adisa would have liked to eavesdrop more but she felt she had taken too much time on her necessary break. Tante would be angry if she didn't hurry up, plus Adisa didn't want to draw attention to herself. She was proud to have made the newspaper take an abolitionist stance but now, suddenly, she knew was in a dangerous position.

The fear of discovery made Adisa afraid all the time. She thought, at first, that Miss Ottilie suspected the writer was her, but the way Mr. Dottin dismissed it, despite admiring the refinement of the writing and perspective, the way he suggested it was written by an abolitionist? She felt she was safe, for now, from the Dottins' scrutiny. But Adisa knew that Elders would read the disposed of paper before he had to burn it. And other plantation owners will have read it, too. Word of it and the new stance of the Trinidad Courant would outrage them, and it would travel fast. Slaves hear everything even though they have to pretend that they don't.

It did not take Tante and Elders long to suspect it was their Adisa who penned the article. She was always writing in her secret journals and they recognised the words she used when she spoke about her condition to them, but they kept it between themselves. They didn't even confirm it with Adisa. They wanted to be able to deny it if they were questioned. They knew that if word got out their beloved Adisa would be in danger and they wanted to protect her. But they also knew, through, they and other slaves had an opportunity to be heard.

When Elders was taking out the papers to be burned one day, he noticed an advert for Faith Nash, a freed mullato slave, who was to give a talk in Port of Spain. Faith Nash was known for her talks about the plight of female slaves, and this attracted Elders's attention.

Since Elders had a certain amount of freedom looking after the buildings and maintenance he was trusted to leave Conquerabia for the Port of Spain every month or so on errands, and to collect mail and packages for Florian. Usually Tante accompanied him, but this time Tante feigned sick and Elders persuaded his master that he needed the help of Adisa to handle some women's duties, like getting fabric and childbirth items. Adisa was surprised at the off plantation work but happy for the adventure.

Once there, Elders snuck the two of them in to hear Faith Nash talk. It proved a turning point for Adisa as she sat intently at the church, listening to the well spoken Nash describe her experience of being a stolen pregnant African slave, who gave birth on the brutal voyage where many slaves grew ill and died, and then she was separated from her daughter upon sale, in Jamaica.

Nash even referenced A Vindication of the Rights of Women by Mary Wollstonecraft! She read the very same book that her former mistress Mrs. Dottin had and that Adisa also found inspiring! She soaked up every word of Nash's talk.

After hastily obtaining the mail, tools, basins and forceps, they were sent to get, they set off. For a short while on the journey back, Adisa and Elders tried to discuss what they had heard, but they soon settled into their own thoughts. The two of them heard Nash's message differently.

Elders drove the team methodically, but his emotions were charging in every direction. He was born of a mulatto mother and witnessed violence no child should see. On a previous plantation when his mother was at her master's mercy he went to protect her but the plantation owner had other ideas. In need of attention, nothing was going to get in his way as he took to his machete and attacked the young man. Recalling this experience Elders placed a hand on the left side of his hip where the cutlass sliced him open. He remembered seeing his blood, such deep red blood pouring from the wound, down his leg and onto the earth. The pain seared through him as he was whiplashed and fell to the ground. He heard a conversation with another female slave talking about her rapes and the theft of her children and he felt the familiar rage rise into his throat again, the rage that he constantly had to drive down. Here it was again. His gut angered.

The fucking sousoute He understood the righteous violence of the slave rebellions elsewhere. Right now he could kill. He knew he could kill. Listening to the story of her babies being ripped from that young mother's arms threw him into a whirl of anger. Deep breaths. Deep breaths. They long had helped Elders push his rage down. In and out and in and out. He needed to push it down again. He'd made his choice, long ago, and now he had so much to lose if he followed that anger down the road it would lead. It wasn't just him anymore. He thought of Tante. He looked over and saw Adisa. He closed his eyes and saw his bible.

Adisa contemplated what she'd heard and she was filled with a desire to gain her own freedom and that of others. She knew she had to write again for the Courant. The fear she had been feeling was fast subsiding. Adisa knew she would get into serious trouble if it was revealed she was the article's author, but seeing Nash speak of the danger she faced speaking out in public? Hearing Nash talk about how close she came to death escaping? How often is she threatened now? If Nash was brave enough to risk her life in the name of freedom then Adisa was going to be, too. She started composing her next instalment for the Courant for the rest of the ride back to Conquerabia.

-o0o-

After their marriage, Florian and Ottilie had frequent evenings with Aubrey, Ottilie's father, who owned a neighbouring cotton plantation. That is how they all met, with Florian going over to meet his new neighbour, and to check out the new competing plantation, truth be told. It was Florian who took Aubrey to the Plantation Owners' Alliance, before things grew contentious there.

Aubrey was a learned man who studied and practised law in France before emigrating to Saint Domingue with his wife and young family to gain his fortune, much like Florian's father had when he came to Trinidad. Aubrey moved his operations to Trinidad due to the revolts, with his now 16 year old son Toby and two older sisters, Ottilie, 19, and Therese, 17. His wife had perished of an island fever long before their plantation was imperilled by the unrest and they were forced to move with so many others likewise evicted by the marauding former slaves. However it came to be, he found he loved Trinidad and settled in quickly.

It was a lucky meeting for both. Aubry needed a nearby friend to help him adjust to his new homeland and to introduce him to the Alliance in these troubled times. Florian considered it an unexpected windfall that his new neighbour came with a lovely daughter to take his mind off his mother's death and to fulfill her dying wish, that he settle down, Aubrey was delighted to marry his eldest daughter off to a landed gentleman. And the men had much in common. Florian gained a wife and a friend.

Aubrey respected Florian, whom he came to view as a son. They often sat on the Conquerabia verandah when the sun went down, putting the world to rights, and discussing the abolition movement. How could they remain profitable without slaves, but how could they justify the current state of plantation culture? They both believed in humane treatment of their labour but they knew there were many plantation owners, like Brodie Henderson, who were brutal and gave them all a bad name. They blamed the likes of them for the revolts.

But now the revolts seemed to be spreading, even to slaves who were otherwise content with their lives. Both of them wanted to help make a difference for everyone by finding ways to placate the labour by offering them things that would confer upon them a sense of self reliance, maybe even the opportunity to buy themselves. Perhaps offer the talented ones some free time to earn money through private work or through a craft. Some of their slaves had learned skills on the plantation they might be able to ply. It was the humane side of Florian that touched Aubrey and convinced him he was worthy of his elder daughter's hand in marriage. A man who treats his slaves well would surely treat a wife well.

Ottilie loved Florian, his worldly knowledge and ways. Her parents took them from France when she was very young and she missed out on the things that Europe could show a young woman. Her father assured her that they were all lucky to be away from France during the revolution but she wondered, and she fretted about meeting a suitable husband. With Florian she found both a bit of the culture she craved and the good marriage she hoped for.

Ottilie felt no immediate need to put her own stamp on superficial things in Conquerabia. She did not feel compelled to redecorate or change all the menus. With no mother in law to impress she soon fell into the role of lady of the house. She liked Tante, and quickly took to Adisa, whom she inherited from the deceased Mabel. For her part, Adisa loved having a mistress closer to her own age. And with such a sunny disposition, too. She especially liked to spend time dressing her and looking through all the beautiful gowns, necklaces and lace garments she had. Ottilie would have liked to entertain more, but relations between many of the plantation owners were strained because of the slave revolts, so Ottilie decided to make her mark as the new woman of the house in other ways first.

It was Ottilie's idea that the women slaves on the plantation enjoy more freedom and family time. That article in the Courant written by the mulatto slave girl really touched her. She insisted that Florian allow them to finish working on Fridays at dusk and to end work on Saturdays by early afternoon. It was unheard of but in return morale improved. Sundays were sacrosanct and work on Conquerabia ceased for most. They were permitted to attend to their own gardens, church or relax at will.

Ottilie also encouraged Florian to give appropriate time off for pregnant women to sit more. She told him she always felt sorry when she saw pregnant slaves struggling, especially the ones in the fields. And for women who had recently given birth, she wanted to give them more time to spend with their newborns, and then return to work when they were fully healed. Even then they should have more time to nurse and care for their babies.

Florian had honestly never given much thought to the pregnant slaves, other than they provided future workers. It seemed to him that things had been working well enough. But his young new bride was adamant. She told him the central longhouse, where the working slave mothers left their children, was used for too much. There was no specific quiet area for the smallest babies to sleep, and the older children, the ones still too young to work, were often shooed away. Ottilie had a large separate nursery built where the mothers could leave their children with a few workers who looked after them during the day and a place for mothers to nurse. She loved the newborns and often went to the nursery to fawn over and hold the babies. She encouraged the parents to have their children baptised. At times, Florian felt her generosity went too far.

But Florian also thought that perhaps Ottilie was onto something, making things a bit nicer for the slaves, and interacting with them so sweetly. News of the growing revolts in Saint Domingue and elsewhere was continuing to reach Trinidad and Florian became increasingly concerned. Aubrey's stories about his family fleeing for their lives as their plantation was burned and ransacked made Florian try to come up with ways to pacify any unrest that might be brewing, which helped prevent Florian's extended eviction from the Plantation Owner's Alliance. Aubry assured them that Florian's ideas were not radical but practical, and often spoke out in favour of him. Trying to persuade the owners, at the national alliance meeting, owners like Brodie Henderson, who ruled with whips and threats, their treatment was inhumane and was rejected as foolhardy. Suggesting that their cruelty made them more vulnerable to revolt and slave uprising brought curses and disdain. Their response to the threats was to redouble their ways. Fear was the only approach they meant to use and use it they did and would continue to do so. With Picton as governor, they felt they had the King's blessing and damnation to those who suggested otherwise. With the revised Code Noir published, which justified their cruelty, it was confirmation they owned property, not human beings.

After changing almost nothing about the big house, Ottilie asked Adisa to help her clear out Mabel's old room. The room had been left untouched since the old woman died and no one, not even Tante, dared go in to change anything, not wanting to upset Florian. But today, a year on, Ottilie felt that she needed to update the house with new furnishings, paint and the odd item of new furniture.

She and Ottilie cleaned the room from top to bottom and switched around the decor to make it more inviting to their guests for lunch tomorrow.

With the room complete, Adisa and Tante were instructed to collect a new dress for Ottilie from the neighbouring seamstress which Ottilie would wear for mass.

For Florian the changes are equally positive. For the first time since he arrived, the big house was lively and often full of excitement. Ottilie's younger brother and sister often came during the day and laughter became a regular sound in those halls. Out on the verandah with the French doors open, where his mother used to lay, the house seemed so different that it was almost unrecognisable. He felt her presence as he listened to the hustle and bustle and excitement of the kitchen. It was a presence of her approval.

Ottilie asked Adisa to help her get dressed. Adisa was flattered and ran up the stairs to the master bedroom where she saw Ottilie in her beautiful, white dressing gown. She took the new dress, which she brought back from the seamstress, and laid it out onto the bed. It was stunning, ivory linen and lace, with a pretty high neck.

Ottilie pinned her hair up and just a few curls released themselves and framed her face. She gently perspired and used a white cotton handkerchief to mop her brow and neck.

Adisa ran back downstairs where she placed a jug of water on a tray and returned. Ottilie was very grateful. Ottilie watched Adisa go about her work. She was meticulous and took great care.

"Adisa, would you mind getting me the pearl necklace from the top drawer of the dressing table? The shorter of the two?"

Adisa did as she was asked and felt the smooth pearlescent texture against her fingers. It was delicate and thrilling to hold the pearls between her fingers. Ottilie watched her gently hold them out to her.

"They are pretty, aren't they Adisa?" She nodded. "Why don't you try them on?"

"But M'm, I could not. I could get into so much trouble if they saw me." Adisa bowed her head. Ottilie got up from the corner of the bed and closed the door gently.

"This will be our secret!" and she placed the necklace around Adisa's neck, turning her to see her own reflection in the mirror. Adisa's golden, mixed race complexion lit up with the pearls. Ottilie pinned her hair up.

"Wait there." Ottilie reached into the wardrobe and brought out a pink dress and held it in front of her. Adisa saw herself as a beautiful young lady. It reminded her of the day she waited on Felix and Peggy and she felt as smart as they looked on the day. A ripple of excitement ran through her - an imagery of equality. She felt foolish thinking such thoughts and remembered where she was. Embarrassment overcame her.

Ottilie studied her too, amazed by the transformation in her slave. Her beauty was remarkable and Ottilie realised how plain she looked in comparison and then caught sight of something in Adisa's features. The cacophony of outside's activities nudged her out of her concern and she dismissed the notion.

"Oh, Miss Ottilie. I look so different. Thank you!".

"Let's keep this between us. You can have the dress. It's a bit old but if we shorten it, we can make it look like new on you. I can't give you the pearls, but when you have a very special day of your own, I promise I will lend them to you."

"But Miss Ottilie, I couldn't accept it from you. I will get into trouble for sure. I appreciate the thought, but no. Thank you!" Adisa dropped her head in sadness.

"Well, how about this Adisa? I have given you the dress. It's yours and when you need to wear it, just whisper to me. I'll take it down to Mrs Brown the seamstress and tell her that you'll collect it, once it's been shortened. What do you say?"

Adisa had never known such generosity from either Florian, Mabel or Ottilie and was moved to tears. She picked up the corner of her apron and wiped her face.

"This is just our secret, OK?" Ottilie kneeled down before her and assured her that the dress was hers.

"Miss Ottilie, I better go or Miss Tante will be wondering what's taking me so long. Thank you!"

Adisa composed herself and asked if Ottilie wanted the tray removed. She took it with her back downstairs and headed off to the kitchen, where Tante asked what had kept her.

"Miss Ottilie needed help getting into her new dress. There are so many buttons up the back. It is so pretty."

"Well never you mind Adisa, please help to finish laying the table. Florian and Miss Ottilie will be going off to church soon and her family will be coming back for lunch. We are getting behind."

"Yes, Tante. Sorry Tante."

Adisa settled back into her role and thought about the dress that was hers, hanging up alongside her mistress's. She smiled to herself, went to the porch and laid up the table for twelve guests. The roses that Tante had cut looked beautiful against the muslin tablecloth.

It was not long before the carriages returned full of gaiety. Adisa watched as everyone arrived and admired the beautiful dresses that Ottilie and her sister wore and two of their girlfriends.

Lunch was a tremendous success and the party dispersed to playing croquet or cards. The men went inside to drink and talk and the women sat with Ottilie and gossiped. Every now and then a shriek could be heard as the women laughed together.

Adisa wondered if she could ever have a life like that. She recalled her reflection in the mirror and then realised that she is a slave and fate dictated she would remain a slave; she could never buy her freedom.

Later that afternoon, high tea needed to be prepared. Adisa lacked the heart to do a good job, Elders and Tante noticed.

"My girl. What has happened to sadden you? Now is not the time for feeling sorry for yourself. Stop your nonsense. We have to serve tea out on the lawn. Adisa? What is it,"

"Oh, nothing Tante. I'm sorry. May I be excused for a moment?" Tante nodded and Adisa ran to her room. She looked in the broken mirror on her makeshift dressing table and imagined herself in the dress and pearls again. She felt the injustice of her situation and considered her position. All that she had to look forward to right now, was getting married to another slave and having children of her own. That would not give her the lifestyle she momentarily tasted and now longed for.

She pulled a box from under her bed and removed the paper she retrieved from the garbage. She read the headline again, which spoke about Florian's remarks at the last Plantation Owners meeting. She admired something about his taking a strong stance for her and others like her. It showed his compassion and humanity. She also saw her stories in the Courant, the national paper which she kept. Adisa raised her head, inhaled deeply and stood in front of the mirror. In that moment she saw the woman she was determined to be. A free woman among free people.

Tante called for her and she quickly folded the paper back and returned it to its home. With a new found conviction, Adisa stood up tall, smiled and went to help Tante and ensure the late afternoon tea went smoothly.

As dusk arrived, Ottilie gathered her family and friends to make a special announcement. She invited Florian to stand with her at the top of the verandah and everyone else, seated in the shade on the lawn looked on in anticipation.

“Dear friends and family. It has been a wonderful Easter Day. Florian and I hope you have enjoyed your Easter Sunday. We are so lucky to have you as our family and friends and …”, Ottilie reached for Florian’s hand. He looked bemused. “My dear, devoted Florian, we are going to be parents!”

Florian looked surprised. His wife is pregnant. It took a moment for the news to sink in, but he was overjoyed and hugged and kissed her.

“Really?” I’m going to be a father?” Ottilie nodded, wearing the biggest smile. “Dear Lord, I’m going to be a father!” Aubrey was the first to congratulate the couple and the women shrieked once again in excitement.

Tante looked at Florian with disdain which Adisa caught. "Miss Tante, what's wrong. Why do you look at Master Florian like that?" Tante, rumbled.

"Nothing, child." The term irked Adisa. "I guess the news just surprised me too." She attempted a smile. "Go about your business and don't mind me." Tante tried to calm herself. Florian caught her eye and immediately understood.

Chapter 20

The day Ottilie and Florian found out it was Adisa who wrote the articles for the Courant could have gone in a different direction. Ottilie had found the paper cuttings and Adisa's writing in a box in her room when Adisa was working in the kitchen. She took her find to Florian and closed the salon door behind her.

Florian read the items carefully and considered Adisa in a different light. In one respect he felt impressed by the young girl, on the other, angry that it was one of his own slaves that was writing her thoughts for the island to read. It felt like betrayal.

Ottilie reasoned with him that it was time they considered what one of their own slaves was thinking and feeling, that her words were powerful and struck home. It wasn't meant to read as an attack but to be enlightening to those who never considered life from a black, let alone mulatto's perspective.

Florian had to admit some of her comments were quoted at the last meeting of the Plantation Owners' Alliance gathering and had the effect of forcing those members to think seriously about the wave of abolitionist activity crossing the island. He told Ottilie her plans, particularly where the pregnant women and women in general were concerned, were making a difference in the demeanour of most of their negroes. But he was concerned as to how he should handle Adisa. More so how his colleagues at the Alliance would treat him, based on his previous comments when he was initially evicted should it become public knowledge it was one of his slaves. He would have to bide his time.

Fortunately Ottilie helped him see reason; that accepting Adisa as the author of those opinion pieces would prove what he proposed as proof he could be right, the tide was turning for the abolitionist movement. It was a huge gamble, but one he was prepared to take on.

He looked at his beautiful wife and thought how did he get to be so fortunate to have such a bright, clever wife who supported him, unlike his mother, until her dying day.

Both took Tante and Elders into their confidence - Ottilie suggested it was best they knew and fortunately Florian did not remonstrate with them, preferring to allow them to appear ignorant of the situation. Tante acted surprised whilst inside feeling relief that it was out in the open at long last. However, Florian felt that he needed to speak with Adisa personally.

"Please, sit down." Florian invited Adisa and Ottilie sat next to her husband and smiled reassuringly. Adisa then saw her collection of cuttings and writings and gasped in shock.

"It's alright Adisa, we're not here to reprimand you." Florian was blunt. "Though I have to say you've really taken me by surprise. Whilst it was a shock to discover the author of those newspaper articles is by one of our own slaves, we just wanted to discuss this with you. I can assure you, you're not in any trouble from us. If this becomes public knowledge, then I do have concerns for you and your welfare." Adisa, wide eyed in fear, was silent.

"When Ottilie and I first read these in the paper, we were delighted to learn of the thoughts from a house slave. It gave us a lot of thought and I personally felt the time of this was paramount, considering how the abolitionists movement is advancing. We have to consider not just our safety but yours and all our labourers on the plantation. This could put us at huge risk, especially if the Plantation Owners Alliance finds out it is I who is harbouring the author."

Adisa felt Florians words cut deep and she thought she should stop writing. She felt disappointed to be called up in this manner and wanted to cry."

"Do you have anything to say for yourself?" Florian asked.

"Master Florian, Miss Ottilie … ." Adisa tried to compose herself. She straightened her back, took a deep breath and stood up. "I am sorry if you feel I have brought ignominy to your household. From what I understand, these rumblings about a possible uprising here in Trinidad are well founded. No one seems to consider how we slaves feel and why some of us have taken such drastic action, though I condemn such actions that harm anyone or anything. I've been reading. Mr Elders gave me a book your mother had by Mary Wollstonecraft and I was taken to hear Ms Nash, a woman not unlike me, but free, speak. I found both enlightening. I felt a sense of relief writing my own words and to hear other slaves speak in a similar light on their own experiences made me proud. I never intended that such an exercise should cast a shadow over you and Miss Ottilie or anyone else and I will stop. Master Florian you can sell me on or move me elsewhere on the plantation and I shall accept what punishment you feel appropriate."

Florian was moved. "Let's just stop and think for a moment. What you are doing is remarkable. Yes, it will take some time to process this, but I cannot stop you from doing something that gives a voice to another; and your musings have caused the Courant to support the abolitionist movement. I suggest we see in what direction this moves. Only we know as well and Elders and Tante whom I know will not speak publicly of this. My primary concern is your welfare". Adisa was dismissed.

"Well," said Florian. "We find ourselves in an interesting situation. I will be evicted once again from the Plantation Owners' Alliance, but I'm not too concerned about that. I think the time is right, but will let this find its own course. Who am I to stop progress?" And with that Adisa was dismissed, relieved but with a heavy heart.

“Darling Florian. I think you handled that very well and I’m so proud of you. What an amazing surprise to find out the author of those editorials is one of our very own negroes. And you thought it must have been a man’s composition. Ottilie tried to lighten the moment. “I’m with you on concerns for Adisa and our own welfare and I have to say reading her columns has given me a lot to consider.”

“Let’s just hope for the best, shall we?” Florian kissed his wife.

-o0o-

Over time, there were rumblings as to who the author of the Courant columns were. Walking through the plantation Florian overheard some of the slaves discussing the author and the remarks within the latest editorial in the Courant. A year had passed and Adisa was still anonymous although suspicions were aroused.

Discussions were held in Church, on trips to Port of Spain, in taverns and other social settings as more and more people read the essays.

When Adisa’s last essay was published, there was a box below it inviting the author to speak the following month at the Caroni Abolitionist Movement held at the Roman Catholic church. Ottilie, Florian, Tante and Elders discussed the implications of going public. Elders and Tante felt the decision had to be Adisa’s; Florian said it wasn’t the right time, but when would be the right time Adisa asked.

Florian paced up and down. He didn't like how this made him feel and what his friends and family would say. Ottilie reasoned with him, that it should be Adisa who decides so long as she understands the repercussions.

Elders and Adisa sat in the front pew as part of the congregation. To help calm her nerves Adisa looked at the beautiful church, its altar settings, the flowers arranged with an array of purple bougainvillea, deep red poinsettia, pink hibiscus, croton leaves, carnations and Ixora. To look at them made her smile, they were glorious arrangements.

The upright piano sounded at the start of the service and everyone stood as the recently installed priest, Father O'Leary led the procession to the altar.

Adisa loved church. It is where she felt a sense of peace and love. It is where she felt a tangible sense of equality. Everyone sang from the same hymnals. Everyone stood at the same time. Everyone kneeled together, prayed together to the same God who loved them all equally.

Father O'Leary's sermon reflected on life and forgiveness. He spoke about goodness being white like a dove and badness in the world as black as a thunder cloud. He felt that soon Trinidad would fall to the hands of maroons, like Saint Domingue, if plantation owners did not adhere to the revised Code Noir. It caused a commotion amongst the congregation. His message was protectionism and he made it very clear he would not hesitate to take up arms and quoted Luke 20:21 - when the strong, armed man guards his domain his property is safe.

His sermon infuriated Adisa who quickly thought through her own talk to make sure it had a strong, uplifting message. She could tell Tante was also riled by the Priest's comments, she was not alone and it was not the place or time to address him. It appeared he was not really aware of what he was saying. When he finished his sermon, there was an uncomfortable silence, which ended when he announced the next hymn. A number of people took the opportunity to cough and clear their throats before singing one of Adisa's favourite hymns - The Lord's My Shepherd.

Elders left his seat before the end of the hymn so that he could circulate a plate on which the collection would be taken during the last verse and final chorus. Then they all took their seats once again as silence descended on the church and Father O'Leary asked everyone to bow their heads in final prayer, and in closing, the pianist played as the church was emptied and refreshments were enjoyed outside. The children, relieved, ran around playing tag with each other.

Adisa and Elders were standing by the lemonade and ginger beer table, waiting for glasses to be poured. "Are you ready Adisa? Do you need to add any final touches to your speech?"

"Well, I am very nervous and unhappy about Fr O'Leary's divisive comments. I hope it doesn't overshadow what I'm trying to say. I think I have it all together. Fr. O'Leary's sermon has certainly unsettled me, but I think I will deliver something more on point. I know that current times are tense but we have to try and make something of a difference."

"I am so proud of you Adisa. You're the daughter I never had. You have turned into a beautiful young lady. I wish Evelina, your mother, could see you now." Adisa looked up at Elders. He had a tear in his eye.

"Thank you Elders. I owe all that I am to you and Tante. I hope I am serving my mother and her memory well?"

"Ladies and gentlemen, The Caroni Abolitionist Movement is about to commence its meeting. Those of you who wish to attend, please take your seats now. Refreshments will be provided after, so if you have not finished your refreshments, please do so now. Thank you."

Ashton Nicolai, who was chair of the Caroni Abolitionist Movement, led the proceedings and introduced Adisa. As she stood up, she smoothed out the skirt on her dress and took the note from her stringed purse standing tall at the lectern.

"Ladies and gentlemen, distinguished guest, Father O'Leary, I would like to address you today, to state my case and reasons for the abolition of slavery in Trinidad. My name is Adisa and I realise that

I am more fortunate than most. Although I am still considered a slave, I have been surrounded by people who took care of me; educated me through the church and the bible and taught me to think for myself.

"I too have witnessed and experienced injustice. The brutality meted out to those who sought freedom through illegal means. My God teaches forgiveness. He teaches us that we are equal in his eyes and that we should turn the other cheek. Let's recall the story of the Good Samaritan. I believe we are all, at heart, good people. To an extent we are a product of our time and society.

"Very recently, when on a shopping trip into town on behalf of my mistress, I was accosted by a young man of whom I am acquainted purely because our paths have to cross. I shall not say who this young man is. He knows who he is.

"But, on this particular shopping trip, the wicker in my basket had become worn and broke, spilling my goods onto the ground, in the street. This man quickly came to my aid, for which I was immediately grateful and surprised that he should willingly assist me.

"I took a seat upon the bench in the square to see if I could repair my basket. It was successful, if only temporary. The young man saw me and asked if he could join me. I agreed. I thought nothing of it. He had been my samaritan after all and I was grateful.

"We then got into polite conversation. He asked me on which plantation I worked and I answered, to which he remarked that he thought it was a beautiful house. He informed me that he would like to own such a beautiful house one day and I assured him that through his hard work, he may well own such a beautiful house.

"I thought that the conversation would end there and was about to leave. He asked me pensively if I could ever see myself owning such a house to which I replied that perhaps, one day, I would.

"What happened next appalled me. He looked at me and said that I could never own such a house because it just would not be right, that someone like me could never be seen in that situation. I asked him why he felt that it would be impossible for me. If he could dream, then so could I, at which point he laughed at me and said negroes can't own property, even if they are half caste. He told me that no matter what, I am still considered a negro and therefore I needed to be reminded of my position.

"I feel in that moment, my samaritan as I thought he was, needed to feel better than me. To feel superior to me. To know that I was not a threat to him. You see the only way in which I was threatening him was purely by the colour of my skin. Society has taught him that I am supposedly inferior, not his equal. This young man is afraid, insecure because society tells him he has to be better, bigger and the oppressor because his country, England, does not practise equality, when it plunders Africans to sell to plantation owners to work for free to provide the lavish lifestyles and therefore entitlement".

Many in the congregation that remained stood up in applause, many negroes, plantation owners and white women. Adisa was amazed at the response.

"For many decades now the slave trade has shown him, my detractor, and other men like him, that it is acceptable to treat others differently. He has brown eyes, I'm told mine are grey/blue. He has dark hair. Mine is black. He has a brain and blood which runs as red as my own. I have a heart. One that is filled with love, compassion and understanding. His, is cold."

"A few of the older men and their wives at the back of the church began to shout out in disagreement. It unsettled Adisa but she calmed herself.

"The more we negroes receive an education we understand and learn about the inequality in life. It is not justice for a man to hang a slave all because he ran away in search of freedom, as he no longer wished to be considered 3/5th of a man. He, we, wish to pursue our own lives as we chose to live. To take children away from their parents, sent to another country, island or plantation? To beat the slave, woman or man, for wanting to speak their mind and question ill-guided authority or for daring to make unintentional eye contact." The commotion amongst certain parts of the congregation was growing. A voice shouted out "let her speak. Let her speak." Fr

O'Leary moved towards the congregation waving his hands in a downward motion to help quell the disorder.

"May I remind you all, you are in a Christian place. We do not behave like this. She is a guest of this church and we show the same courtesy to her as we do any other speaker. Please take your seats." He nodded towards Adisa to continue and she managed a nervous smile to thank him.

"Where in the bible is this criminal and abhorrent behaviour ordained? Where is it morally right to dispense such violence against minor crimes to men, women or children?" Adisa's voice began to falter and her eyes welled up. She told herself she had to be strong.

"The tide is turning. If we do not take measures to prevent what has happened in Saint Domingue, Jamaica or elsewhere, the same could happen here. The movement for the abolition of slavery is growing in momentum. We need to be treated better. To be respected for who we are and what we are, not just abducted black people, and what we all contribute." There was more booing, which was met with pro-supporters cheering at Adisa.

"Ladies and gentlemen, I ask you to see reason and find your moral compass to join the movement to bring an end to the abomination that is slavery and the mistreatment which comes with it. The revision of the Code Noir benefits a minority. Think on it. Thank you!"

The cheers and applause erupted loudly and took Adisa by surprise, overwhelming the dissenters. As she took her seat by Elders, Adisa straightened her back and looked down at her hands, twisting her handkerchief tightly, listening to the reception she just received. Tante reached over and took her hands reassuringly. This gesture gave Adisa the strength to look up at the audience and nod her appreciation.

Fr O'Leary addressed the congregation and raised his hands to silence everyone once again. A few departed noisily in disgust of what they just heard but the majority of them stayed and sat down.

"Miss Adisa, thank you for that heartfelt story. I am very saddened that it should happen at all. You're a very brave young woman and I commend you." Adisa nodded in acknowledgement. As he dismissed everyone from the event, several went up to Adisa.

"That was a very powerful talk. Thank you for your courage." A young man of dark complexion shook Adisa's hand. Others took her left hand just to have something to hold and by which to congratulate her. Adisa was overwhelmed by the response. A number of white land owners congratulated her and complimented her on the clear delivery.

It took more than thirty minutes for the church to empty. Everyone set off in their carriages to enjoy Sunday lunch and family time. Adisa went to the front of the church where she took a candle and lit it in her mother's name, knelt and said a prayer.

Elders and Tante waited for her and together they rode back to the plantation. Later that evening, a rider came to the house and delivered a letter addressed to Adisa. She read it and had to sit down because its contents surprised her. Meanwhile Saint Domingue was in flames.

Chapter 21

Once again Florian found himself evicted from the Plantation Owners Alliance since they were unhappy with the author of the essays being one of his slaves and he refused to discipline her in the extreme way they wanted her taught a painful lesson. Adisa was a valuable worker and Florian did not want to lose someone who knew the family well, especially with Ottilie now pregnant and a personal maid to his wife.

Adisa too had received mixed comments from her peers who were surprised to discover it was one of their own writing for the Courant. Florian had also received death threats and on one occasion Tante had opened a parcel sent to Ottilie; a dead rat with all its entrails removed. It was a stark message and Florian promised Elders and Tante not to speak of it to Adisa or the fragile Ottilie. Security was enhanced across the plantation and Cornelius was instructed to make wooden and metal spikes to be placed atop the fences surrounding the land.

It was an unsettling time and Florian made provisions for some disruption. Adisa refused to let naysayers distract her from what she felt compelled to do. Yes, it was hard, but she wasn't hurting anyone. Why couldn't they understand?

The morning sickness Ottilie experienced in the first trimester did little to dampen her excitement of becoming a mother. She had been recommended bed rest for most of the initial term and when the sickness subsided, Ottilie felt strong enough to take short walks in the early morning or later afternoon to avoid the heat of the day.

She passed her time embroidering or crocheting. Her sister began making a christening gown in ivory silk, taken from Ottilie's wedding dress. Adisa became her personal maid and looked forward to feeling the swelling stomach.

One day, when Ottilie had returned from her walk, she stood on the verandah, looking out onto the plantation and watched the negroes at work. She felt happy.

"Good day Ma'am." Adisa was polite.

"Good morning Adisa. Would you be so kind as to bring me some water?" Ottilie sat on the deck chair, cooled by a gentle breeze. The flowers that adorned the verandah, the poinsettia, hibiscus and croton plants in the ground looked rich in colour. To her right, on the stand, was her bible. She reached for it and opened it in thoughtful prayer.

Adisa arrived with a carafe and glass filled with water, on the side she placed slices of oranges and lemon to flavour the water as

Ottilie chose. As she poured, Ottilie watched how daintily she moved and she smiled as she saw her favourite maid then turn, and leave.

"Thank you Adisa. It's most welcome," she rubbed her belly. "Adisa, will you read to me please? I can't concentrate on reading and the text is a bit small for me right now. Please?" Adisa felt delighted to be asked and to be relieved of her domestic chores.

"Where do you wish me to start ma'am?" Adisa asked.

"Oh, why don't you start from the first of the gospels? I feel in need of some inspiration. Hopefully I can get something from them."

Adisa began to read, slowly and surely. Eventually she picked up momentum and her reading was more fluid. Her lilting voice sent Ottilie off to a light sleep as she cradled her stomach. The plantation activities made distant rhythms.

Tante called out for Adisa and found her sitting next to Ottilie on the verandah. She was taken by surprise with the close proximity she was sitting to Ottilie.

"It's all right Tante. I asked her to sit and read to me. It was so pleasant on the verandah. I hope you don't mind?"

"Mistress, that is fine by me. I don't want her to tire you out."

"Oh, hardly, Tante. I'm relaxed at the moment. Do you need Adisa for anything urgent? Perhaps she can sit with me for another half an hour?"

"Yes ma'am. Adisa, please return when you have finished. I need you to sort out the laundry." Adisa's heart sank as the prospect of proper work loomed. She returned to her reading as Ottilie poured herself another glass of water adding a slice of lemon. Ottilie found it more refreshing as a result. Tante was irritated that Adisa was afforded such close proximity with Ottilie.

A dark cloud loomed on the horizon. Ottilie grew anxious and sat forward in her chair. The wind was picking up.

"Maybe we should leave it there, Adisa? I think I'll go back inside. Have you seen Mr Florian?" Adisa shook her head and curtsied. "If you do, please tell him I wish to see him?" Ottilie went into the living room where she lay on the caban as the wind rattled the shutters. She felt fearful and clutched her bible and unborn.

"My darling Ottilie. What's wrong? Adisa said you wanted me."

"Yes dearest. I'm feeling anxious right now. It's gone overcast all of a sudden and the wind has picked up. What's the weather forecast? Do you know?"

"No need to worry. We're due the back end of the hurricane which is out in the north Atlantic ocean. You'll be fine." Florian kissed Ottilie reassuringly on the forehead. "I should go and help bring in the animals before the winds start to damage the plantation and animals in turn. Get Adisa to call me if you need anything, my love." Ottilie felt calmer although the winds grew stronger.

Outside, the negroes and Florian tried to round up the horses, chickens and goats. The dogs began to bark and the birds flew from the trees sensing trouble. The sky grew darker and the humidity increased.

Florian instructed the carpenters to board up the windows on the house. This terrified Ottilie who had not experienced severe weather like this. She wanted to be with her father, but was advised not to travel in her condition. Ottilie grew fearful for her family's safety, despite Florian's assurances.

By nine o'clock, the animals were secured in the barn and the windows bordered up on the house. Florian was home and sat with Ottilie, still holding on to her bible for comfort. Her pose reminded him of Mabel before she passed. Florian took Ottilie's hand. She looked pale.

"We'll ride this out. Don't worry darling." Florian tried to reassure Ottilie, but she could sense he too was concerned.

The shutters rattled on the windows and the wind whistled through openings in the wood and floor boards. The cats sheltered under the house, along with the dogs. The horses whinnied in the distance and one broke free of its reigns, screeching and running around. A couple of the negroes tried to capture it, but it reared and kicked out in fear.

A woman's scream sliced through the air and Florian ran to the verandah in its direction. In the distance he saw flames. The dormitory and huts nearby were on fire.

Florian called on Elders and they both ran with bales of water. Fortunately the building was near the river and a line of men conveyed the buckets of water to and from the river. The flames, fanned by the winds, spread and women and children screamed and ran from the disaster.

Cornelius suggested they stop trying to extinguish the flames as their efforts became futile and it was best to let the buildings burn down. Elders and some of the men searched for anyone who may be trapped. Florian instructed another group of men to disperse and check the other buildings. Filaments of flame were being carried on the wind and could cause fires elsewhere.

Soon, the boiler house was on fire. Then the barn. The animals were set free to escape by instinct. Many of them broke through the wooden fences and ran into the next field. The young sugar cane, corn and cotton were trampled on.

Florian looked back towards the plantation. He heard Ottilie scream. The house was on fire. He ran towards it. Ottilie had collapsed on the verandah and he picked her up, calling out to Tante and Adisa to meet him at the entrance to the plantation and to bring a blanket, where he rested Ottilie by a copse of palm trees on the ground away from any building.

As he looked towards the house and the buildings beyond. He watched as his livelihood burned. He was helpless. The negroes were helpless. He sat on the ground next to Ottilie, a broken man and sobbed. Elders came to him with the wagon. Wracked with guilt and helplessness, Florian did not notice the adverse weather had subsided.

"Sir, we must take Ma'am to the church. She and the domestics will be safe there. There is no need to expose them to this. They need shelter. I'll come back and fetch some of the other women too. They can make sure Miss Ottilie is taken care of."

"Good idea Elders. I need to stay here and make sure no one is hurt."

"I believe everyone is accounted for Master Florian. When I return, I too will help you inspect. The wind is dying down now so let's hope that the rain will help to quell the fire. Are you OK sir?" Elders asked.

"Yes, Yes, Elders. I'm OK. At least I'm not hurt. I need to find out how this started. Go with Ottilie. I'll see you back here. If you can look in on her father on the way back, please let him know Ottilie is safe?"

“Yes, sir.” Elders led the buggy with Ottilie who was unconscious. It was a slow walk to the safety of the church with a heavily pregnant, scared woman on board.

The wind subsided but the path was strewn with branches and debris. Florian stood up and looked into the distance at the orange glow where buildings used to be. He felt angry. This could not have been an accident; several fires all at once? Someone had started these deliberately and he was determined to find who was responsible.

Elders returned. He was soaked through.

“Sir, Miss Ottilie … I went to see her father on the way back. His plantation is burning. He sent Miss Therese to the safety of the church too, and to help look after Miss Ottilie.” Elders was breathless.

“How is he?” Florian asked.

“Yes. He’s fine, if a little shaken.” Elders offered.

“I wonder who is behind this. Two plantations on fire? This is no accident.” Florian said under his breath.

“Do you have any idea who may be behind this and why?” Florian asked Elders so directly that it unsettled him.

“No. No sir. I cannot think who may be responsible. To inflict such damage is unthinkable." Florian looked at Elders and believed him. “I have not heard any rumours about factions stirring up trouble like the other islands. Let's see if and what it leads to and if we have a group looking to start serious trouble here on the island. I'll also keep my ear to the ground but nothing, I've not heard anything or witnessed any suspicious behaviour here on the plantation sir,"

"I will find out who is responsible and believe me, they will pay!" Florian stood up tall. He and Tante set about clearing what they could.

-o0o-

The eerie quiet of dawn was broken with bird song and cockerel calls. Florian had dozed off on the ground. The day was beginning to heat up. Sitting up he remembered the events of the previous day and, leaning on his right elbow, looked out to the fields. Buildings were smouldering and the dead animals were placed on a pyre, others in the ground. Some of the men were already up, helping to clear what they could.

The main house had burned down. Florian's head sank. Overseeing what the negroes were doing he felt he had to check on Ottilie at the church. He saw one of the horses roaming free, eating at the grass. It looked calm and walked towards Florian seeking reassurance. Florian stroked it and realised that it would be fine to ride. Without saddling the horse he rode it at speed into town and the church. He passed Aubrey's plantation and saw similar carnage, but he needed to see Ottilie.

As he entered the church the first thing he saw was Ottilie, Therese and Adisa helping to sort out food for the children, including negro children. All that was available was rice and beans. It was something. Ottilie looked up and saw Florian and ran to him. He was relieved to see she was fine and focusing on others, not herself.

"Darling, it's so good to see you. I've been keeping myself busy here. How are you, you look terrible?" Florian held Ottilie in his arms then motioned to her to sit on the nearby pew.

"It's all gone Ottilie. All the buildings have burned down. Everything we had is lost." Ottilie gasped in shock.

"Everything?" She asked. "Anyone hurt?"

"No, fortunately no one was hurt or lives lost but yes, we have lost everything!" Florian repeated.

"Well, we have each other darling and that's fine with me. We'll get through this. Was anyone hurt?"

"Not as far as I know. I've left Elders in charge. I, I just needed to see you and make sure you've come to no harm, you and the baby.

"Don't worry about me darling." Ottilie caressed Florian's dirty cheek. "I'll stay here with the women and children and make sure they're taken care of. I'm sure you can get the men rounded up to rebuild what's necessary and start to produce sugar again. It just means it's going to take time, Florian. I made a commitment to you.

I'm going to spend the rest of my life with you. We'll get through it. In some respects, this will be our new start."

Florian was taken by surprise at Ottilie's optimism and positivity. She was stronger than he thought. He took both her hands in his and kissed them.

"How did I ever deserve you? You are extraordinary." Florian was touched. "If you're sure you're fine here, at least there is a roof over your head, I'll speak with the vicar."

"There's no need, Florian. The vicar and his wife have already offered me a bed for as long as I need it. The vicarage was hardly damaged by the winds and I'll be fine for the time being. Please go and attend to the plantation, that's more important right now. Tante told me about my father's plantation too. They walked past it last night. He's got my brother. I'll see them later, when I've sorted out everyone here. We will be three in two months time. We need somewhere to live as a family. Go. I'm fine."

Florian kissed Ottilie and hugged her. Tante looked on disapprovingly. Recalling how Adisa saw her reaction last time, she raised a false smile and focused on handing out the food to the women and children in need.

Chapter 22

Florian went to check in on his friend Aubrey two weeks had passed since the storm and Aubrey appeared a shadow of his former self. His house too had burned down and he was forced to take shelter in what remained of his boiler house along with some of the livestock that sought shelter. He had commandeered one of the slaves huts for Therese and his son as he focused on rebuilding and reclaiming what cotton and cocoa he had that was still viable. He was walking back to where the house was when he saw Florian ride up.

"You don't look like you've slept at all, Aubrey." Florian remarked. "I'm sorry it's taken a while to come and see you, we are as devastated as you and, I see your house also burned down. This is terrible! Seeing it, I'm convinced this was done intentionally."

"I'm inclined to agree with you, too many fires occurred at the same time here, we could not attend to each and every one and resigned to just let things burn, so long as the negroes …, Therese and Toby are safe. How's Ottilie?

"She's doing well, Aubrey. She's staying with the vicar and his wife who have kindly taken her in, and in turn Ottilie is focusing on the needy. She really is a remarkable young lady." Aubrey smiled.

"Look, I have something on my mind. I've not seen Toby around for the last couple of days, you haven't seen him on your travels, have you?

"When did you last see him?" Florian asked.

"Two days ago, he was helping out clearing the land from the debris and I sent him into town that afternoon to purchase timber. He never came home. I'm rather concerned."

"I'm sure he's safe, but if you have not heard from him this time tomorrow, maybe you should report him to the local constabulary?

"They've got a lot on their plate with all these fires although I did send my house boy to let them know and I've explored the grounds as best as I can. There is a lot of damage and so much clearing up needs to be done. This is so out of character for Toby."

"Who's your best worker? Can you get them to go and search?" Aubrey shook his head.

"I need all the manpower on the plantation, so I can't take him away. I need to get this up and running as soon as I can. My finances won't survive Florian. We have lost a lot of money fleeing Haiti as it is!"

"I understand Aubrey and don't worry, Toby will soon turn up safe and sound "

"Sure Florian. Thank you for stopping by. It's going to be an uphill struggle, but standing around talking about it's not going to help. I'll see you soon. Again, thank you for checking on us." Aubrey fanned himself with his hat.

"If it's money you need, don't hesitate to let me know Aubrey." Florian offered. Aubrey choked, touched by the gesture and waved Florian away. Florian got back on his horse and looked at the damage across the plantation. He wished he could help but knew he had similar concerns of his own.

The countryside was devastated, dotted by blotches on the horizon of burned buildings still smouldering. Over the years Florian had grown to love the island, but nature could be brutal. He had truly settled there. It was his entire life and livelihood. He and Ottilie would soon have a child of their own and, if it were a boy, would inherit everything.

He passed a negro man selling coconuts and grilled corn. He opted for the sweetness of the coconut milk, paid and went on his way.

In broad daylight the plantation looked ravaged. The existing house, sad as it looked, was to be left, for the time being, as a new building was being erected nearer to the river. It was Florian's dream to build a house next to the water, providing a much better view.

What could be taken from the old house to be used in the new building would be salvaged. The foundations had been laid and the main structure was being built and the land had been cleared from all the debris. Florian inhaled deeply. It was indeed another new start.

He sent Elders into town to collect his own order of timber, nails and steelworks for the mills, along with new copper urns for the sugar cane and summoned Cornelius to repair his buggy.

When Elders returned, he found Florian by the lake and gave him a note. The Plantation Owners Alliance had called an emergency meeting in two day's time to discuss recent events, Thursday at 5pm. Why would they call him when they evicted him for a second time? Perhaps they need someone to blame, thought Florian.

Aubrey had grown weary, trying to clear the land as best he could. His manager rode towards him at pace. He looked troubled.

"Mr Aubrey, you must come with me quickly. It's Toby."

"Where is he?" Aubrey asked nervously.

"I think you should come urgently." The manager held out his hand for Aubrey to jump on the back of the horse and sped off, outside the plantation down the main road which led to town.

In the distance, at the side of the road was a group of people. Two women were looking into the corn with handkerchiefs over their mouths, and were in distress. Two young negro men were on their knees beside what looked like a body.

As they arrived, Aubrey dismounted and joined the group. Immediately he saw his son, laying on the ground. His throat had been cut in such a savage manner, and in his chest was a gaping hole, by the body was the heart. It was a clear message.

Aubrey collapsed on the ground and held his son’s body, a last desperate act of love.

-o0o-

The funeral of Toby took place a week later. It was a small ceremony. Florian attended to support his wife Ottilie, her sister Therese and Aubrey, a broken man. The funeral cortege headed back to the plantation and the river which ran through it. Underneath the palm tree Toby's body was laid to rest

Chapter 23

Mrs Brownlow, the vicar's wife, sent her footman to get Florian. He found him in the mill, along with Florian's driver and a handful of negroes, unloading the sugar cane not burned in the fire, the air acrid with the sickly sweet smell of boiling cane. Florian was instructed to return with the driver immediately as Ottilie had gone into labour. Therese was by her side.

Florian was allowed to see Ottilie briefly. He was torn by the excitement of becoming a father and by the pain of Ottilie giving birth. He could not comprehend how God could allow her to suffer.

He was swiftly ushered out of the room and invited to sit in the parlour. Reverend Brownlow offered him a glass of sherry which he declined.

After twenty hours of labour Florian heard the last scream that would bring his son Baxter into the world and he stood up, unsure what to do. His instinct tells him to run to Ottilie's side and protect her, but he knew this was ridiculous, she had all the help she needed.

About twenty minutes later Florian was invited in to see his radiant but tired wife, holding their son. The child, asleep, was so small and fragile that Florian thought he may hurt him. This was the first time Florian had held a new-born. So delicate and such a marvel he could not stop staring at the sleeping child.

"He's perfect." Florian said and kissed Ottilie. "I have never felt so happy."

-o0o-

Within two years, Conquerabia shone with a new house and the sound of eighteen month old Baxter at play. Baxter was the image of his father at the same age, with long blond curls.

Ottilie was a natural mother, nurturing without stifling. In time she would teach Baxter how to read and write. She taught him, along with four other negro children. Florian marvelled at her patience and love of what she did.

By now Adisa was her personal maid and in charge of Baxter when Ottilie had errands to run. She spent the morning with Baxter, playing games and reading to him. They had walked hand in hand around the vicinity of the house. Baxter chased after the butterflies or the two Kings Charles spaniels, Buttons and Patch.

His calls to Adisa to swing him around were heard and she took him by his hands and swung him around to screams of delight. Ottilie looked at them from the table on the verandah where she was writing letters. It made her happy to see her favourite maid having fun with Baxter.

Tante called out to Adisa to get some water and she looked at Ottilie for permission to leave Baxter's side.

"Go on Adisa. I'll watch over him." She smiled at Adisa. "Baxter darling, why don't you come and draw with me?"

"Yippee!" he responded. He liked to draw and was very good at it.

Adisa returned to the kitchen to grab the milk maids' pales and yolk and headed off to the water pump to fill them. There, she removed her shoes and stood in the nearby stream to enjoy the cooling sensation on her feet.

"Look who it is? It's the hoity-toity Miss Adisa . The one who thinks she's better than the rest of us." Scipio scorned.

Adisa quickly gathered the buckets to fill, but Scipio kicked them away. His presence intimidated her and she felt threatened.

"What do you want? Please leave me alone." Adisa quietly asked for fear her voice would prove how scared she was.

"We can never be like them, child" Her voice, a serious whisper. "They make it so. Only someone like you can get the benefits and privileges, unlike us. You think you talk good for us? Look at yourself. Your pretty little face, so angelic …". He cupped her chin. "Maybe I should bring you back to earth, how would you like that?

"I, I don't know what you mean. Please leave me alone." Adisa went to push him away, but he was strong and grabbed her wrists, pulling her towards him.

"Who's going to come and rescue poor Adisa? If anyone sees us, it will just look like two negroes courting and your screams just playful cries." He was menacing now and Adisa understood him.

He could tell she was scared and smiled at her; her fear aroused him. She was unsure what to do. Her first thought was Tante. She would be angry if Adisa did not come back with the water. Scipio stepped closer to her and she could smell the musky sweat on him.

"Why don't you just give me a little kiss, girl? I know you'll like it." Scipio put his hand around her back and pulled her tighter towards him. He was strong. With his left hand he grabbed her right hand and pulled it around her back he held both. He lifted Adisa up and walked toward the trees, where they could not be seen. Adisa tried to scream but fear had taken her voice.

He lay her on the ground where he now had both her hands above her head and was kissing her intently so she could not scream, even if she tried. She tried to wriggle out from under him, but he was too strong and too heavy and it only aroused him further. With his right hand, he was fumbling for her under garments. Her fear increased. Suddenly, Scipio's limp body rolled next to her on the ground.

"Get up chil' and finish your chores. He'll be out of it for a while, that's if he wakes up again. You OK?"

Adisa sat up and rearranged her clothes as she looked up and saw Elders. She nodded at him, took his hand to help her stand up. She was shaken and unharmed, relieved the ordeal was over. She looked at the limp body of Scipio, now unconscious.

Elders helped Adisa refill the two pails with water and she walked back to the house, her legs shaken and unstable. The house was in sight. If she could just focus. Elders knelt on the ground and tried to awaken Scipio, who rubbed the back of his head as he regained consciousness and looked at Elders, puzzled.

"Listen man, if you ever go near that girl again, I'll personally chop it off. Do you understand me!" Elders meant what he said and Scipio got the message.

"Yes, yes sir!" He nodded to Elders.

"Just go tell them you fell and hit your head, they should not question it. But if I …", Elders held up the cutlass towards Scipio who ran off in fear.

Tante saw Adisa arriving and knew that something was amiss. She was in distress and trying her hardest to hide it. Adisa placed the two pales in the kitchen and took the bar to the outside shed where it was stored. There, away from anyone's gaze, she broke down in tears. Elders, having arrived with two freshly plucked chicken for Tante, heard her.

"Don't worry. He'll not do that again. Wipe your eyes and let's forget about it?" Adisa looked at Elders, She knew he meant well.

"Let's go, Adisa", Tante shouted. "There's work to be done." Elders left. Adisa followed.

Chapter 24

Ottilie and Florian were complete with the addition of a daughter, Isobel, two years after Baxter was born.

The restoration work on Conquerabia and its environs was finished. Its grandeur was similar to the day Florian arrived all those years ago, but it was larger and the home was filled with the laughter of children.

Florian doted on his children. He became passionate about the need for change and built a school house on the land for the children of his slaves and it would be a place for his own children to attend, when they were older.

He corresponded with one of his former tutors at Eton, asking if he knew of anyone who wished to teach in Trinidad. He received several applications, including one from a young man, Willem Lizt, who along with his wife, was looking for a new challenge. Willem was well educated, having graduated with a Latin degree from the University of Brussels. He taught Theology at Eton before moving to Belgium where he served as a missionary. His new wife Cecily taught mathematics and English along with Religious Studies.

Florian was very impressed with his resume that he wrote immediately to invite the couple to take up posts at the school. A horse and carriage was sent to Port of Spain, and the couple was brought to the Plantation.

Ottilie was excited to have the couple to stay and was hard at work making the house presentable. Tante and Adisa made various jellies and pickles and the main meal that would welcome the couple that evening.

It was a particularly hot day and the atmosphere was electric. Adisa was preparing Ottilie's dress when she arrived in the bedroom. She caught Adisa by surprise.

"I'm so sorry Ma'am. You frightened me. I was not expecting you."

"Don't worry Adisa. I don't mean to alarm you. I just wanted to change the necklace I'm wearing this evening. Can you find me the pearls, please?" Adisa curtsied politely and went to the bureau where the jewellery was kept.

"Do you remember the pink dress you tried on a couple years ago, before the fire, Adisa? And how beautiful you looked?"

"Ma'am, that was so long ago, I can barely recall that." Adisa took the short pearl necklace, wrapped in tissue out of the draw and passed it to Ottilie.

"How we got through those dark times … . I never thought we would. The loss of dear Toby and my father, taken to drinking." Ottilie was sad.

"Miss Ottilie, don't look back, we need to look into the future and believe that all will be well. There are bad people in this world, but most of all, I believe there are some good people. People who like to make trouble for others when it is not necessary. Our lives can be difficult but we need to be thankful for what we have. And Miss Ottilie, you have young Baxter and Isobel to be most thankful for. Just look at how happy and beautiful they are. They are what's important right now. The good Lord has provided you with two beautiful children … and a man you love. I hope one day I too can find someone to love me the way Master Florian loves you!" Adisa blushed. She had overstepped the line.

"Oh my dear Adisa. You know you can speak freely to me, especially when we are alone. How did you get to be so wise? You speak truthfully, my girl. Is there someone in your life to whom you wish to give your heart?" Ottilie had a twinkle in her eye.

"No ma'am. I have no interest, nor time for any one. I don't think there is anyone there with whom I can consider my equal. You may recall the abuse I received in the wake of my last talk in church?

"Firstly Adisa, I think Trinidad is nervous. Nervous of what's happened in Saint Domingue and the other islands. We could potentially see an uprising here. Perhaps we have begun to see the signs with the arson on our plantations before Baxter was born? Florian assures me that the Plantation Owner's Alliance has not received any knowledge of rumblings for a potential uprising.

"With regard to the abuse you have received, you should try and understand where it comes from. Some people fear change, the loss of their livelihoods and you are unique. I know of no other, forgive me, mulatto woman in Trinidad embarking on talks in favour of abolition, you're something of a pioneer."

"Don't forget, you'll find someone special for you in due course. It wasn't until we moved here that I met Florian. I thought I'd never find 'the one', but here I am, married with two children, a handsome husband, and a beautiful home."

"Miss Ottilie, please don't take this wrong, but other than your children what are you passionate about?" Ottilie looked puzzled. She had never been asked a question such as this. "If I could wear such beautiful clothes and jewels such as this, to be free to come and go, as you, I couldn't be happier, but I doubt I'll see such freedom in my lifetime."

"Adisa, I understand that, but this is the world in which we live right now. It takes time for change. You know that Florian and I are doing everything in our power to improve your circumstances and those who work on the plantation? I don't know if you know but Mr Florian was thrown out of the Plantation Owner's Alliance for suggesting improvements to worker's rights?"

"I do ma'am, but we need to do more for ourselves. I think this is where education is important. That's what I am passionate about ma'am. About being active and vocal on behalf of my own people to forge an understanding between all of us. I know I'm better off than those who work on the land, but I'm not here by choice. My colour dictates where I work." Ottilie looked at Adisa and saw how beautiful she was, blossoming into a young woman.

"Adisa, do you know who your father was? Is he still alive?" Ottilie asked.

"No Miss Ottilie. All I know is that my mother Evalina was a young slave here and that she died in child birth. Miss Tante took me in and brought me up with Elders. I owe everything to them."

"Adisa! Where are you chil'?" Tante called out irritatedly.

"Miss Ottilie, please excuse me." Adisa scurried off to see what Tante needed.

Ottilie reflected on the conversation and was impressed with Adisa's conviction. She did not appear to be concerned about her paternity, but focusing on the future and possible change. She sat on the end of the bed and contemplated the building of the new school house as an exciting prospect to help deliver change.

The children's' squeals heralded the arrival of the new couple as Florian and Ottilie went to greet them on the verandah.

Adisa stood to offer cooling drinks as Elders and the young house boy helped with luggage and securing the horses. Ottilie, excited to have a new female with whom to talk, quickly took to Cecily.

As Florian greeted Willem, he recognised him immediately. Time had fared well as he had changed very little, just the dark curls he recalled Willem had when he was a young boy, were now grey, short and he was balding at his crown.

"I knew it was you Florian and I'm thankful you chose us. I guess we have a lot on which to catch up?" Florian felt at ease immediately and he took to Willem.

"Well, maybe you can tell me about my own parents? I've longed to know more about them." Florian shared.

-o0o-

Conquerabia Plantation was thriving and the school was now over subscribed. Conquerabia was not without its own issues. Scipio was causing trouble. He took out his frustrations on the machinery, by breaking the vat and blunting the cutlasses needed for the cane. He often found himself in fights, threatening to band together a group to overthrow Trinidad. Adisa disliked him, he frightened her but when he escaped, no one really missed him, taking one of the gallon bottles of rum with him when he escaped to join rebel negroes as he once threatened.

Aubrey's manager had found the escapee in Port of Spain, drinking with some of the freed negroes, quite publicly. He had become drunk and was protesting when he collapsed on the street. The constables picked Scipio up and dumped him on the back of the wagon, along with several other reprimands, on their way to the prison.

When Florian heard about Scipio, he sent Elders to collect him. Scipio looked terrible and miserable that he had been sent to prison. As the wagon turned into the plantation Scipio saw Adisa sweeping the verandah and she looked at the sorry state of him. She pitied him. She knew Florian would be kind towards him, to give him a chance to become better, but he did not deserve such kindness. Scipio would be left for a week to consider his actions and the impact on others.

Tante's arthritis was getting worse and her chores, especially in the kitchen, became harder. She was very fond of her charge and realised that soon enough, she would be 18. She sought counsel from Florian and Ottilie to mark her birthday. Ottilie was obviously delighted and took herself off into the local town.

The plans were to be kept secret until the day, two days later Tante was in the throes of polishing the brass door plates and handles as Adisa was dusting the mantles and surfaces when she collapsed on the floor clutching her chest. Adisa ran for Elders, instructing the house boy to send for the doctor. She returned to find

Tante on the floor, awake, her breath shallow. She looked at the tearful Adisa, taking her hand and knelt down beside her.

"Don't worry Tante , the doctor will be here shortly. Are you in pain?"

Tante nodded. She was panting. "Do you think you can sit up? If I help you, can you sit on the chair?" Tante closed her eyes momentarily and nodded. Gently Adisa helped her up and made her comfortable on the arm chair. Elders stood in the doorway looking at his wife. He did not know what he should do and watched Adisa as she cared and comforted her. Tante stretched her other hand out to Elders.

"Don't be so frightened, Elders. It will pass. It will pass." She tried to smile at him but he was unconvinced.

"Mr Elders, please can you pass me the smelling salts. Just in case. Miss Tante, can I get you some water?" Without waiting for her to respond she rushed to the kitchen to get a wet towel. Adisa rested it on Tante's forehead to cool her down. "Miss Tante, how are you now? Does that help?" Tante smiled at Adisa.

"Thank you. You are kind. This will pass, just give me a short while and I'll be back to normal."

Elders and Adisa looked at her. Tante was ashen and concerned. The pain in her chest was severe. Not like she had previously experienced. Momentary respite from the pain allowed her to smile and she tried to reassure Elders who sat next to her. He kissed her on the forehead. Cecily arrived and looked at Tante, as a sharp pain shot through her chest.

"Tante you need to rest. I think it may be your heart and until we know what the doctor says, please rest." Cecily was insistent.

"But Miss Cecily, who's gonna get the tea ready for Miss Ottilie? She needs me ...!" Tante could only just manage a whisper.

"That can wait. I'm sure Ottilie would rather you were able, than unwell. Do you need anything?" Tante shook her head. "Then close your eyes and just rest. The doctor will be here shortly!"

There was a matronly tone in Cecily's voice that Tante understood was well intentioned. Adisa felt that she needed to leave Elders and Tante alone with Miss Cecily, and returned to the kitchen and her chores. Very soon she heard the sound of the horses arriving with the doctor.

He rushed into the living room where Tante was taken. The door closed behind him. Adisa was concerned for her surrogate mother. All of a sudden it went quiet. Adisa went to the door to see if she could listen. Cecily opened the door, making Adisa jump. She smiled at her.

"Tante's doing well, Adisa. She just needs complete bed rest for the next couple of days and she should be better."

"Thank you miss Cecily. Can I see her please?"

Cecily signalled for Adisa to enter as she personally accompanied the doctor to his horse and waved him off.

"Thank you Adisa. You acted very quickly. I'm sorry to have frightened you. I"m going to rest here a moment longer. Don't you worry about me. I'll be good." Tante's smile was of relief this time and Adisa and Elders believed her.

Adisa had never known what it was like to lose someone that close and the thought of losing her surrogate mother frightened her. Adisa felt she owed Tante everything. She took Tante's hand again and hugged her.

Adisa lifted the small bell from the bureau and left it on the side table by Tante's chair. "Ring this if you need anything Miss Tante and I'll come quickly." When Tante saw the bell, it immediately recalled memories of another sickly lady. She looked at Adisa who recalled the same situation and both laughed.

That night Adisa knelt by her bed and prayed hard that Tante would be safe. For the next two days, Adisa managed the kitchen with the help of one of the young girls.

It was now three weeks since Tante had her scare. She was up and about but still rather frail. Adisa tried to take on as much of the workload as she could, but Tante, ever the fighter, was determined to fulfill her role. After all, today is an important day.

It was not long past six in the morning. The air was humid. Tante reached into her drawer and removed a small package, wrapped in muslin. She held it carefully and went to Adisa's room. The door was ajar and she saw Adisa writing in her journal. She gently tapped on the door.

"Come in" Adisa responded and closed her journal.

"Good morning Adisa. Today's a very special day." Tante smiled at her.

"Yes, it's the day Isobel gets baptised. It's sure to be a lovely day for the family." Adisa agreed.

"Yes, it's also a very special day for someone else." Adisa looked at her very puzzled.

"I don't understand Tante. What do you mean?"

"Chil', eighteen years ago you arrived into this world. A beautiful little girl. Your mother made something similar to this but it was lost in the fire here, many years ago. I made these in the likeness of the original, with your name embroidered on them. Tante presented the parcel to Adisa, who gently unwrapped it and found two cotton handkerchiefs with her name embroidered in blue thread. The stitching was neat and they were ironed to perfection. Adisa was moved to tears.

"Thank you Tante. Sometimes I wish I knew my real mother, but when I think about all that you've done for me, it goes away.

You have been more than a mother to me and I'm very grateful." The two women embraced. "Thank you so much Tante. Thank you".

"Well, let's not forget what we have to do today. It's an important day for two very special people." Adisa looked at Tante and smiled.

Adisa went to Ottilie's room to serve her breakfast and knocked on the door. She was invited in. Ottilie was already up and almost dressed. She placed the breakfast tray on the bed.

"Adisa, I gather today's your birthday. Is that true?" Ottilie had an impish glint in her eye.

"Well, according to Miss Tante, yes. I am eighteen years old."

"In that case, I think I may have something for you. Do you remember all those years ago, you tried on my pink dress? You looked so beautiful in it?"

"Yes, ma'am. I do. Before the storm. It was such a pretty dress."

Ottilie got up and went to her wardrobe and took out a large parcel presenting it to Adisa. She wished her birthday blessings. Adisa was surprised. She did not feel she could take anything from her mistress but Ottilie insisted. Unwrapping the package, there was a pink dress, similar to the one she recalled trying on.

"This is your dress. I promised you then it was yours, but now, I feel you should have it. But wait, I have something else." Ottilie removed a box from the cupboard and handed it to Adisa, who was filled with excitement. “For you!” Adisa placed it on the bed, stood up and removed the lid. In the box was a beautiful pink bonnet, to match the dress.

“In honour of your day, I want you to wear this to the church for Isobel’s baptism. Miss Tante has given you the day off, so that you can join us for the service and then back here for the celebrations. The negroes will join in later this afternoon. I want you to enjoy your day as much as possible. I hope that’s fine with you?”

Adisa could not breathe with excitement. She put on the dress and bonnet in her mistresses' room. She was amazed at how grown up and pretty she looked.

“Miss Ottilie, I don’t think I can wear this. I may get it spoiled.”

“Don’t be silly Adisa. I want you to wear it. You’ll be the prettiest girl in church, that’s for sure.”

All Adisa wanted to do was run out into the fields and scream with delight but she maintained her composure. She loved the reflection in the mirror and felt it was someone she knew but did not recognise.

Ottilie rounded up the children and Florian joined her on the verandah. He was impressed with the image before him and could not quite believe how stunning Adisa had become.

As they entered the church, they were met with whispers. Adisa felt awkward but chose to ignore them. She sat behind her master and mistress as Baxter and Isobel chose to sit with her.

Aubrey looked at her, her face familiar. Then he recalled who she is - a slave girl as part of the family in church? This was not a good look at all, but the girl he knew as a domestic slave was a stunning young woman whom he found attractive. It was at odds with his views and he was most perturbed.

Lunch was busy. Florian and Ottilie entertained the vicar and his wife at Conquerabia, along with Therese and Aubrey and the Doctor and his wife, Willem and Cecily. Aubrey was imbibing a bit too much that he became rowdy, much to the chagrin of his daughters, not helped by Aubrey's loud vulgarity. Therese suggested she take him home but he would not be drawn.

Aubrey stood up and swung on the wooden column by the balustrade and caught sight of something in the distance. He looked at the young girl as he struggled to maintain his composure.

"Who's that young girl there, with the two children?" He asked drunkenly. Florian went to help support him, bothered that he should take such interest in his slave.

"Why don't we get you home? Elders!" Florian shouted for him to get his landau and take Aubrey home.

From the field, Adisa looked up to see some commotion, but was too far away to discern what was going on. Baxter and Isobel stopped playing, aware that all was not well. Swiftly, Adisa tried to distract them by trying to throw horseshoes at a peg. Baxter missed and threw a pretend tantrum which made Isobel laugh.

Back at the table, all was quiet again. Having resisted Elders, Aubrey wandered inside the house and into the salon where he slouched on the chair in the living room, semi conscious. The heat and alcohol were getting to him too. He fell asleep and it was thought best to leave him there, at least he would be out of sight.

Baxter grew bored and found a steel ring, the lining for one of the wagon's wheels. He wanted to run with it but the ground was uneven and he could not get sufficient roll.

Ottilie invited the remaining guests to join her on the lawn for a game of croquet, with the children, where Isobel ran towards her for a cuddle. Ottilie swept her up to Isobel's delight.

"Adisa, would you please be so kind as to fetch us some fresh mauby?"

"Yes ma'am." Adisa responded and went to do as she was asked.

Ottilie quickly signalled to the other domestic negroes to gather themselves beyond the fence. Elders and Tante walked towards the water's edge where a long table of food and drink was displayed. Ottilie, with Isobel on her hip, walked towards Adisa as she returned with the tray of juice and placed Isobel down on the ground taking the tray from her.

"Adisa. Thank you for all that you've done today. I think Elders and Tante have another surprise for you?" Both women turned towards the end of the lawn, beyond the fence to see Elders and Tante beckoning to her, to join them. Adisa looked at Ottilie, puzzled. "Go on. It's time for you to go and have fun. Enjoy the rest of the day. We'll be fine." Adisa raised her hand to her mouth in delight that her mistress had given her time off.

"Thank you Miss Ottilie." Adisa ran towards Tante and Elders and the gathering by the river. She could smell the familiar fried chicken and it made her hungry. She had been so busy with her Master and Mistress that she forgot to eat. Ottilie and her guests watched as she joined everyone and the music and dancing began.

"Let's enjoy the early evening sun. How about a glass of Sherry, anyone?" She took the decanter and poured several glasses. The children had fun playing and chatting with their guests and Aunt who doted on them.

Florian checked in on Aubrey who was gently snoring in the armchair. He returned to join everyone in the garden and took a glass of Sherry, and kissed Ottilie.

"So Florian, tell me how you've managed to remain profitable? The vicar asked.

"How about I give you a tour too?" Florian asked. The vicar agreed and both excused themselves from the others. "Willem, why don't you join us?" They started at the mill and Florian invited his guests to try some of the sugar cane. It was juicy and sweet.

They discussed the recent spate of revolts around the Caribbean and got lost in conversation over coffee served back on the verandah as the evening drew to a close. The guests made their excuses and left, followed by Therese, without Aubrey, who was still asleep.

Ottilie bathed the children and put them to bed. They had exhausted themselves on the lawn with Adisa and Ottilie read a passage from the bible to them. They fell asleep before she even finished. She kissed them both, placed the mosquito nets around them and left. Glancing back, she felt herself brim with emotion. Her two sleeping angels.

Soon, the house was quiet. Florian and Ottilie could hear singing and dancing some distance away and surmised that Adisa was having fun. Ottilie sat on the swing on the verandah. A cool and gentle breeze blew and the cicadas' song could be heard.

"I'm going to bed, would you care to join me?" Florian asked.

"I'll be up in a minute . I should clear away some of the mess." She said to Florian.

"Don't be long my love. By the way did I tell you how beautiful you looked today?"

"No, you did not, darling and I never tire of hearing it." Ottilie kissed him on the cheek.

Adisa was weary and decided to head back to the house. She was happy. Playing with Baxter and Isobel, attending Isobel's baptism. Not forgetting the beautiful dress Ottilie had remade and given to her for her birthday. Tante's gift of the embroidered handkerchiefs. She had also been given bracelets made by some of the negroes and an embroidered bookmark for her bible. It was a good day.

The moon was high in the sky, clear of any cloud. It was still quite humid. And the fireflies danced around the light. The house appeared to be in darkness. Perhaps Florian and Ottilie had gone to bed, already. She had to be silent. Her room was at the top of the house.

On the verandah, Adisa looked back at the lake and saw the fire's embers glowing. It had gone quiet there too. A couple of people were still dancing to the solo fiddler, too drunk to care.

She closed her eyes and said a prayer to God to thank him for such a wonderful day. She noticed that the table had been cleared and the chairs placed tidily away. How kind of Ottilie to do that, rather than leave it for her or Tante. She must remember to thank her in the morning.

The house was still, the cicadas and crickets singing outside. A stair creaked under her as she headed up stairs. She stopped momentarily to see if anyone stirred. Silence. She carried on and thought she heard something. She dismissed it. In her room she placed the handkerchiefs on the bedside table. There was just enough moon light to see what she could.

As she stood up to undo her dress, Aubrey stood drunkenly in the doorway, wavering.

"So, it is. The slave girl wearing that dress. Who does she think she is?"

"Excuse me … Mr Aubrey. What are you doing here? I thought you left?" Aubrey stumbled into the room and placed his weight on the closed door. Adisa looked at him terrified. Memories of Scipio's attack came flooding back, along with the fear.

"You're just a nigger, a mulatto, a pretty one at that" He slurred. "You do what you're told to do. You're only good for one thing." Adisa recoiled as he advanced and fell across the bed, tearing her dress in the process. Aubrey looked at the moonlight on her skin. It piqued his interest.

"No, sir. Please stop." Adisa's pleas were futile. He smelled of sweat and rum and his jacket was wet through. Adisa screamed.

"Be quiet or you'll make it worse for yourself." He placed his hand over her mouth, stifling her cries. He was clumsy and knocked the table over. Adisa bit his hand, which he felt. She screamed again and he slapped her face. She was momentarily dazed. Aubrey tore the remaining dress off and she screamed again, terrified. His limp body collapsed on the bed beside her as she saw Florian standing in the doorway. Adisa crawled away as he jumped in, angry by what he saw, he grabbed Aubrey by his shirt collar and punched him in the face. It surprised him.

"What the hell do you think you're doing Florian? She's just a negro and a pretty one too. Come on, you and I know she was asking for it." Aubrey rubbed his sore jaw as he eyed her up. Adisa sobbed in the corner.

"How dare you treat her like this. Are you bloody insane?"

"She's just a domestic girl Florian, what's it to you? I bet you've had some good times with her too?" Aubrey rubbed his chin and saw that his nose was bleeding and felt the cut on his cheek sting. Florian threw the bed sheet to Adisa and picked Aubrey up by his jacket collar, so much so that Aubrey knew he was serious.

"Let me go. You don't know what you're doing. She just a bloody darkie, a slave. Property. What does it matter to you?"

"She's my daughter!" Florian seethed at Aubrey. "How dare you go for her!" And he threw Aubrey to the ground pointing his Flintlock duelling pistol at him. "If I didn't know any better, I'd be well within my rights to use this on you! Get out!

Ottilie gasped in the doorway, confused. What did she just hear? She looked at her father, at Adisa, naked in the corner of the bed, but for a sheet draped across her, and then at Florian. The declaration rang in her ears. Without thinking Ottilie turned on her heels and ran. She ran and ran not knowing where she was going. She ran until she could not, finding a tree beneath which she sat too exhausted to cry.

Chapter 25

Adisa woke up with a start and realised she had to keep moving. Ahead she saw the sea and decided to walk north, following the coast. It was still dark and she needed rest but knew she needed to get further under the cover of darkness. Adisa decided to press on, trying hard to ignore the blisters on the soles of her feet.

Very soon she heard activity. It appeared that men were trying to load a wagon, near to a church. If the church was open, she could possibly rest inside. She approached it carefully, trying not to draw attention to herself. The two men appeared to be black, possibly freed negroes. She knew she could not trust them, and waited for them to leave, the sun now about to rise.

They left quietly leading the horses so as not to make too much noise. They appeared to be working covertly. As soon as they left and had put sufficient distance between them and her, she headed towards the church. It was locked. Damn! Adisa rattled the brass handle, but it would not open. Disappointed, she left.

Further up the road she passed the vicarage which had a chicken coup in its yard. Could she try and grab some eggs? It was still quiet.

It did not look as if anyone was around. She found a mound by the fence. It would help her climb into the yard and to the coup. It was a successful grab and she passed a sack of potatoes leaning against the vicarage wall. If she could get a couple of potatoes for later, she would have a decent meal. But she was being watched.

The vicar's driver, a negro, had seen what she did and confronted her as she attempted to leave the grounds. He called out to his master. Adisa was frightened. Unsure what could happen to her. The prospect of being sent back to Conquerabia was not an option. She struggled to get free but the driver tied her up and sent for the constables.

In goal, Adisa was placed in a cage until the court opened later that day. Still hungry she felt more miserable and scared. She was in a cell with five other people who were due to be tried for petty crimes. It was dirty and smelled, roaches and the occasional rat, braved the dirty ground. Her cellmates looked like they had been there for days already with dirty faces, soiled clothing. She saw the driver and the constable talking to each other, but she could not hear what was being said. The driver nodded and left.

Sat on the dirt floor, with her hands tied. In her string purse were the handkerchief's Tante had made for her. She wore the slip from the dress torn by Aubrey. It was blood stained and dirty, the skirt wet from wading in water.

The driver went to the house of the slave merchant and was informed about the new addition whom it was thought could be of interest. Mr Bancroft wasted no time in getting to the cells to see his potential new earner and was delighted to see his latest prospect.

He spoke with the constables and a package exchanged hands, but Adisa could not see what it was. She knew it was related to her. Bancroft wasted no time in retrieving his new negro prize. He felt sure he could get a good price for her and took her away from the prison to his barn.

Bancroft chained Adisa in order she not run away. Apart from the odd livestock and dog, she was alone where he undressed and examined her. He opened her mouth to check she had all her teeth. Her tongue was a good colour with no sores. He was relentless in being thorough and derived great pleasure in doing so. Adisa wished it could end. Perhaps hell is a better place than this? When finished Bancroft threw a sack dress at her and made notes in his book.

"Have you eaten?" Bancroft asked. It was curt. Adisa shook her head. "You'll be given some rice and beans. You may have a long journey ahead of you today, if I think I can sell you for a good price." He walked her to the wagon inside the barn and chained her to it, along with the other three women and a man, and left. She looked at everyone.

"What's happening?" Adisa whispered as the humiliation of what she experienced brought a tear to her eye. The older woman, who looked about thirty-five to forty years of age responded.

"We are to be sold. There is a sale at about 2 this afternoon. That man thinks he may get a good price for us. I'm Esme and these are my two daughters Norma and Patti. We came here three days ago by ship from our homeland. Where are you from?" Adisa was able to understand a little of their language.

"Really? By ship? Where is everyone else?" Adisa asked.

"He sells them. Mostly men and boys, everyone including my son and my partner. We don't know where they are going." Esme added.

"I was born here! I was caught stealing eggs." Adisa did not wish to further discuss what brought her to this point "Where will we go?"

"Child, we don't know. We don't get told. It could be anywhere. Be warned the man likes the whip too much." Esme turned her back, as best she could, to show Adisa the lines cut through her gown and the raw marks on her back and arms, many of them still seeping. "When he comes back, you will be quiet. Don't back-chat. What's your name child?"

"I'm Ad .... Adisa. Adisa!" The second time she said her name made her feel proud and strong. It helped her stop crying. "Yes, I'm Adisa and I was born on the Conquerabia Plantation in Caroni.

"Pretty name, Adisa, that means nothing to me. You know this place better then. We come from far away. I lost count of the days that turned into night on that seuwiere of a ship. We went to two other islands where many were sold. We're all that remain."

"What's going to happen to us? Will they kill us?"

"No child, we are to be sold, to a slave owner." Adisa soon realised she liked the woman, she could talk and make sense, and tried not to feel so scared, for the sake of her and her two children. They talked further until they were disturbed once again by Bancroft.

"It's time to get into the wagon. You're up for market." He pulled Patti and Norma away from Esme and both started screaming, kicking at Bancroft who used his bullwhip to control them, despite Esme and Adisa's protestation.

The sisters were soon bundled onto the caged wagon and taken into Port of Spain's market place. An hour later Bancroft was back for Esme and Adisa. The afternoon heat was oppressive and Adisa looked at the streets they passed bustling with people. It was busy and noisy. The dust from the wheels was being stirred up and the wind blew it back into their faces, and with chained hands could not wipe the dirt away. It stung their eyes.

A strong crowd had gathered to watch the sale. A number of men in their smart suits, fanning their faces with their hats, some older, rotund women and children playing in the dust, unconcerned with what was taking place.

The auctioneer commenced proceedings, whilst behind the screen the women's faces were being cleaned. They were then marched up to the dais and prospective buyers ogled, touched and manhandled the women.

Bancroft kept Adisa until last. He sensed he may get a good price for her. Esme was sold to one man. Due to her wounds she didn't get him a good price but he was glad to be rid of her. Esme did not see to whom her children were subsequently sold, and it was only upon hearing their cries, she looked around to see them heading away from her. She will never forget the fear in their eyes as they went their separate ways.

It was Adisa's turn to be paraded. Bancroft wet a cloth and used it to wipe the dust and dirt from her face, to reveal her natural beauty. Several men came closer to inspect her, poking and prodding her all over. The humiliation was degrading, but she could do nothing to prevent it, her hands were tied tightly behind her back. She recalled the strength she gained in saying her name as one man felt it necessary to come close to her and grope the goods on offer, showing his two remaining rotten teeth and bad breath which made her eyes sting and sick to her stomach.

As he put his fingers into her mouth to examine the health of her tongue and teeth Adisa attempted to bite his finger. Bancroft saw it and called the man off in order to strike her on her back, so she fell to the ground. He needed to be careful not to mark her or it would devalue her price, but he also needed to demonstrate he could control his chattel.

The auctioneer began at a very low price. Firstly it was three reales, then it went up to five. Adisa lost count and the gavel went down on a figure much higher. The most Bancroft had earned from one slave sale, which delighted him.

As she was taken away, Adisa realised that she would be joining Esme. Once again her hands chained to the wagon so she could not comfort her friend, but Adisa managed to put her head on Esme's shoulder, until it was pulled away so harshly it made her wince; a metal collar was installed on her neck.

"I hope this means we're going to the same place. If it is God's plan, at least I feel I know you child." Henderson and Bancroft exchanged money for the goods and soon Henderson was on his way with his new property.

Henderson liked what he saw in Adisa's spirit and thought she would be good on the land. Young, healthy and potentially hard working.

Brodie Henderson had lost his plantation in Saint Domingue in the slave revolt and had left the island in fear of his life. He was a shrewd man, having invested in land across the Caribbean, taking advantage of the land available to prospectors. Some thought him a maverick, others knew the truth. He did things his way, regardless of the consequences, but the plantations were making a healthy profit and that meant he had power.

Little did he care that he was removed from the West Indian Owners' Alliance, the governing group for all groups on the island, since his views were extreme of the revised British ideology in the face of the advancing abolitionist movement. Sir Thomas Hislop, the latest Governor of Trinidad, liked him very much and they became friends and card buddies. He gifted his friend an additional 100 quarries of land in Siparia.

Henderson was a burly man who was fond of the drink. Though fond of the girls, he was now single. Married once, she had died in the uprising that took his plantation in Saint Domingue, along with his son. He didn't miss her. He was controlling and dominant.. All he focused on was the money.

The journey seemed endless, as Esme and Adisa fell to a rocky sleep, which was interrupted when they finally arrived at a sugar, coffee and cotton plantation. The Folly, in Siparia. It was already dark and not much to see apart from the occasional flame from fires, scattered around the site. There was an odd silence apart from the animals in the distance and the wagon was brought to a halt by the main office.

The sky was cloudy. It felt like rain was due despite the already humid air, Rain would be most welcome. The newly purchased slaves were brought down from the wagon by Henderson's plantation manager. Mr Grey. His front two top teeth were missing and his brown eyes deeply reset. His brow furrowed from constantly squinting in the hot sun. Fleeing Saint Domingue under such violent and hasty circumstances had aged him significantly..

Esme looked at Adisa. She had fear in her already bloodshot eyes. The pair was lined up in front of Mr Gray, and inspected again then assigned their roles. The two men who accompanied the women were to work in the field, and would be introduced to their group tomorrow. Esme was to be placed in the house on domestic duties, and Adisa, assigned to the land. The news hit her hard. She had been used to domestic life and knew how to cook.

"Sir, I think you will find my skills better served as a domestic. I can cook. I can sew …". She pleaded. This was met with a hard strike on her back and shoulder which threw her to the ground. The pain was severe. She struggled to find her breath, but was abruptly grabbed and raised up on her feet, the metal collar on her neck cutting deep and she began to bleed.

"You shut your mouth." Mr Grey seethed and marched both of them off to the dormitory. "Another word out of you girl and you'll be in solitary."

Esme looked at her, unable to speak any words of comfort, for fear of the same treatment. She mouthed to Adisa 'I'm sorry. Be strong, child'. Cook was sent for and took Esme to the house, on the other side of the plantation, which overlooked the sea. She looked back to send signs of sympathy, but Adisa was on her way, being shoved and pulled in varying directions.

Inside the dormitory, the spaces were divided. On one side were the men's cots, the other the women's. Separated by a large curtain, which had been torn and repaired numerous times. It gave basic privacy.

In the side room they were given potato sacks and towelling, or makeshift pieces and told if they were destroyed, those found guilty would be fined. They were allocated their cots and had to report at dawn for their jobs. Adisa found her cot, and sat on it, holding a piece of cloth to a wound. There were some other women who watched her arrival. One lady sewing, another platting a little girl's hair into cornrows. On her bed, she placed the sheets and towel and without making it, lay on the straw and cried.

"Girl, don't let them see you cry. They enjoy it. It makes them more wicked. Master Henderson doesn't care. Don't give Master Grey reason to beat you. He will and he will enjoy it."

-o0o-

A tap on the shoulder woke Adisa. Her eyes were sore and puffy from crying the night before.

"You better get up. You don't want to be late on your first morning, do you?" The lady had kind eyes, but she was firm. Adisa went to the outside hut to wash and tidy herself and presented herself for instruction as directed.

She did not see the two men with whom she was brought, neither did she see Esme. It was all very strange. There were about twenty other workers, all lining up to be sent out to the field. They were each given a sack and a pruning knife and Mr Grey told her to follow the others, who will show her what to do. She would have to fill her basket per day or she will be fined or punished or both. She will have to work until she's made the amount before she can be released.

Most of the workers were young. There were a large number of children, the youngest looked like they could be about seven or eight. Adisa was possibly one of the oldest.

She watched some of the young men approach the tree and cut down the pods. It was an automatic, well practised routine. They were obviously experienced and made it look so easy. Billy saw that Adisa was watching him and he stopped what he was doing.

"You got to hold the tool like so …. Don't let it master you, or you will lose. Don't be scared of it, once you know how to use it, it will be your friend and you can do so much with it." Adisa noticed that he was firm of grip and how different the weight of the tool was, now that he had instructed her how to use it. "Once you feel confident, you can cut through the stems much quicker and fill your bag with the pods."

"You make it look so easy and you're much stronger too. I don't think I could ever be as masterful as you at this." Adisa said.

"You will. It takes a bit of time and perseverance, but you will. And, you don't really want to give them a reason to beat you. Come on, let me see you try. Look for the darker coloured ones. These tend to be riper, leave the whiter looking ones." Billy had a kind face and the best of intentions. As he turned away to give her access to the tree, she saw the welts on his back. He noticed. "It ain't nothing. Don't worry." He tried to smile.

Adisa shook as she tried to approach the tree, holding the tool up as she was instructed, became heavy and looking up, made her feel off balance. As she lifted it to hook around the base of the pod she dropped it. Fortunately it fell in front and away from her. Billy smiled and picked it up, handing it to her again.

"Don't worry. We all start at the beginning." Those words were sufficient encouragement as she realised, of course, we all have to start learning at the beginning, something that is new to us.

"Thank you Billy. You're right." Adisa added.

It happened several more times as she got used to the weight. The sweat poured down her forehead into her eyes. Billy offered her a cloth to mop her brow.

"I got to get on with it. I need to fill my quota today. Don't worry, I'll keep watch but I need to get on." Adisa nodded her head in acknowledgement. “You’re not expected to reach the quota set for us, until the end of the week. New ones are given time to learn.”

It took two weeks for Adisa to get used to the weight of the pruning tool, despite her arms aching horribly. A sense of achievement ran through her, but she knew there was a very long way to go. To rest, she picked up the pods that she felled. She rubbed her back. The different position was welcome but short lived. She had to keep going. Grey was watching.

Already she had cuts and bruises with blisters forming on her hands. Her muscles ached, but she could not give in. Mr Grey was on the prowl and looking at her progress. He noted how tired she was, it was back breaking work, and he knew she feared him, as most of the negroes did. That’s one thing Brodie Henderson liked about him, he could scare the slaves just by looking at them.

Mr Gray leaned on the fence watching, taunting the slaves, sniffed and wiped his nose with the back of his hand and spat. Billy saw him and moved quicker. The welts on his back a raw reminder of the punishment Mr Gray was too happy to administer.

Adisa took a moment to stretch her muscles.

“Oi, stop slacking!” Shouted Mr Grey as Adisa heard the crack of his whip.

“Keep going. Please miss. He ain't' worth it!” Billy whispered to Adisa. She did as he said. Ignoring her aches and pains, she grabbed the pruner and started hacking at the pods and branches as dust and leaves fell in her face. All she wanted to do was rub her weary arms and legs.

Grey looked on, a brutal smile crossed his face. He was amused that the crack of the whip aimed at Billy she thought was for her. She learned fast, he mulled over to himself chewing tobacco.

Adisa began to cry. She did not want Billy to see her crying. She needed to be strong. For his sake, not just hers.

Chapter 26

Ottilie had left Florian, taking Baxter and Isobel with her. She moved back in with Aubrey. Florian had been the target for anything Ottilie could throw at him. She had been betrayed. She had been lied to. No matter how hard Florian tried to apologise, he could not get her back.

Florian loved his children with Ottilie and never once thought that Adisa would come between them. She was, after all, a mulatto, born to a slave mother. That's the life she knew. She was a slave.

Ottilie was fond of Adisa until that fateful day. She was the perfect maid and the children loved her. Their half sister a negro! She felt she could forgive Aubrey his actions towards the girl that night, due in part to the amount of alcohol he consumed. But she could not cope with the shame of having a darkie member in her own family. Florian's first born. The indignity. She felt unclean. Having lain with Florian when he had already sired a child.

Therese awoke early and sensed something was not right. Aubrey was still in an alcohol induced sleep and the children were fast asleep. She tied her robe and went down stairs. Her father's office door was open. How odd she thought to herself. As she walked in she found Aubrey's display cabinet door was prised open, the contents strewn over the floor. On the desk was the previous day's newspaper open to an article on Aubrey Frederickson and his recent fall from grace due to disclosure his son-in-law sired a daughter with a slave. To see it in print made Therese's heart sink.

Therese grew anxious and headed outside to see if she could find where Ottilie had gone. Her robe was on the ground, a glass tumbler, some distance beyond. Therese smelled the glass, it was rum. Panic gripped her as she realised Ottilie had gone towards the river. It was there she found her sister's body.

-o0o-

Time went by and Adisa grew stronger. She found a rhythm to her days and soon became one of the top grossing pickers. It was harvesting season and they were not even allowed to go to church.

Most of her days were spent working, with little time to eat or answer the call of nature. She was working well into the late night and six months had already passed. Provided they all managed to gather the target, they would have the next Sunday off to go to church; all day to themselves once mass had been celebrated. It was on these days she saw Esme and sometimes they would sit together.

Esme was unhappy. She walked with a stoop and had aged. She longed for Sundays when she could meet with her friend Adisa and read the bible together. Adisa saw the wounds on the back of Esme's hands, back and face. It appeared that Esme was being frequently punished but she would never discuss it. Neither would Adisa dream of confronting her about it. Esme had to trust in her. She could not force her to discuss it, and what could Adisa do anyway?

Adisa saw how the workers lived in fear of Brodie Henderson. He was a ruthless and brutal man. There were an abundance of stories about his brutality and evidence too. Amputees and injured roamed the plantation, walking without purpose. Their spirit, broken. They would eventually be put to work as any other or left the plantation under suspicious circumstances.

More time transpired and with good will Adisa went to church. She longed to teach Sunday School again. Her Sunday afternoons, when possible, were spent helping those in church who wished to read and write. Gone were her days of writing to the newspaper, as well as her inspiration to write. She had no privacy anymore to write, nor the energy. With little time to eat nourishing food, she lost weight.

It was a beautiful day. The flowers were colourful and bright and the sky was clear. The sun is hot and direct. She relished having a few precious moments to sit and think. She found solace in reading chapters from her bible.

A humming bird flying past distracted her and she looked out from the church to the sea beyond. She recalled the last time she had an article published about her experiences as a young girl working as a domestic in a plantation house and felt compelled to write once again, about her new experiences and brutality she received.

She asked to speak to Reverend Willis and confided in him her previous life and articles written. He was surprised by her admission and knew the articles of which she spoke. He had been inspired by them as an abolitionist. He proposed that if she could get the stories to him, he would willingly send them on and she agreed, on the provision that the money earned would go to the church; she could not be seen to be speaking out against her master and profiting from it, so both agreed.

He also asked if she had ever given a talk about her articles and said that there is a growing movement amongst the slaves to hear people from their own kind speaking, offering hope and showing other slaves what was going on in the world. She shared the experience of her last talk and how she longed to return to such times, but it would be nearly impossible for that to happen on this plantation, with little time to herself or privacy.

She learned that once a month Reverend Willis held an open service at which anyone who wished to give testimony could do so and she should use that platform if she felt confident enough to do so. She longed to speak once again, but felt she didn't have much confidence to resume her meetings. Reverend Willis left it to her to decide when she felt able to do so.

So it was agreed, if Adisa could get the time out, she would attend the next service the following month and if confident enough, give testimony.

As she walked back to her dorm, Adisa realised this was the first time she felt happy in months. Recalling the same feeling when she had her birthday. Almost a year since she arrived. She had changed drastically but found her calling once again.

Chapter 27

It was a relief, at long last, to sit in the church and sing her heart out knowing she had the day to do as she wished. She had earned it, finally. At prayer, Adisa was on her knees as was the rest of the congregation. She prayed hard to God seeking forgiveness for being such a poor Christian and vowed to do better. As worship ended she went to thank Reverend Willis for the service, and he asked her to stay behind if she could, he had some news which he felt may be of interest.

Adisa walked outside and into the hot sun, feeling His glory on her face. The chance to stop and think and to be free, if only for a short period of time, reminded her of Conquerabia. The freedom she had to go to church some Sundays and of an evening too, when there was a bible study group or meeting of the Abolitionist Movement.

She missed those days. The conversations that went with them. The discussions, what is going on in the news. She realised how odd her current environment is. No one to share her interests or conversation. The atmosphere on the plantation was oppressive and reflected in most of the workers.

Adisa looked down at her hands. They were calloused and rough. Her nails once elegant and pretty, now gnarled and ugly. She did not recognise them as her own. Then her back began to ache. She was standing up tall and straight singing the hymns. No heavy weight from the baskets of cocoa pods she had to carry. She offered up a prayer of thanks. 'Dear God. Thank you for the opportunity to appreciate you and all that you do. I am grateful to serve you; to worship you in your House and for the strength and understanding you give me to get through each day.'

"Adisa! Adisa!" She heard Reverend Willis call her name. "You must have been far away then."

"Yes Father, sadly it is only in my mind, not reality. However I am delighted to speak with you. You said you had some news which I may find of interest?"

The church and the surroundings were nearly empty of worshipers, making their way back home. "Yes, This is Lester. He's a free negro working on the neighbouring plantation to Mr Brodie Henderson. He spoke with me. He said you used to give talks for the abolitionist movement back in Caroni. I've been collecting these papers for you. I hope this won't get you into trouble, as I am familiar with Mr Henderson's ways and deplore him for it. There is hope, Adisa."

Adisa looked at the cuttings Lester held in his hand. She hesitated to take them knowing the consequences if she were caught with them in her possession, but it was too tempting to decline. She longed to read the newspapers to find out what was going on outside her secluded world on the plantation. She longed for the life she knew well. She thought about Ottilie and the children, recalling the laughter they all shared until that fateful night. Reverend Willis was offering her hope. She shook in anticipation, nervous to receive the papers in front of her.

She looked up at Lester to see if he disapproved. His smile was encouraging and his eyes were kind.

"I would like to invite you to have lunch or dinner at the parsonage when it's convenient with you. I will formally ask Mr Henderson if he can spare you for a bible session. I know I am going to have to stretch the truth a little but, we will of course have time spent in bible study. There is also something developing which I would like to bring to your attention. I shall not bother you with it here, I don't want you concerning yourself until such time - we can talk later, but I think your background may help our cause."

"Father Willis I don't know how I'm going to contain myself until then. I'm intrigued. I would hate that such pretence could adversely impact both of us, or those to whom you have also entrusted with such a generous invitation."

"I can assure you it is part of God's work and we need change. I would like to present you with this bible. I can see yours is well loved, but you might enjoy having something new?" Reverend

Willis pressed the papers and bible into both Adisa's hands with such significance Adisa could not refuse. "I will send word for when I will arrange the next group meeting. I welcome your thoughts on this and I am sorry for how it may affect you.

It was now dark and Adisa had to get back before 10 pm or questions would be asked.

Back at the plantation she found herself locked out. One of the foremen was on night duty. She felt uneasy.

"Good evening Miss Adisa. Why are you late? Did you get a pass?" Simeon asked.

"No, Mr Simeon. I'm very sorry. Church duties kept me later than I anticipated." Adisa responded.

"Well Miss, you will have to go to Mr Grey's office and let him sign you back in." Adisa nodded as the kindly foreman opened the gate to allow her entry. She headed off to the Manager's Office but no light was on. She headed over to the main house to see if Mr Grey was there. She rang the hand bell on the table and Esme came to the door.

"Evening Adisa. How'r you girl?" Due to the informality she whispered. Adisa nodded and smiled at her.

"I've been sent to see Mr Grey to let him know I'm here, but there's no one there. I thought it best I call out to let Mr Grey or Mr Henderson know that I'm back."

"Wait here chil'. Let me go and announce you."

"Before you go, could you take this for me? Esme looked at her friend concerned to handle some contraband. "It's my bible, honest." Esme hobbled off, her stoop became more pronounced and Adisa watched her go. As she came back Esme did not make eye contact.

"Mr Henderson has asked you to go to his study. Please, follow me?" Esme shuffled off again, with Adisa in tow. She grew more nervous. She experienced Mr Henderson's temper and fearsome way and her heart beat faster.

"Esme." Adisa whispered. She didn't look up. "Esme, please can you look after this for me?" She offered her friend the bible she'd been given, wrapped in a string purse. Esme hesitated. The two reached the study door. Adisa held out the purse and Esme took it, hiding it as she turned to go back to the kitchen

"You may go, cook. And close the door behind you!" Mr Henderson barked, standing up from behind his desk, adjusted his trousers and walked toward Adisa.

"Well what do we have here? Brodie drew up to his full height and bulk. Adisa felt like he towered over her and she dropped her eyes to the floor. "I remember you. I bought you in Port of Spain. I hear Grey says you're a good worker."

"Master?" Adisa uttered.

“Well, why are you here?” Brodie was now enjoying his intimation of her.

“Sir, I was late back from church duties and I seem to have lost my late pass. I was not expecting to be this late, five minutes over, if that. I am very sorry, Master.” Adisa could barely speak for fear. A gentle breeze blew in from the patio doors and the net curtains danced. It caught Adisa by surprise.

“Why didn’t you tell Mr Grey? He should have been in his office?”

“No Sir. The foreman on duty sent me there but there was no sign of Mr Grey, so I thought it better to come here instead, thinking he might be here. I want to do the right thing, Master.” Adisa could feel her heart pounding in her chest and her hands began to shake, her head felt dizzy.

Brodie looked at Adisa and could see terror in her eyes. He wanted to have a little fun at her expense. He reached his hand to her chin to take in her features but she recoiled. Without missing a beat Brodie slapped his hand across her face. As she placed her hand to rub her cheek, a tear rolled down her face and her cheek smarted. Brodie grew more aroused.

“You are so beautiful. Beautiful eyes, delicious lips. Just beautiful.” Adisa knew the door behind her was closed. She could either try and reach for it or make a run for the patio doors. That looked to be a more direct exit but she was no match for Brodie and she struggled to release herself from his clumsy embrace. She scratched her nails on his face and drew blood. Brodie finally won. His musky smell of sweat, alcohol, unwashed clothes and hair made Adisa nauseous but shock left her numb.

She tried to compose herself and felt wetness on her leg. She looked down and ran her finger through it. It was blood. Adisa tried to cry but she had no tears. She could not draw attention to herself in this state either. Brodie was asleep on the floor where he slumped snoring deep, ratched snores, aided by alcohol and his sheer size. She knew she had to get out of there quickly. She removed the handkerchief from his jacket, wiped her legs and ran as fast as she could to the women's wash area where she scrubbed and scrubbed at her unclean skin. It made her sick.

"Adisa, Adisa. It's Esme." Came the whisper.

"Yes?" Adisa stopped crying momentarily and looked up.

"Child, I have something for you. It's a towel." Esme said quietly. Adisa looked over the wooden door and saw Esme who placed the towel over it, grateful for its use. She noticed it hid the bible she asked her friend to conceal. Adisa quickly wrapped the towel around her and stepped out. "I am sorry child. He's a bad man. A nasty man." Finally the tears came as, held by her dear friend, she was given permission to weep.

Chapter 28

Adisa was restless, she didn't sleep. She was hurt and spent the night in a state of pain and sadness. She was alone. When she could sleep she saw Aubrey and Brodie Henderson's eyes and the smell of their bodies or the touch of their hands on her skin. No one could comfort her. Mr Grey saw her on the bed in the dormitory and realised what had happened.

"If you don't get up and onto the field, I will beat you like the dog you are!" he threatened. Adisa who just looked up at him as he slowly and dramatically gathered up the bullwhip, ready to strike. Her eyes puffy and red. "You look a fright, but we need you out there." He then cracked his whip next to her cot which made Adisa jump. She stumbled to her feet. The pain in her abdomen bent her double and she heard the crack of the bullwhip again. "Next time I won't miss." Mr Grey raised the whip in determination.

Adisa forced herself to get dressed as Mr Grey looked on, taking in every single feature of her body. He was waiting. She hobbled out to the field and he followed. She went to pick up a pruning knife, a sack and a basket. It was hard to function, let alone concentrate but she was determined not to be beaten in every sense by Mr Grey or Brodie Henderson.

"I thought the Code Noir protected us negroes from such violent abuse? You're breaking the law!" Adisa whispered.

"You what!" Mr Grey was somewhat stunned to hear her speak to him in such a manner. "What would you know about the Code Noir? You're nothing but a no good mulatto. You're neither one thing nor the other." He raised the whip in his hand.

"We can punish for any good reason" He gloated. "You're less than one of us, you're - what is it they say? Yes, you're 3/5th human. You are no better than a dog to Mr Henderson. He is using you just the same."

"Look at me. I am white. I'm better than any of you. I get to look down on you, spit on you if I want", and to add effect he spat out his chewing tobacco. "That Code means nothing. It was destroyed ages ago. We have a new law now and it says we can do what we like to our negroes. You see, the old law was unprofitable … ." His voice trailed off as he brought down the whip to strike Adisa. "Why the fuck am I explaining this to you dumb nigger?" It was caught by Lester.

"Sir, I think you've made your point. Give her time to compose herself and she'll be back at work soon enough. As a Christian man, you know when you may have gone too far. Don't make this personal." Unbeknown to Adisa, Lester was holding a knife at Mr Greys' side.

Mr Grey was taken by surprise. The audacity of a negro speaking to him like that. Adisa got up. She was shaking from the encounter and tripped to the ground again. Mr Grey pulled down his shirt and straightened his hat.

"Mark my words Lester". Grey spat out his tobacco. "I will not forget this! You can wait." Mr Grey stormed off.

Adisa looked up at her saviour and mouthed her thanks. Lester gave her some privacy to make herself decent. Adisa wanted to cry her heart out but knew this would make more trouble for herself and she needed to get up.

Mr Grey stood, leaning on the fence some distance away and watched Adisa work. Now, more than ever he felt compelled to break her. Adisa kept cutting down the pods. The pole she used to bend the branches was too heavy to lift as her whole body ached and trembled.

"Adisa. Adisa, are you OK?" Lester called out as he watched her collapse on the ground. She was unconscious. Grey looked over his shoulder at the commotion and blew his whistle for help.

Chapter 29

Three more years had passed and Adisa now wore her troubles on her face. The pretty bright eyed girl was now much older, in appearance. Her body ached and her hands and feet calloused beyond recognition. Her back crisscrossed with welts from the numerous beatings at the hands of the controlling Mr Grey.

The wind shook the trees. As soon as the sun shone through, the earth was dry again. The humidity was high but work had to carry on.

Adisa struggled to work. She felt spasms of pain in her side and the brief rest she took eased the discomfort but as soon as Mr Grey saw no work being done, she soon heard the crack of the whip and forced herself to continue. Then, one strong shooting pain sliced through her body, she thought she'd been struck by the whip.

The wind rustled up outside the sick house where Adisa was taken. She lay in a state of confusion and pain and suddenly calm descended on her body.

Adisa's outstretched hand gently turned with the palm facing up and the fingers unfurled, waiting for a greeting of some sort. Esme instinctively reacted and took the hand in hers, noting the smile across Adisa's face.

"Mother, what are you doing here? They told me you passed on the day of my birth." Adisa said.

"That is true my child. I left my body soon after I held you for the first time. As soon as I set eyes on you, I knew you would be special. You are the only thing I ever wanted. The only thing I ever valued in life. Everything else did not matter."

"Look at you!" Evalina said. You're not ready to join me. You have to return. Your work is not done. You were put on earth to make a difference and I will not let you join me until your work is done. I was not given long on earth, but I watch over you every day. I am proud of what you have become. Don't be mistaken, I feel your pain. I also feel your happiness and you will enjoy it more. Your life will be the beacon of hope to others, but you have to go back and finish your good work."

"You are of me. Strong and a leader. You will make a difference." Evalina held Adisa's hand and gripped it firmly. Esme felt the grip tighten and it gave her hope.

"Adisa! I named you. It means 'the one who is clear'. Your life and purpose will be clear to others. We are not ready for you."

Evalina looked at her child as her grip tightened on her hand. "Always remember how much you are loved!"

With that Evalina let go and faded away. The further into the distance her image faded and Adisa's grip on Esme eased.

"We sit and wait. Adisa will come back to us. Just wait." Esme was hopeful.

Two days later Adisa stirred. She was confused and disorientated. She immediately felt she was back at Conquerabia but her surroundings were unfamiliar. She tried to sit up and drew the attention of one of the ladies who watched over her, who ran to her side.

"Gently, gently! You've been out for a few days. I am Mina. Are you OK? Adisa was too weak to sit up and Mina gave her another cushion under her head.

"Where am I? What's wrong with me?"

"You took ill Miss Adisa. We have been taking care of you. I'll send for Esme, I think she'd like to know you're awake. Here, have some water." Mina helped Adisa lift the cup to her lips. It tasted so good.

"Not too much, you might make yourself sick. Just sip it." Mina's sister came in the door and saw Adisa awake. She looked at Mina who nodded to get Esme.

"How …? What …?" Adisa tried to make sense of things.

"Let's just wait for Esme. All in good time. It is such a relief to see you open your eyes. We really feared you would not make it."

As Adisa rested back on the pillows, Mina took a cloth from her shoulder and wrung it out in the pale of water nearby and mopped Adisa's brow.

"That feels so nice." Adisa remarked. It did feel good and she was grateful for the care. The door opened. It was Esme. Adisa's eyes lit up at the sight of her good friend and the two women embraced.

"Why am I here Esme? What's going on? What happened?" Adisa asked.

"Chil', how are you feeling now? We were so concerned for you." Esme held her friend's hand as a tear rolled down her cheek.

"I'm fine. I think. What's going on? Please, tell me!" Adisa was insistent.

"You took ill a few days ago. You collapsed and were brought in here. You lost a child, a boy child! Esme stated. Adisa looked at her in disbelief.

"I was with child?

"Yes. He was only about six months in the womb and was still born." It slowly dawned on Adisa what happened.

"I must have been working in the field and passed out. I don't remember much, but I recall feeling a pain in my side. It went blank after that."

"Adisa, I am sorry for your loss. He would never have made it. When you have your strength, I can show you where he is buried. Right now we need you to try and eat something and get your strength back. Do you think you can eat?"

"I am hungry. I'll try. Do you think you can help me sit up?" Esme and Mina went to Adisa's aid as the third woman went to get some cassava and chicken.

The food tasted good but Adisa could only eat a small amount. It took a lot of energy out of her and Mina took the platter away from her before it fell to the ground.

"Miss Adisa, you will be slightly dizzy for a few days. Please try and rest. We will look after you."

With a change of clothes and a makeshift wash Adisa felt better. It was only later when all that she had learned sunk in, Adisa, feeling sorry for herself shed a tear for the little boy she would never know.

Several days later Adisa tried again to stand up and, for the first time, she did not feel weak on her feet. She drew a long, deep breath and reawakened her lungs and stretched until she thought she was touching the sky.

She moved towards the mirror hung on a nearby post in which she saw her reflection. Despite the mirror being cracked, she looked into her eyes and recognised someone.

It was Evalina who came to her in her dream. She recalled it moment by moment and the earnest way in which she was told her work was not yet complete.

My mother came to me. It was wonderful. She said she has been watching over me, Adisa thought to herself. From beyond this world she knows and spoke to me. She came to me! Adisa had to sit down quickly, at the validation she received in vision. She shook with excitement.

I have to continue to speak up! I have to help teach those who wish to learn, about how they too can support the mission. This will be to honour my mother and many like her. I shall do all of this in her name and memory.

With her resolve strengthened and her determination renewed, Adisa allowed neither Mr Grey or Mr Henderson to weaken her purpose, and fought hard for it not to show on her face. She knew when she was called to service Brodie Henderson and resigned herself to it. In time Brodie Henderson soon moved on to someone else, someone younger.

Adisa became something of a matriarch amongst the other women. She led readings and prayer sessions in the makeshift church since they were not permitted liberty to leave the plantation on Sundays anymore. These occasions afforded Adisa the opportunity to look to the sea in the distance and long for her home, and imagine a world where she is free.

When feast days and holidays arrived, other negroes from neighbouring plantations would visit and she would sit with them and hear the latest news. Who had been lynched, who had been maimed and for what fabricated reason. She could obtain snippets of news from Britain and America on the developments of the Abolition of Slavery. Each time she was filled with more hope and gave thanks to God for the favourable news.

Brodie Henderson banned newspapers from being circulated on his plantation. But occasionally Adisa was passed clippings from papers fellow negroes and visitors left, particularly when it became known she was an admirer of the American Quaker Anthony Benezet who was succeeding in his abolitionist mission. She was handed tracts or writings on slave revolts, which she hid in the ground, behind the dormitory, along with the handkerchiefs Tante embroidered for her 18th birthday.

Most of the negroes had something hidden in and around the back of the dormitory, by bushes of croton which was close to the latrine.

That evening, Adisa lay in her cot talking with Esme.

"Have you read this? Governor Thomas Picton has been accused of the torture of a young girl, around 13 years of age. My word, it's terrible to read." Adisa looked up at her friend.

"You know I can't read as well as you. I'm a slow reader and I still struggle with some of those big words they use in the newspaper. I've heard something, what is the latest?" Adisa read the story aloud.

"Governor Thomas Picton has been accused of the torture of a young girl, believed to have stolen money from a Mr Pedro Ruiz' home." Adisa stopped and observed how interested Esme was, who asked her to continue. "To elicit a confession, it is alleged that Governor Picton had instructed Miss Luisa Calderon be tortured by 'picketing' and imprisoned without recourse to trial by jury."

"What!" Esme said. "For truth …?"

"According to this article it is. What young person at this age knows as much as a man his age? This is shocking. Not to be heard by a jury and convicted without evidence …" Adisa looked up at Esme. "The poor child."

"What else does it say? Read on." Esme encouraged.

"Governor Picton, acting on advice of Alcalde Sainte Hilaire Bergorrat, commenced the case against Luisa Calderon, who acted in response to her proposed marriage to Pedro Ruiz who said that he understands the money, around 2755 reales was stolen from Mr

Carlos Gonzales, a friend of Pedro Ruiz. Whilst there was no evidence, he said it was Miss Calderon and only she knew where the money was stored, as she and her lover were frequent guests of his.' This doesn't sound right. She is so young too. I remember being 13 and I knew little about life, let alone be someone's mistress. I was still playing with my straw dollies. Adisa, why do you think there are men like this? Like Mr Henderson?"

"It is down to the white man but I have seen some terrible things amongst us coloureds too. You have to recall, many of us were brought here against our will and those of us with a dark complexion lack the liberty, the free agency, of the white man. Perhaps it is about fear, control and image, like when the peacock spreads its feathers to show off? When threatened I think we all have the capacity to strike out, but some of us can control ourselves.

"Let us consider our situation. It is the white man who owns us and what is it they have to lose that causes them to be so afraid? Money, status and everything which makes them protect it. Why do you think there are so many slave revolts like in Saint Domingue and Jamaica? The coloureds there are tired of being suppressed." Adisa stopped in thought and looked at Esme. "We have not seen anything like what's happened in Saint Domingue as yet, but there is still time. I need to get more newspapers to see how this Calderon case is developing. I read elsewhere he was also convicted of her torture in England."

Adisa stood up and put the newspaper cutting in a handkerchief momentarily on her shelf and tidied the clothes away.

"I wish there was something I could do to help Luisa, and others like her who are taken advantage of but sadly I am a mere slave. I have no freedom. She has freedom in her favour, but yet the colour of her skin means she has less freedom than the white man."

Adisa woke early. Her night was restless, thinking about the young girl being tortured. She got up, choosing to put the time to good use, and headed off into the cocoa field where some of the men were already gathering the cocoa.

Six of them sat in a circle cracking then head and tailing the pods with their cutlasses, then holding them lengthwise and slicing into it again with two more strikes, twisting it just enough to expose the rich creamy pulpy seeds that were placed on the ground to dry. Two young boys carried the baskets on their heads over to the expanse of land where the seeds would be added to those already out to dry in the sun.

It was hot and the straw hat Adisa used to fan herself was ineffective. Two women were bent over drawing their hands across the pile of seeds to level them off after the men dumped the contents of their baskets on the existing pile.

When the large square area of sacks was sufficiently covered with the seeds, banana leaves were then placed on top to start the fermentation process. To the right of this new pile was another and two more women were tending it.

After about seven days, the aroma from the fermented pile would be familiar. It would take about another ten to twelve days for the beans to fully dry. This second pile was going to be placed on a third, that of bamboo mats, for the drying process to be complete. These beans on the raised mats would be turned and sifted through to remove any bad seeds. Adisa often found this process soothing as she listened to the dried seeds rubbing together as if rattling a child's shaker.

Strong men then had the job of filling jute sacks with the dried beans, which would be despatched first to Port of Spain and exported. Henderson's plantation made the most profit in the south west of Trinidad, an achievement for which he was proud, whatever the human cost.

When not harvesting cocoa, Adisa would be required to go and work in the corn field, adjacent to the cocoa fields.

There was nothing Adisa liked better than roasted corn and as she reached the fence, she looked out onto the tall plants, ladened with ripe ears. She joined several other women already at work, cutting down and stripping the corn wrapped up in the leaves. A number of butterflies were dancing around the purple flowers of the plants. It reminded her of the hair on her first dolly.

As she got to it, she searched out the brown cobs, these would prove to be the most ripe. Fortunately there had not been much by way of rain and so most of the plants looked like they were ready for harvest and they should get a strong crop.

When younger, she used to imagine the cob with its brown silky tassel as a toy and made up families with several of them. The first one she picked was firm to touch; a promise of juicy yellow corn hidden under layers of wrapping. She could not resist undoing the cob in search of the delicious kernels and biting into the juicy goodness. It was a treat the pickers allowed themselves, provided they were not caught. Fortunately the plants and their fronds were sufficiently tall, they could walk into the field of corn and hide, momentarily.

-o0o-

"Miss Adisa, I have someone who'd like to meet you.

"Yes, of course Esme." Adisa adored Esme and knew that the personal request was important. She got up, brushed her hair and washed her face with a cloth, which she hung out to dry on the nearby line. She made sure she looked decent and went to meet Esme by the river, where there was a gated fence.

In the distance was a striking looking man of about 30 years of age. He was tall and commanded attention. Adisa recognised the face, but couldn't place him. He looked friendly enough and he was heavily into conversation with Esme. 'My word!' thought Adisa to herself. 'I do believe Esme is smiling for the first time I can recall.' Adisa caught up with them both.

'Adisa, I want to introduce you to Lester Pearce. Lester is a carpenter and occasionally stops by when he's finished delivering items of furniture for Reverend Willis and Mr Henderson. Lester offered his hand to Adisa, who found Lester charming, she too found a smile on her face.

"Pleased to meet you Mr Lester Pearce. Your face is familiar." Lester studied Adisa's face and saw the weary burden she carried.

"I am pleased to meet you too under more favourable circumstances." Lester responded. "Esme tells me great things about you. You both share some history. Esme credits you with keeping her morale up, when she felt she could no longer care. Your reputation precedes you!" Lester still held her hand. "I'm delighted to see you under more favourable circumstances." Immediately Adisa recalled their first meeting and felt embarrassed for the occasion.

"You came to my aid. I recall. Thank you Mr Pearce. You surprised me. I have no reputation to speak of. But thank you."

"I have known of you for some time and was delighted to learn you are here. I understand you speak on all matters to do with freedom of the negroes and mistreatment of them. You have been quoted in my mother's letters to me. She too worked on the

Conquerabia Plantation about five years ago. Sadly she died before she could taste the sweet nectar of freedom."

Adisa's heart sank and she heard the name of her former home and she studied Lester's eyes for any betrayal of what he said. There was none. His eyes were warm and kind.

"Miss Adisa, would it surprise you to learn that I am a free man? About six years ago, under manumission I was able to buy myself out of slavery and set up my own carpentry shop, mainly for the churches in the area," Adisa looked up in surprise.

"You're a free man? Don't tease me, your wickedness is not needed here. We have enough of that. Plenty to go around, from the staff alone." Lester laughed.

"As I live and breathe, Miss Adisa. It is true. There are few of us on the island, about 100, if that. A tide of change is coming, but not soon enough. Here, here is a copy of the Trinidad Courant from a few days ago. There is mention of a talk we gave at the Savanna Grand Park in Port of Spain - a group of us free negroes speak and campaign for the government to hear us. We'd like you to join us. Come and speak at one of our conventions. It would be most powerful for you to speak alongside us and for others to hear what you have to say!"

"But, how can I when I am not free? Surely they will not believe me, if I'm a slave, speaking at a 'freed slave gathering'. What weight could I have to speak with authority? Plus, I don't have such free agency here. You'll learn all in good time Mr Brodie Henderson can be something of a tyrant. He will never grant permission let alone for me to go and give a talk. Are you mad?"

"Indeed, Miss Adisa. I understand what you're saying, but as far as we know, you're the only vocal woman who has spoken out over the years. You have already been quoted in the newspapers and Parish circulars. You're quite legendary, can't you appreciate it, people will listen to you, more so than to us men?" Lester tried to reason with Adisa.

"But the life I have here is nowhere near as good as it was in the days of growing up and living on Conquerabia Plantation. For a start, I worked in the house, not on the land and Master Florian, a rather enlightened man, gave me the room to speak freely after church meetings.

"Here, I will be flogged with Mr Grey's whip which he now uses liberally. Then there is also the problem of Mr Henderson. We don't even get to see any newspapers but some people have kindly saved bits and pieces for me. If I'm caught with this or any other contraband, my life will be a misery."

"Then I will see to it that you can have access to our meetings, say about once a month. We have another in just under two and a half weeks. Now that I'm working for the church, I won't let any harm come to you.

"Please say, you'll speak at our next meeting? It will be under the premise of you attending a baptism and celebrations. There will be a baptism on that date. You don't need to say anything now, but at least by Thursday, in three days, I'd like to hear your favourable answer. Is that fair?" Lester smiled at Adisa and she felt weak at the knees.

"Yes, Mr Pearce. I think that's most agreeable. I will meet you back here on Thursday about 7 in the evening, if that works for you?" Lester's eyes sparkled and a warm feeling washed over Adisa. It was like nothing she had ever experienced before and she could not make sense of it. How silly she felt, thinking that she was 16 years old once again.

That evening, feeling somewhat elated, Adisa, having eaten, reclined to her dorm. A small candle on the table next to her cot she lit and pulled out of her pocket on her dirty frock some of the newspaper cuttings Lester gave her. She made out the headlines. They were hopeful. Headlines about the Luisa Calderon case saddened her; Headlines about the progress of the abolitionist movement in Trinidad; government meetings disrupted by opposers. Another cutting's headline read 'Freed Trinidad Negroes Fight for Equal Rights'. They spoke of four men, including Lester Pearce, Carpenter, formerly of Toco and now of Siparia, inciting fear amongst the land and plantation owners and calling negroes to revolt. It talked about Chef Doxey of Saint Domingue and his group of maroons and urged the Government of Trinidad to prepare for war.

Adisa's heart beat loudly in her chest. It was almost painful. She could not believe that these men, including Lester, were getting such negative coverage in the newspaper. She read on: "Lester Pearce and his henchmen, claim they believe in the power of words and non-violence to persuade the Government to follow in the footsteps of Britain and The Americas, to consider strongly supporting the proposed abolition of slavery." Adisa read and re-read those words 'supporting the abolition of slavery.' At long last there was hope. She had her answer.

She heard someone outside and hurriedly hid the papers. In the process some of the papers fell to the ground and Adisa caught a headline that sent a shudder through her body. " Scipio 'Skip' Alvarez along with two accomplices hung for the murder of Toby Fredericksen, son of plantation owner and chair of the Plantation Owner's Alliance, Aubrey Fredericksen. Present at the sentencing were Aubrey Fredericksen, whose eldest daughter Ottilie May Dottin, who was mired in scandal, committed suicide some years before, and his daughter Therese Peters. Both were relieved by the judgement passed. Toby Fredericksen's body was found by a brook having had his neck slashed and his heart eviscerated. The body had been removed from the original site of death, in a premeditated attack. Scipio Alvarez, Pauly Newell and Gideon Johnston were tried and found guilty and were hanged within the week."

Adisa read this with shock. Since that day back in Conquerabia Plantation when Scipio had cornered her, she despised him and thought he had the potential to do harm. In some respect, it did not surprise her. She read on:

"It is thought the attack was due to Scipio Alvarez' frequent attempts to escape, unruly behaviour, laziness and theft from his master's and Aubrey Fredericksen's plantations. The attack on an upstanding member of society's son was seen as a message of defiance for which the three accomplices were hanged as a deterrent to others."

Sadness overcame Adisa. Of what she knew of him he did not deserve to die and wondered if the charge was false.

Chapter 30

Florian was still troubled by nightmares recalling that fateful night when Ottilie found out about Adisa; the shock on her face and Adisa's as the stark realisation and betrayal set in. Ottilie screamed and lashed out at Adisa with the heel of her shoe, angered by the love and attention she had showered on her trusted and favourite maid, working so closely with Isobel and Baxter. Her idyllic life is a lie. Florian was ashamed, betraying everyone except his mother who, on her deathbed, pleaded for Florian to recognise his daughter. Only Tante looking on felt that time had at last come to pass, held no sympathy for her master, just relief it was all now in the open, no more deceit.

Therese paid Florian a visit and recounted how over a period of time, Aubrey had become an alcoholic recluse, fearing he could no longer show his face in public. Disgraced! The plantation was saved by the attention of his overseer. She too had become a social pariah and decided to move to Port of Spain with Aubrey, where they rented a house and placed the children into a new school.

Therese felt sorry for Florian and was the only link between him and his children. She had to inform Florian that Aubrey had banned him from the funeral and burial. He went on a rampage destroying anything Ottilie left in the house.

He became delusional thinking he saw visitations of Mabel, her face sad, disappointed. On one occasion he thought he saw her so clearly, hovering over him and saying, "Pick yourself up Florian. This is not how I expect you to behave. You roll the dice, as your father did, and you play to win. No son of mine is going to ruin everything over one mistake. One slave girl. Get up and find your dignity!"

Florian shot up, his head throbbing. The vision was clear and it frightened him. He shook his head and squinted his eyes. Mabel was there in the room. Now, she is gone. He swore he could have touched her. Her perfume, the one with lilies she always wore, lingered. He sat there all through the evening, staring into the space where Mabel appeared. He was too frightened to move, or so he thought.

"Master? Mr Florian. Are you alright?" Tante knocked on the door. He did not move. Tante placed the dinner tray on the table next to the chair where Florian sat and shook him. He jumped. "Master Florian sir, I'm so sorry. I didn't mean to surprise you. Is everything alright sir?" Florian slowly turned his head to where she stood and looked up at her.

"Go fetch Father. O'Leary. Quickly!"

-o0o-

"But I saw her, Father, just as if she was still alive! She even spoke to me." Florian was confused. The priest was with him as he spoke of his loss, his drinking, and his vision.

"It has been a stressful time for all, particularly you and Aubrey. I think in time, you will come to terms with the loss of Ottilie. Perhaps you should have a Memorial service of your own, to mark her passing? It could help you start to grieve and to heal. It is understandable the need for a drink but it is not the answer. You still have two beautiful children who need you. Time is a great healer, Florian. I understand what the discovery of Adisa as your first born meant to Ottilie, as you need to see things from her perspective." The priest, Father O'Leary, sat on Florian's left. He did not want to make things worse for Florian, but the longer he denied the truth, the longer his misery would endure.

"Florian, forgive me for saying this, as I don't wish to cause you any more pain, but where Ottilie is concerned, she's lived a lie. She married you in the knowledge that she would give you your first child. And she believed you to be a man who would never lie with a slave, as you would your wedded wife. She knew men can be weak. Perhaps you should have told her at the beginning? As Christians, we are far more forgiving than we imagine." Father O'Leary looked at Florian, who did not flinch. He remained sat up in the arm chair staring into the distance, absorbing what the priest had to say to him.

"Florian, only you can make amends. In time Aubrey may learn to forgive and to understand, as he too has lost children in terrible circumstances. You must remember him in your prayers but mostly you must seek forgiveness from God and then from Aubrey.

"But Father. I cannot imagine anyone, even God, forgiving me for what I've done." A tear gently rolled down his cheek.

"In the blood of Christ you will find forgiveness. He sacrificed his life to save you. You must beg his forgiveness but you must also follow this up with deeds. Live in confession and contrition. Perhaps the vision from your mother was a way for God to speak to you?" Florian did not respond. "How was your relationship with Mabel, Florian?" Florian inhaled deeply, recalling the taut relationship.

"That is a hard question. If I can say this without sounding mad, our relationship improved towards the end of her life. I was an arrogant young man when I came to Conquerabia, fresh from witnessing the capitulation of the Spanish. I was hardly disembarked when I found out, from the wagon driver no less, that my father had died unexpectedly. Was awash in conflicting emotions. I had indescribable grief at the loss of a father I hardly knew, indescribable joy in being reunited with a mother whom I had missed since childhood, and an urgent sense that I needed to assume the role of a plantation owner. I didn't even ask her about running the place. I assumed that my father had been in charge and that she was merely the lady of the house. I deferred to my father's longtime manager. I had been hearing about this manager for many years and it was in him that I placed my trust”

“I imagine I would do much the same, Florian, who would know more about the place than your father’s right hand man?

“I appreciate this thought, but you asked me about my relationship with my mother. So yes, going to the manager, Diego, made sense in many ways, and indeed Diego taught me everything about managing the machinery of a sugar plantation, and managing imported labour, and getting the crops to port. It was an intense learning curve in such a short period of time. But it took a while for me to appreciate my mother’s role in the on-going management of the accounts, the finances.

“Well, again, Florian, it sounds like you took your responsibilities seriously, and from the prosperity of the place it appears that you would have made your father proud, and I am certain that is how your mother saw it.”

“But that is just it. Yes, I learned how to manage Conquerabia as my father did, but when I discovered what brought them here to Trinidad - when my father lost the marital home in Peutie, Belgium, I saw mother in a very different light. I warmed to her even more, but I learned of this only a short time before she died. Truly, conversations from her death bed turned my entire understanding of having both her and my father on the land registers, so she too owned land. It was remarkable for the time. She even took over the books for the plantation and ran it profitably.

"I wish she was still here to help me. She was strong. It could so easily have been a different situation for her, but she chose to stand by my father and give me the best possible upbringing. I owe her that, at the very least. When she sent for me after my father died, I came as soon as I could. I gave up my dream and respectable career in the Royal Navy to look after the plantation, in order that she could live out her life in the manner in which she was accustomed. I have little to regret, I owe her, or rather I felt I owed her."

"Only mother could get me to do most things". He smiled recalling the letters in which she said she was proud of him. "All that I became was mostly down to her. We had this tense relationship but I know deep down she knew I loved her deeply, and vice versa."

"How do you feel now, talking about Mable?" The priest asked.

"Father, I'm feeling somewhat better. Thank you for hearing me talk. You've made me realise I need to value what I have now - the children, my health. I should put more stock in my faith and the church which I know I have neglected."

"That's understandable Florian." You have to do this in your own time." Father O'Leary was sympathetic. Both sat in contemplative silence.

Well, Florian. If you have no objection I suggest we meet once a week at the church. I feel it best I should hear your confessions. That will help you. How does that sound to you? Florian felt he had no choice. Too many people depended on him, let alone his two children.

"For now, let's kneel in prayer and give thanks for His grace and mercy Florian!" Florian nodded his head in agreement and joined the minister on his knees. Father. O'Leary led the prayer as Florian started to cry. Fr. O'Leary placed his hand on Florian's shoulder and continued. After they finished, both sat in their respective chairs in silence until Florian fell asleep.

Quietly Father. O'Leary left and gently shut the study door behind him. He sought out Tante and told her what took place. Father O'Leary knew how much Florian relied on her and Elders, and Tante would not betray him, at any cost.

She gathered a fresh platter of cheese and cold meats, dry biscuits and fruit along with a glass of Sherry, which she took to Florian and laid on the table by his side, removing the earlier untouched plate. When he wakes, he need not seek out fresh sustenance.

The plantation ran with relative silence as Elders kept things going. The morale was bleak as everyone felt the sadness and loss of Ottilie. Her energy and love would be missed by many. Adisa too, he missed. Perhaps he really did care for his daughter? Perhaps he really knew he could not just dismiss her as the daughter of a negro woman who bore his child. Who was he to deny her?

After a brief slumber Florian woke to the food Tante left on the table by his chair. He was thankful she had been so considerate at his time of grief. All along she knew, but she never betrayed me, he thought. There was singing in the distance, he had to see from where it came. Father O'Leary was right, grief will take time. I will take this one day at a time. I can't fix things immediately, I need to earn everyone's trust and I vow to do so.

Florian's recovery was slow, and he lost a lot of weight, visibly ageing. He had no news of Adisa or where she was, or if she were alive. All he could do was to immerse himself in work and to build the extension to the school house.

Chapter 31

Willem and Cicely had become close to Florian. It was Willem who tried to broker an olive branch to Aubrey, who was still grieving for Ottilie and still seeking solace in drink.

Therese took charge in raising the children, maintaining a routine for them. But it was Baxter who was most affected by the loss of his mother. Isobel was too young to fully appreciate the loss. Baxter became rebellious and lashed out. He could not understand why he moved home or lived with his aunt. He wanted his mother and father and the familiarity of Conquerabia and the nice maid he used to play with.

Florian missed the children deeply and wanted to see them. They had attended a new school in Port of Spain, where Therese was now living with her husband, a French diplomat and Aubrey. On days when he had business in the Capital, Florian would ride past their school in anticipation of catching a glimpse of the children.

On one occasion Baxter saw him and screamed out in delight at seeing his father, but one of the nuns, who witnessed the incident, picked Baxter up and ran inside the school, as he was kicking and screaming. They had been instructed by Therese and Aubrey that Florian was not to be anywhere in sight, it was too disruptive to Baxter's well-being. Seeing his father and then being whisked inside, traumatised the young boy.

Florian was in constant emotional pain, however immersing himself in work helped but was also a reminder of that eventful day but neither could he let the plantation flounder. He was grateful to Elders and Tante for taking in hand most of the duties in running the house and plantation. He had promoted Elders in the process, to become the overseer, with pay since Diego's son had moved to another plantation in Barbados.

Tante, who continued to experience poor health, did not let her ire towards Florian show and made every effort to support his rehabilitation. The pain left from Adisa's departure ran deep. They grieved for her. She and Elders would often sit in evening prayer with Adisa very much in their thoughts.

One afternoon, after Tante and Elders returned back from church Florian invited them to join him on the verandah, asking if they heard anything to do with Adisa's whereabouts or heard anything that might give them a clue to finding her. Both denied any knowledge and hoped Adisa had not been kidnapped and taken from the island.

Tante returned to the kitchen in order to prepare for his dinner guests Willem and Cecily. It was just the company he needed. He finished his work early and sank into a long cool bath Tante had prepared for him. He enjoyed the sensation of water on his skin. He shaved and began to feel more like his normal self. As he dressed he tried on several items of clothing which he realised hung on his frame and made him look gaunt. Each item that was ill fitting found its way onto the bed. He needed his clothes taken in.

On the verandah, Tante was laying the table and dropped a tumbler, which shattered on the wooden floor. As she bent down to pick up the larger shards of glass she saw something white in the flower bed and realised it was a pouch with a label attached to it. It bore Adisa's name. It contained 5 reales, 'Happy Birthday. Florian and Ottilie Dottin'. She placed it in her apron pocket and cleaned up the rest of the glass.

As he finished dressing, Florian saw Willem and Cicely walk towards the house and took a moment to survey the view. It never ceased to take his breath away. He truly loved Conquerabia. He finally realised he could call it home.

At the bottom of the stairs, Tante was waiting for him. "Master Florian, I've just found this." She handed him the pouch. "I don't know how long it's been there, but I think it's a good omen!" Her smile was encouraging.

"Thank you Tante. I'll look at it later. My guests are here and you could be right about a good omen." Florian tucked the pouch into his waistcoat pocket. “William! Cicely! How lovely to see you? How are you both?”

“Ah, Florian. Yes, we’ve not long returned from Port of Spain, I attended a synod and Cicely came with me to join the clergy’s wives. It’s been interesting, for sure.” Florian shook Willem’s hand and kissed Cicely on both cheeks.

“What can I get you to drink? Tante has prepared a suckling pig for dinner”.

“That does sound good.” Cicely added. “We enjoy her cooking.” The trio sat down for a relaxed dinner and discussed the plantation’s school extension. Work was going really well.

“Florian, I’ve heard some troubling news today. It appears our Governor is in disagreement with His Majesty’s Government in London. I fear our stability may be at risk. There have been rumblings that Picton is not quite the man we would like him to be.”

“I’m not with you, Willem, what do you mean?” Florian appeared concerned at this news.

“See here, reported in the Courant, this young girl Luisa Calderon has been reported as being a thief. She allegedly stole a significant sum of money, something like $2,000 from one Carlos Gonzalez, a Government Contractor and shop owner in Port of Spain.

"It has become known in certain quarters that Picton's rule of law does not align with the King and this story, here in the paper about Luisa, has me concerned." He showed the article to Florian.

"This girl can't be more than 13 and they're painting her as a criminal before any real evidence is brought forward. She is now in prison without trial, and I understand Picton has been torturing her." Florian looked at the image of torture. Only a monster could come up with that method of hurting a child, he thought to himself. It made him recall Adisa at that age and just how fragile a person she was with those bright eyes and happy disposition.

"I met with her mother Maria, to offer some comfort." Willem added. "Cicely was with me too. She is inconsolable and swears Luisa is innocent. I think what I'm really getting to is that there are a number of stories I'm hearing about our Governor that gives me great cause for concern.

"As you know so well, he revised the Code Noir which until a few years ago gave the negroes protection. It stated that 'no one could punish a slave other than the master or his representative and that punishment could not draw blood. If so, then the master or his representative will be fined $50'. I have seen the document that removes this clause and the slave owner is now entitled to punish at extreme cost with no risk of penalty. I feel this is a grave error. In Port of Spain there appears to be a growing concern of a revolution like in Saint Domingo. It appears Governor Picton has become a law unto himself and is on his way to England for his own trial regarding this matter. We are unsure if he should return, but if he does, what's next?"

"Yes." said Florian. "I am fully aware of this and it is part of the reason I was barred from the Plantation Owner's Alliance. I disagreed with the revision and we have seen that this gives people like that brute Brodie Henderson licence to continue to abuse his workers or anyone who gets in his way, ad nauseum." Florian added, looking at Cicely whose eyes pleaded with him for guidance.

"I have to admit Willem, I've let things go. I've lost touch with the Plantation Owner's Alliance and need to pick up on what I've missed out on over the last few months. The local Alguida, Quinton is a good friend. I'll speak with him and see if he can shed some light. Leave it with me Willem."

"We understand Florian. We are not here to make things more difficult for you, but our livelihoods may be at stake if we live under a potential despot. For the sake of Baxter and Isobel's future, we need them to be secure."

"Yes of course, you're right." They continued to dine in silence.

"Oh, yes, some good news Florian. Cicely's mother is coming to visit very soon with a friend of hers. I don't know if you recall Father Maxwell who ran the parish where your parent's lived in Peutie?. We're quite looking forward to seeing her. It's been some time." Willem smiled and gently squeezed Cicely's hand. It did not go unnoticed by Florian. Cicely smiled at Florian. It was a genuine, warm smile.

"I am with child Florian! We are to be parents!" Cicely looked at Florian and waited for the news to register.

Florian jumped up at the news. "Congratulations to both of you. It is good to have some wonderful news to celebrate at long last. You must think terribly of me. I am delighted for you both." Florian raised his glass. "To the happy couple, may you be blessed with a healthy child, or children!" Florian's heart sank. He missed his own children, but could not let it show. This was their moment.

"Thank you, thank you Florian." The couple said in unison and the conversation turned to lighter tones. Florian sat back in his chair and realised that this was the first time he felt content in quite some time.

-o0o-

Adisa's back was sore. Work was relentless and it was already humid. A number of negroes were already working the land. She realised it was Sunday, and closed her eyes to see if she could catch a bit more sleep. She bolted upright. Today is an important day!

Lester had secured special dispensation from Brodie Henderson for Adisa to go to church for a special baptism of one of his friends and to stay for the celebrations afterwards. What he omitted was that the celebrations would be for Adisa to make her debut speech to the

Trinidad Freed Negroes Movement for the Abolition of Slavery meeting, which would take place in San Fernando. They would attend the baptism first then head on to the event. Lester allocated an hour and a half to get there by buggy, so they needed to leave early. Adisa preferred not to rush and laid out her papers, bible and purse on her bed. Her nerves began to jangle and she went over her speech in her head.

Lynchings were becoming commonplace amongst black negroes or even those who had already sought freedom. The militia and constables were running scared so Lester ensured he had the invitation to baptism on him should they be stopped, en route. Every black man, woman or child out in public needed to prove they had the right to be there. Those without documentation from their owners were thought to be runaways and were often jailed until their innocence could be proven.

The island's constables had a stipulation of 3 days for ownership to be declared or those jailed would be sent to the island prison or killed. However, all too frequently, the militia out patrolling the streets in the capital or towns, became jittery, particularly when they encountered a black man or group of black men. Reports of shootings or hangings were now all too frequent and the island was becoming lawless such was the threat of an uprising.

More and more freed negroes, inspired by the Saint Domingue maroons, started to take action against those they believed were killing negroes indiscriminately; their bodies thrown in the back of the military or constables' patrol wagons or left where they were killed, by the side of the road.

Trinidad, once an idyllic island, now smelled of blood, gunpowder and burning flesh.

Chapter 32

Cecily and Willem made such a success of the school; it was over subscribed. Freed negroes now applied to have their children educated there. Florian had to create a separate dirt road for access to accommodate the varying buggies and wagons transporting children of all ages eager to learn.

In fairness, priority was given to the children of workers on Conquerabia Plantation. 10% was allocated to freed workers who paid a nominal amount to have their child educated. The school catered for children from 8 years of age to 11 after which secondary schooling had to be arranged elsewhere.

The Plantation School had developed good relationships with local schools and, as well as an increased number of children, additional teaching staff was sought. The school now had a complement of seven members of staff, teaching Latin, English, History, Religious Studies and more.

Willem went to speak with Florian to confirm the arrangements for Cicely, her mother and the priest. They would be guests of Florian and stay in the main house. This meant that the building of the school extension could continue without interruption. Florian was delighted to make his home available for the guests and within six weeks, they arrived.

The elderly Rayne had lost none of her 'joie de vivre', and accompanied Father Maxwell in her professional capacity, her duties were basic now that he had retired, and would offer his ministry as a locum should other parishes need cover. Rayne was delighted to be with her daughter once again, and with nothing to keep her in Belgium, relished spending time with both Willem and Cicely and doting on her new grandchild.

Maxwell suffered with arthritis and the warm weather was advised. He had all but lost his hearing and now walked with the aid of a stick and horn to aid his hearing. He had to take to his bed shortly upon arrival due to the overwhelming heat and arduous journey.

Rayne fussed over Cicely and soon joined in the fun and games at the school house and both Florian and Willem welcomed her administrative skills where the running of the school was concerned. And in time, at her instigation, a summer school was founded for those who needed revision skills with a second, evening summer school specifically aimed at adults who wished to improve their education.

On Saturdays, the school house was used by the community for other classes such as sewing or embroidery. Every year the school house held a fair to help raise much needed money to continue its development.

Florian was too young to remember Rayne, however he had some memories of attending the church fair back in Peutie. He would have been no more than ten, Florian found that in time, the presence of Rayne and Maxwell proved a welcome distraction. There was so much that needed his attention and Rayne's social secretary skills ensured Conquerabia, Florian and she became the talk of the town.

Despite the warmer weather easing his ailments, Maxwell took ill and sadly passed four months later. Upon his death, he left instructions for Rayne to write to and notify his Bishop back in Belgium. He requested to be buried in Trinidad and Florian kindly allocated a plot of land for him in the plantation's cemetery for him to be interned, that had views across the adjacent fields.

Florian offered Rayne the services of his lawyer to write to the Bishop with news of the death, and to contact the solicitor to set about the sale of what little property Maxwell had. What few belongings that remained in Peutie were packed and shipped off to Trinidad. Rayne would later gain a small windfall; Father Maxwell remembered her in his will as recognition of her years of devotion working for him and the church.

Weeks after giving birth, Cicely became more active, taking the twins for walks around the plantation in the perambulator and meeting with the plantation children and young students excited to see the new arrivals.

At her own instigation, she had decreased her teaching time in the school preferring to enjoy spending time with the babies. She was a natural mother. With Rayne's help the young couple, and their twins, thrived.

One day, Florian called upon the couple and asked if he could speak with them privately. Although Rayne appeared to be put out at this request, she happily took the twins off to the garden, where she sat sewing.

"I apologise for asking to meet with you like this, but I have a proposition for you, that I think could be mutually agreeable?"

"This sounds intriguing." Willem added. "Yes, what is it about?" He sat opposite Florian.

"I've been observing things lately and feel that you, Cecily and the twins should move into the house. I can move into the apartment over the school as you obviously need more room.

"I can speak with Tante to extend her help with domestic issues so that Cecily and Rayne can focus on the boys. It's just me rattling around this big house and it's delightful to have Rayne stay, but you all need to be a family together." Florian offered. "You don't need to make a decision now, but think about it. Honestly, you'll be doing me a favour."

"Florian, that's very generous, I think I can speak for myself to say, that's a lovely idea provided my mother is in agreement. However, I think Willem and I would of course pay you rent. It is the right thing to do." Cicely was close to tears, moved by Florian's gesture.

"Well, I think that answers the questions. If my dear wife is in agreement and then Rayne, it would be wonderful to accept your kind offer. That's more than generous of you Florian. Thank you so much." Willem stood up to shake Florian's hand as Cicely kissed him on the cheeks. Cicely went to the window to call her mother who came quickly pushing the pram, anxious and excited to learn of what was making them so excitable. Rayne was overjoyed at the news.

"I'll ask Elders to help move your belongings into the house at a time convenient with you all, and you are to avail yourself of the house as if it were your own." Florian suggested.

"I would be delighted, Florian. Thank you once again for thinking of us all. It's a tremendous help." Rayne playfully curtsied at Florian, rocking the pram in the shade with the twins still asleep.

A celebratory meal was enjoyed by all the following week, once the move commenced. Having Rayne's presence helped change Florian's mood. She was an interesting companion to him and he admired her wisdom. He looked forward to the dinners she organised at the plantation, which proved entertaining for all. In some respects Rayne reminded him of Mabel and he especially loved the evenings they both sat on the verandah talking long into the night as she recalled her stories about Mabel and their friendship and Florian as a child.

Florian correctly surmised Rayne was still unaware of the true reason Mabel and Johan moved to the island. He decided it was best not to shatter the fondness Rayne had of her dear friend.

It had been some six months since Rayne had moved into Mabel's old bedroom and she asked Florian to excuse her for two days, so that she could go into Port of Spain to finalise affairs with the solicitors that handled Father Maxwell's estate.

Elders prepared the horse and buggy and took Rayne to the station where she boarded the early morning landau to the capital. The driver led her onto the carriage placing the luggage in stowage. Elders agreed that he would arrange to meet her back there, in two day's time, for her 8:40 pm arrival. She was too distracted to read, staring out to the passing countryside, thinking about all that she had done within the last year and mourning Maxwell.

"Ma'am!" A gentle male voice brought her back to reality. A hand was held out towards her with a crisp cotton handkerchief. "I don't wish to embarrass you, but I think this may come in useful!" Rayne looked at the gentle man sitting opposite her with kind, tired eyes.

“Thank you sir. I’m terribly sorry you had to witness this. I was mourning the loss of someone very close to me, who recently passed.” Rayne took the handkerchief and elegantly dabbed her cheeks from the tears.

“I’m so sorry to hear,” he replied sympathetically.

She extended her right hand. “I’m Rayne Jensen. I apologise again.”

“I was the same when my own daughter and son passed. Children should never pre-decease their parents. Grief is tough, but I prefer to focus on the wonderful memories I have. It does get easier with time. I’m Aubrey Fredericksen. I’m very pleased to meet you. I’m travelling up to Port of Spain to visit my other daughter and her husband for a couple of days. How about you? Do you have any children too?” Aubrey’s mood improved.

“My only daughter Cicely is married to a former missionary who now runs a school in Caroni. Not that long ago, she made me a grand-mother with the birth of adorable twin boys, Oscar and Hugo. They are about four months old now and the apple of their parent’s eye. I’m very much a proud grand-mother, as you can imagine.” Rayne enthused.

“You said you live in Caroni? I am surprised we have not met before, I have a plantation there.” Aubrey stated.

"I live in Conquerabia!" Aubrey visibly bridled to hear this. He managed a smile. "I have heard so many great things about events held there, recently. I am pleased Mr Dottin is doing well, especially after we experienced severe damage a few years ago due to the storm and arson attacks." Aubrey became lost in his thoughts and the remainder of the journey was spent in silence. The landau arrived at its destination and as Rayne departed Aubrey addressed her.

"Rayne, are you doing anything for lunch tomorrow? If it's not too much of an inconvenience? There is a lovely Spanish restaurant not far from where my daughter lives and I would welcome the opportunity to get to know you. If you don't think it's too much of an imposition?" Rayne was surprised by the invitation. Ever the social butterfly she accepted. "Perhaps, you may allow me to take you to see Mozart's The Magic Flute at the Concert Hall tomorrow evening? I have tickets. My friend broke his leg last week and is unable to join me. You'd be more than welcome?"

"The opera? How wonderful. It's been a long time since I attended the opera and I love the music of Mozart. He's quite a genius, don't you think? I would be honoured." Rayne was excited at the invitation.

"Excellent. Where can I pick you up and at what time? I suggest we dine first, if that fits in with your schedule?" Aubrey relaxed.

"Mr Frederickson, I'm staying at the Fleur de Lys Hotel on the Sangre Grande Road. I'd be delighted to meet you at 5:30pm. I'll be in the salon. I look forward to it." Aubrey took her hand and, as was the custom, kissed it gently.

The following morning Rayne arrived at her solicitors Weller & Davidson Associates, close to the Savannah Grand park. Outside she arranged her hair and hat and re-tied the silk purse to her wrist. She looked remarkably striking. It was warm already and busy.

Rayne left the solicitors office and the bellboy hailed a hansom cab to take her to the hotel where she changed. Another cab was hailed to take Rayne to the fashion district where seamstresses had their workshops and showrooms to see if she could find something new and pretty to wear. She had arranged to have the afternoon sightseeing but told herself it would have to wait for another occasion. She arrived back at the hotel by 3pm, ladened with boxes of shopping.

She unpacked her new pastel blue dress, ready for the afternoon's entertainment. Rayne felt giddy with excitement to be out at something so civilised, it was a welcome distraction.

Chapter 33

The Magic Flute was a success and Rayne and Aubrey decided to take a stroll in the Savannah Grande. It was late and many people were also enjoying an evening stroll in the cooler night air. They talked long into the night about music and family.

Aubrey was taken by Rayne's spirit and her independence. They did not notice time passing, so engrossed in conversation. They shared their own life experiences of love, laughter and loss. Aubrey was monotone, trying not to get emotional, which Rayne noticed. She did not think it wise to enquire further. His eyes lit up when he spoke about Therese and how supportive she and her husband were. He told Rayne how he never expected to see so much strength in Therese and how she has blossomed as a surrogate mother to his grandchildren. When he spoke of them, he looked into the distance and a smile danced across his lips.

It was two o'clock in the morning when Aubrey looked at his pocket watch. He apologised to Rayne for keeping her out so late and offered to walk her back to her hotel. He agreed to collect her in the morning and they would spend the day together and travel back later that afternoon.

Rayne spent a restless night lost in her thoughts about Aubrey, the loss of her dear friend Father Maxwell brought a tear to her eye. The small clock's alarm rang, waking Rayne from her slumber. She had to get ready swiftly in order to have breakfast before she departed.

Aubrey was early. He too had little sleep and it showed. He took a copy of the paper and sat in the corner of the salon and stood up as Rayne arrived.

"Good morning Mr Frederickson, I hope you slept well?" Once again he kissed the back of her hand in greeting.

"I think you can call me Aubrey now we have shared so much", he smiled warmly. "I can see you've got considerably more luggage than when you arrived," he joshed. Rayne coyly smiled at him. "I hope you enjoyed shopping?" Aubrey looked more relaxed."I had a wonderful evening last night and did I tell you how lovely you looked? I suppose this beautiful hat, the one you wore last night, is one of your new purchases?"

"Need you ask my dear Aubrey?" Rayne emphasised his name and it felt sweet on her tongue and she entwined her arm in his as the pair walked towards the carriage where he helped her into her seat. "And you can call me Rayne!"

They were to spend some of the day at the botanical gardens and then a late afternoon lunch would be enjoyed before travelling back to the coach station in Port of Spain, to get the carriage back to Caroni.

Knowing Elders was to pick her up at 8:40pm she invited Aubrey to share her ride back to the plantation. Aubrey's plantation was not far away and it allowed the pair to continue talking quite animatedly. As they neared Caroni, Aubrey became rather restless.

"Aubrey, is everything all right? You know you're nearly home now?" She once again wrapped her arm in his as the carriage pulled up.

"Rayne. If I may be so bold, would you care to take dinner with me this coming Saturday? It would please me immensely." Although somewhat off guard by sitting outside the familiar plantation, he felt compelled to see this extraordinary woman again.

"Aubrey, I would be delighted!" He got off the carriage and took Rayne's hand in his to bid farewell and before he could even speak, Rayne gently kissed him on the left cheek." "Goodbye Aubrey", she emphasised his name. "I'll see you at the weekend." Aubrey was pleasantly taken by surprise at this gesture, and felt his mood elevate. It has been a considerably long time since he was kissed so tenderly by a woman and he swung his portmanteau as he walked all the way back home.

-o0o-

Although Trinidad was flourishing, it also gained notorious attention due to the Luisa Calderon scandal. The scandal reached England, and Luisa was summoned to give evidence in London at the Court of King's Bench before Lord Chief Justice Ellenborough. A jury found Governor Thomas Picton guilty of torture.

As unease grew, English settlers sought to exploit the island's resources before its ownership was finalised. By 1802, and The English Party was established to finalise British rule and compete against the current administration and Picton's unilateral rule. William Fullerton was the first of three commissioners appointed to govern the island, with Picton appointed as Military Commissioner and Commodore Samuel Hood as Naval Commissioner.

Tensions arose between Fullerton and Picton when Fullerton requested an account of legal affairs under Picton's term. This led to Fullerton returning to England to bring his concerns to the Secretary of State. Upon learning of Fullerton's actions, Picton resigned and returned to England, discovering that the Privy Council was interested in Fullerton's concerns, particularly the alleged torture of Luisa Calderon to extort a confession.

After resigning as Governor of Trinidad, Picton fought in the British-French war and briefly served as Governor of Tobago.

In London, Fullerton published a pamphlet detailing his assertions, which generated significant media interest. By 1806, a retrial at the Court of King's Bench ruled out further charges against

Picton, citing that under Spanish law, which governed Picton's actions, torture was permissible and therefore no malice against Luisa Calderon existed independent of the act's illegality.

By 1810, the court declared Picton a free man. However, the trial had been costly for him, despite his supporters in Trinidad raising significant funds to contribute to his legal expenses.

It was a scandal the island would struggle to forget.

-o0o-

At the picturesque setting of Conquerabia, Florian sat down at his desk to open the letters. The first one opened was from his close friend Mr and Mrs James Alton, inviting him to the baptism of their son Charles Alton, it would take place at the catholic church in San Fernando, after which he was also invited to attend the celebratory lunch in the presbytery. It also mentioned guests were welcome to attend the Abolitionist's event in the town hall later that afternoon. Florian was happy, he and James were old friends and he respected him very much for what he had achieved in becoming the Justice Minister. Once he had cleared the letters which needed his attention, he placed them in a pile for despatch.

-o0o-

Esme sat with Adisa securing both plaits with a white ribbon just at the top of her shoulders. The opportunity to get out of the plantation alleviated the stress and strain from her face, although her body ached. She examined Esme's handiwork in a broken hand mirror.

It had been a long time since she felt this happy and she was amazed at how her entire face lit up and decreased in age by about 10 years.

"You look so beautiful child'!" Esme commented.

"Thank you Esme. You have made me look pretty. I don't even recognise the person in the mirror anymore. Please, can you tell me who she is?" It was just the right response to make both ladies laugh and Adisa gave her friend a hug.

"Esme, please would you accompany me today? It would mean so much to me?"

"Really? You don't want an ol' lady like me to be such a bother to you. It's an important day for you. No child. Thank you, but Lester is going to take you himself."

"I have already spoken to Mr Lester and he assured me that it is possible for you to come. There is no other person here whom I would like to accompany me, than you Esme. Please don't take offence, but you have been like a mother to me, and I value you immensely."

"I would be honoured to accompany you, if it means that much to you. Yes, of course".

Esme finished helping Adisa dress, with hat and lace gloves she walked with her to join Lester, atop the wagon, wearing a straw hat, which appeared new and not raggedy like most of the men wore on the plantation. In his hands he took command of the reins as the brown and black stallion respected his master. The horse was still, his head slightly bowed feeling every tweak and pull of his master's command. As Adisa and Esme approached, the horse snorted, which took Adisa by surprise.

Lester saw this and smiled. At that moment, Adisa looked up at him and was taken by his handsome features. Esme noticed the fleeting moment. There was no denying it. Adisa looked towards her friend and realised she had been caught out and blushed in embarrassment.

Lester laughed at the blushing Adisa and held out his hand for Esme and then Adisa to board the wagon and they departed. Adisa prayed for her heart to stop beating so fast partly with anxiety about her speech and second, sitting so close to Lester.

"You look very pretty today Miss Adisa, as do you Miss Esme". Lester toyed with Adisa. However, it made her blush even more. She could not recall ever being complimented by a man in such a genuine way.

"May I say, you look rather fine too, Mr Lester Pearce!" You look very happy. I have to say that at this particular moment I'm feeling far too nervous to be as confident as you look. Perhaps I need to be concerned that you may not be taking this as seriously as I am. Are you sure you're not kidnapping me sir?"

They sat three abreast on the seat at the front of the open wagon, Lester on the outside, Esme on the left with Adisa in the middle. Every turn forced Adisa to lean on Lester or Esme.

"I can assure you Miss Adisa, I have no plans to kidnap you nor Miss Esme. You both mean too much to me and I would never even think to kidnap someone as pretty as you my dear." It was all too much for Adisa and she frantically started to fan herself, which was futile as the breeze travelling through the countryside was sufficiently pleasant.

"So, why don't you two ladies tell me how you met?" This time it was Esme who spoke, giving Adisa time to compose herself and recalled the day the two first met at the slave market, and how Adisa was the calm, reassuring one without whom she would not have made it to Siparia.

The trio laughed together, sharing their tales and woes that were suitable to impart, never wanting to offend or seek sympathy when they all shared many stories.

Adisa marvelled at Lester's positive, optimistic outlook. He had a passion for life that she had not witnessed before in any negro. She was familiar with the drudgery all negroes shared as most of them knew nothing else. Lester was different. He had passion and ambition. She noticed some of this when they first met, and she was excited for what he represented. Today, however, she saw Lester in a totally different light.

He spoke with confidence, sure that the world will change soon, for the best despite the horrors going on around them. To Adisa, he posited why people behaved the way they did. He was educated in a way she was not and that was a huge attraction to her.

“Mr Lester, please may I ask you a rather personal question?” Adisa looked at him, as he concentrated on the road ahead.

“Yes, but first you must call me Lester. Just Lester.” Adisa was flattered that she could be on more familiar terms with him.

“On one condition, Lester!”. Adisa emphasised his name. It sounded rather sweet on her tongue. “You must call me Adisa and she is Esme.” Esme looked at Adisa and smiled in agreement, enjoying a new found sense of temporary freedom.

“Agreed!” Lester accepted. “Please, continue Adisa.” He emphasised her name.

“I find you a rather striking, educated man Lester. You cannot be much older than me, yet you are a free man, you speak well, you are full of confidence and even have a great command over this here horse. May I ask how you became so self assured, when many of us have the confidence beaten out of us until we are no more than a workhorse?”

“Hmm! That’s a lengthy question.” Lester teased Adisa some more. “I soon learned that the plantation and slave owners were running a business of sorts and that I quickly found I have an ability with wood and carving. I’m self taught. I soon asked what else I could teach myself? I used to listen to the older negroes who spoke of their time on the island, and about where they used to live. I became fascinated by the world and life. Also, I discovered that since I had a much needed skill, I became obedient in their eyes, but not subservient ...” Adisa interrupted.

“What do you mean ‘subservient’? I am sorry for interrupting you. Do continue.”

“Subservient" - meaning that I did not necessarily bow down to the owner, acting as if I’m lower than him. Because of the colour of my skin, he may think that, but without my talents as a carpenter, I became something of his equal. He realised that too. Once I understood the power of our relationship, we both knew we needed each other.”

“That knowledge and understanding gave me power, that I started to view the world differently. The church where I was before used to hold meetings of various kinds: literary, legal, arts and music and I used to sit in the back so that I could not be seen and I would leave before the end. I listened a lot, made notes, watched how the ‘white men’ behaved and adopted some of their mannerisms and language.”

"You see, this, in some sense, is old news. It's been going on for a very long time. I quickly learned to read and found an appetite for learning. I was surrounded by people who encouraged me to read and to question what was going around me. I see this in you too, Adisa." Adisa blushed again.

"I was based much further north west of here, in Arima, and got to learn a lot about Thomas Picton our governor. He is a brutal man, but you have to understand why and the circumstances he encountered."

Adisa noticed Lester's tone deepened. She sensed something serious was about to be said and she prepared herself and took hold of Esme's hand.

"I've read about him too. A despicable man. What he did to that poor girl ..." Adisa was interrupted.

"Luisa Calderon?" Lester questioned. "Yes, How could any man treat a young girl, a mere child, in such an appalling manner?"

"I vaguely knew her mother Maria." Lester offered. "She was a free coloured and came to make a life for herself and her family. Then she had three daughters, Catalina, Benacia then Luisa. I gather there was no father or husband, so Maria struggled to raise the girls as best as she could. She then met and worked for Señor Pedro Ruiz by becoming his housekeeper. By this time Luisa was around 11 years of age and from what I understand, he had designs on her, of which her mother disapproved. Ruiz was a wealthy businessman and after a while Maria hoped that, despite her objections, he could provide a life, better than she herself, could give her youngest daughter Luisa."

"How terrible for her. At least she had the best intentions." Adisa added.

"Yes, she did and I think many of us want the best for ourselves and each other. Maria was popular and wanted her daughters to be better educated.

"I understand there was a break-in at Pedro Ruiz' house and a significant sum of money had been stolen. With little by way of witnesses, the only person present, allegedly, was Luisa. According to what I've read, this burglary took place whilst Ruiz was out. Luisa was too young to understand and to appreciate the situation, and it was easy to make her a scapegoat. Perhaps this is what Ruiz wanted, revenge on Maria."

"The poor girl!" Adisa remarked. "So young too." Adisa looked beyond the wagon as they travelled in silence. "When did this happen? How did events unfold?" She asked Lester to continue.

"It depends on what you read or to whom you listen. Saint Hilaire Bergorrat, a friend of Picton's, urged him to place Luisa on trial, without a jury, believing she was already guilty. Picton then questioned her, without a jury. She was tortured by piqueting, as you know. A nasty tourture. It is suggested that Bergorrat also threatened her with the hangman's noose unless she confessed. She's still in jail now, as I live and breathe.`` Adisa looked at Esme who had a tear in her eye. She clasped her friend's hand tightly.

"I am sorry if this has upset you both, but Governor Thomas Picton was not a very nice man. Adisa you asked about how I became the person I am now. I saw the wealth many of my own kind had, through education. There was another man I met, who inspired me to become better. His name was William Dowding. Educated in Classics in England and well travelled he chose to make Trinidad his home and seek his fortune. He is a creole, but I liked what he represented: aspiration, education, freedom and wealth, but he had his own issues under Picton. I wanted to be like him and a number of the wealthy French nobles that moved here in the late 1780s due to the cedula. Trinidad was a land of hope and opportunity. I think it still is."

"At first, it felt foolish, wanting to be like them, but I realised that I wanted what they have and that is freedom, most of all. I wanted to be a free man in every sense of the word and I was determined to get there. I know I'm very lucky and many others will think I have 'become like them'. The trick was not to be threatening but polite and respectful to them as a human being, not just as a coloured man. Now as you can see, I have my freedom and it's been worth it. I'm determined to make it possible for others."

"You're quite a remarkable man Lester and I'm hopeful and inspired by you ..." Adisa spluttered.

"Are you all right Adisa?" Lester asked, concerned by her reaction.

"Yes, I think so, but that smell is making my eyes water and nose tingle. What is that terrible odour?" Adisa and Esme held their handkerchiefs to their noses. Lester drew in a deep breath and exhaled it rather quickly.

"Ah, yes. That's the Pitch Lake over in La Brea, to the west of here." He answered. The ladies looked puzzled. "Are you aware that Trinidad was populated by a people known as the Amerindians? Then, Trinidad was owned by the Spanish, who named that area of the island as Tierra de Brea or in English, the Land of the Pitch. It is an unusual black lake. Story has it that an Englishman called Sir Edward Ralee (Lester mis-pronounced the name), landed here in his search of El Dorado. According to what I have read on the subject, the little I have read, to be honest, he applied the black liquid to his ship, to prevent it leaking and apparently it was successful. I believe this was around 1595 or 1596." Adisa was amazed at this.

"Imagine, people inhabiting this island almost 300 years ago. I've never really considered that possibility before." Adisa added.

"Under Spain, in about 1792, Governor Don Jose Maria Chacon was instructed to build a processing plant but apparently that did not last very long since the island became part of the British empire in around 1797. Eight years later, I recall, a British Admiral was ordered to explore the lake and its potential uses. I am unsure as to what those findings are, or if they have been determined as yet. That smell you notice is what is called the sulphur content of the lake. A bit like the smell of rotten eggs, don't you think?" Adisa nodded in agreement. The strength of the smell is now too powerful to even speak.

"It will soon pass, depending on the direction of the wind." Lester laughed once again. They rode on in silence.

"Lester, you have given me food for thought. May I ask you another personal question?"

"Yes, of course. You can ask me anything you want, within reason!" Lester teased Adisa who did not take the bait.

"Don't you feel that you are being subservient in your behaviour to become accepted? Isn't it a lot of hard work thinking that way and acting out in the same way as the white folks?"

"It can feel like that at times, but I prefer to think about it as my way of navigating life to get what I need, then to get acceptance to get what I want for my fellow people. Yes, it can be tiresome, but change requires a lot of time and patience. I have found that you have to speak with authority and knowledge. Charm and patience, understanding their ways without being confrontational. I cannot say it works for everyone, but so far, it has helped me. I'd like to think that making a way for myself in this world is easy, but I will be telling you an untruth. People need to seek ways which work for themselves without recourse to violence, which in my opinion, is futile. All it causes are dead people, mostly black male negroes."

"You're a wise man Lester." Adisa added.

The rest of the journey to the Church went in silence as Adisa and Esme thought on all that Lester had to say. Adisa was full of admiration. His ethics and moral compass matched hers and she liked him very much. He also motivated her and she brought out her notebook and pencil to make amendments to her speech. It boosted her determination, and she was satisfied she would give the talk of her life.

In the distance, the Cathedral of St Joseph came into view. It looked dazzling with this white exterior, tall bell tower and surrounded by an array of beautiful flowers.

Pulling up outside, was an array of carriages carrying families and couples to the church service. As each wagon alighted, it moved on to the nearby park, where the drivers could secure their horses to railings.

It was very busy, but the order was well coordinated. Lester joined the queue to drop Adisa off outside the church entrance and said he would meet her and Esme inside. He instructed her where there were reserved seats.

It was a particularly bright morning, with no clouds in the sky. The world looked shinier and brighter. The purple Morning Glory outside the church was in full bloom

More and more people were arriving and the church began to fill up with worshipers and celebrants of the baptism. Adisa had never seen so much finery amongst the women, or so many white women going to church. She studied the crowd so hard to see if more black people and negroes were going in to worship. Very few. She began to feel uneasy. Fortunately Lester arrived back and sat with her and Esme, putting her at ease.

This would be a new experience. Adisa took the lead from Lester's conversation in the wagon, and watched everyone closely to see how they behaved.

As the men entered, they removed their hats. The ladies sat very primly in the pews with knees together, hands resting gently in their laps. They looked like statues as they all sat and looked towards the altar.

Lester looked over at Adisa and sensed her unease and placed a reassuring hand on her white lace gloved hands, which she had placed, like the other ladies, on her lap. One or two removed their fans, which they opened with a swift flick to open and fan their faces. It took Adisa one or two attempts to open her fan in the same manner, with some authority as the other ladies did. It made her giggle along with Esme who too was feeling uneasy and grateful for the release through laughter.

The priest, a tall grey haired man walked up the aisle with four acolytes wearing vestments, over which they had white collars, and took their seats at the side of the altar. He announced the first hymn and the service began.

The pianist tinkled an old, but well loved upright piano that had lost some of its notes, as the congregation sang, along with the tenor voice of the vicar. Adisa opened her hymn book and listened to the first verse so that she too, may sing along to the rest of the hymn. There was happiness in her heart.

Many of the ladies continued to fan themselves and little children ran about the aisle, the little boy, whose baptism it was, lay sleeping in his mother's arms, unaware of the major ceremony in his honour.

Florian had arrived late and sat at the back, not wishing to disturb the proceedings. There was mostly standing room left and he was amazed how many people were in attendance.

During his sermon, the priest spoke about forgiveness and understanding. He called for restraint in this time of fear and gave the story of The Good Samaritan, only using himself, not the biblical character, and his experience to give the story more resonance.

Adisa found herself agreeing with the points he raised and the story touched her heart. It made her think of the treatment she receives under Brodie Henderson and his manager Mr Grey. It strengthened her resolve and made her think more about others and increased her efforts to help them, not herself.

The baptism ceremony was performed next and the proud parents and Godparents were invited to gather at the church's font.

The service was then interrupted by the cries of the baby boy startled by the water being poured along his forehead. It received a number of chuckles and 'ahhhhhs'. Vows and prayers were said and the priest announced the next hymn, 'Jesus, Lover of my Soul' and the congregation stood.

After the service those invited to the baptism celebrations were invited to the presbytery for a private party. Florian joined them.

Adisa on Lester's left arm, Esme on his right, were escorted to the Hall where they were offered glasses of sherry or softer drinks, as per the guest's choice. Adisa opted for the champagne flute and the bubbles tickled her nose. It made her giggle. It tasted like nothing she had ever had before, and was unsure if it was something she liked.

"Adisa, please may I introduce you to Dr Ralph Greenford. He is Head of Surgery at The Port of Spain General Hospital. He is also a supporter of the abolitionist movement. Dr Greenford, This is

Adisa Soloman, who will make her debut at our talk, shortly this afternoon.

“I am pleased to meet you Dr Greenford.” Adisa offered.

“And I am pleased to meet you too. Mr Pearce has spoken of you highly. This is my wife Gladys Greenford. She is head nurse in the Maternity department at the same hospital.

“Miss Adisa.” Gladys shook hands, removing it like she had touched something offensive. Adisa was too polite to comment. Lester caught the act and looked reassuringly as Adisa.

"The baptism went well. I was delighted to see Justice James Alton, father of the child. He knew Governor Picton and I understand he wasn’t a fan”. Dr Greenford added.

"Whatever became of him? Lester asked.

“He also served as Military governor here, from what I can gather, then he went back to London for the court case with Miss Luisa Calderon. I've not heard the outcome. No doubt we'll hear in due course." Dr Greenford added.

Adisa looked at Lester and caught his surprise at the news. She continued to be introduced to several dignitaries and high ranking officials and felt that she was not worthy. Adisa watched Lester work the room. He was respected by many of these white people and it baffled her. It was disconcerting to her that he courted such favour with these people and suddenly realised that she needed to pull herself together, or it would affect her speech later that afternoon.

Speeches and comments were made to toast the child's baptism and acceptance into the church. The heat and the wine made her feel light headed and she took Esme with her to stand outside and see if she could feel a breeze across her face.

She confided to Esme that she felt out of place, but Esme reassured her that she was just as good as them, that she had every right to be there.

"You have to be strong. Look at Lester. If he can become free, there is hope. You have a voice and can speak on our behalf. You are gifted and blessed Adisa. Please use this opportunity to be heard and to help make a difference. If I could, I would love to be in your shoes. Adisa took a deep breath, stood tall and walked back in to find Lester.

The town hall was filling up again as people took seats in readiness for the speakers. A significant number of negroes also arrived. Most of whom were wearing their Sunday best. Those unable to afford the best dresses or suits, made sure they looked as presentable as possible. Adisa noted to herself that despite such oppression the negroes would not allow their appearance to deny the pride in themselves.

The Town Hall was packed. A canon who took control of the proceedings outlined the programme for the afternoon's event. He ran through the agenda, and spoke about what was discussed at the last meeting; how William Wilberforce was now taking steps in Great Britain to advance the Abolition bill, which received a thunderous round of applause. There were some dissenters and as Adisa looked around she caught sight of Brodie Henderson, sitting some distance towards the back of the hall. He had not yet seen her. Her fears were compounded by knowing he was there, having obtained permission to leave the plantation. Please God, don't let him hear me speak or my life will not be worth living anymore.

She took hold of Esme's hand and squeezed it hard, and Esme looked at her rather puzzled. Adisa did not return the look. She felt her stomach turn over, placing her hand on it to help calm her nerves.

The Canon introduced Lester who spoke next of his own experience. It was moving and despite hearing some of it in the wagon on the way there, Adisa now found it more moving and inspirational. His key points were punctuated with applause from most of the audience. He spoke with pride and dignity and never once spoke ill of others and asked for understanding. He spoke about education for all, and through education a move towards understanding and forgiveness would be reached. Lester was powerful as an orator and his words touched people

Next Dr Greenford spoke about a change in the world and sought patience and thought before action. He was good, but struggled in the wake of Lester. He spoke briefly and then introduced another man, the Chief Justice of Trinidad, Nathaniel Douglas. A man of some years who spoke slowly and read out the latest bills passed by the British Government.

When it came to the reading of the proposed bill for the Abolition of Slavery, Douglas could not hide his thoughts on the matter. It would be put forward to parliament for debate later in the year. He jumped when the audience rose to their feet in cheers at the news. Douglas walked back to his seat aided by the Canon and his walking stick, shaking as he moved, from age and heat.

Adisa admired him for his erudition, but his demeanour was dark. His way of life was probably threatened by the proposed abolition of slavery. He was very much a Colonialist.

Lester approached the dais once again to announce the final speaker. "Ladies and gentlemen it is my honour to invite you to hear about a remarkable young lady. I had heard of her reputation speaking eloquently on the freedom of negroes, at her local church back in Caroni, several years ago. She had become something of a legend, since it is still uncommon for a young slave woman to have a platform from which to speak."

"You may know my own story very well. I consider myself to be fortunate, not only to have the freedom to stand before you, but to introduce Adisa Solomon, who has been campaigning for the abolition of slavery for the last 10 years. Please be upstanding for

Miss Soloman." Lester stood back and began applauding, looking at Adisa who was overwhelmed by such a glowing introduction.

Esme took Adisa's hands and wished her good luck as she got up, took her notes from her purse and walked towards the dais. She looked into the audience and made eye contact with Brodie Henderson who's anger was apparent. It empowered Adisa to appreciate she had authority, momentarily and was not discouraged by his presence.

"Ladies and gentlemen", she whispered, then cleared her throat. "Ladies and gentlemen,I would like to say thank you to the distinguished panel and Mr Lester Pearce for inviting me to speak to you today. My story is not much different from many of you, your negroes and slaves. I was born into slavery, my mother finding freedom, passing to the next world during childbirth. I was her first born, immediately taken into care by a loving couple who headed up the house on the plantation where I was born. In that sense, I feel privileged to have grown up and worked there, but nonetheless, I am a slave. It's all I have known.

"Sold on to another plantation owner, my life changed exponentially where I was raped." The audience gasped. "Not just once, but several times, because you see the plantation owner doesn't see me as a human, but rather as his property, to do with as he wishes. In his eyes I am considered 3/5th a man. The livestock on his plantations enjoy a better quality of life than us, his labourers.

"It is not for me to judge, but His, alone. It is for me to understand why he feels threatened by the likes of me that he needs to control us in that manner, on the plantation. He is afraid. Afraid to lose what he has. Money! You see, without such wealth he loses his status looked upon as a pauper unable to contribute to society. Adisa looked directly at Brodie who knew she was discussing him and she could see him riling up.

"I am pleased to see an increased awareness and movement for the abolition of slavery. Freedom is on its way, perhaps not in my lifetime, but it's coming. Speaking from a position of understanding, I have chosen to forgive my oppressor". Angered Brodie, left. "My fellow men and women. We hear of the violence being meted out to us. What does that achieve? A great man once told me to observe and to learn and to become better; better in knowledge as that weapon is the most powerful weapon we have."

The audience was silent. Stunned by the delivery of such an honest perspective. Then, slowly the clapping commenced as black people rose up to applause and cheered one of the most heart rending speeches they heard in some time. The ovation lasted for more than 10 minutes. All the members of the panel with exception from the Chief Justice stood in applause. His face was of admiration for the courage of Adisa to speak so eloquently but age prevented him from standing.

General Alton stood by the lectern with his hands raised, calling for silence in the hall. He smiled, admitting defeat and began applauding once again in Adisa's direction and she went to sit down next to Esme, who embraced her.

"Ladies and gentlemen." The Canon called. "Ladies and gentlemen." He repeated. The audience calmed down. "I can honestly say, we have never had such a heartfelt, passionate talk by a woman before and I hope this will not be the last. I would like to thank Adisa Solomon for her contribution today. Indeed, it has touched me in ways I never expected." He turned to Adisa "Thank you so much for being here today and for such an inspiring talk. It was wonderful to hear you speak."

Adisa was overwhelmed. The anxiety of preparing the talk and the speed with which it was all over, left Adisa feeling dazed, as Esme once again put a reassuring hand on hers. Lester swiftly removed Adisa from the hall fearing they may outstay such a warm reception. At the back, too far away Florian saw his daughter.

"Finally, I would like to thank everyone for being here today and for making this event such a success. There are messages we can take from each speaker and I, for one, will continue to fight for the success of the Abolition of Slavery bill here and in Great Britain. Proceedings are now at an end."

"We need to get you back as soon as possible. I saw Mr Brodie Henderson in the audience and he didn't look too happy. Don't worry. I will be with you both." Having raced out of the hall, Lester sped back to Siparia as fast as he could.

On the steps Florian stood as people milled past him. His heart raced. He'd finally seen his daughter.

Chapter 34

Brodie raced back to his plantation humiliated. On horseback he had the advantage as he was not limited to the main paths, he would race back to the plantation through the countryside with greater speed than Lester could with the wagon. He whipped his steed and dug his spurs into the animal to gallop faster. He made it back just as dusk was falling.

"We - have - to - teach - that nigger - a lesson!" Brodie struggled to catch his breath. "She cannot - ridicule - me - in public! Grey, where the hell are you?" Henderson, rubicund and sweating profusely called out to his overseer, as he leaned against the horses' trough.

"What do you mean sir?" Mr Gray was puzzled. "That bloody girl. The impertinence of her speaking this afternoon at that meeting. Had I known, I would never have given her permission to leave today. She will be punished for this. Call me as soon as she and that Lester man arrive and take them to the workshop. And get me the tools as well. I'll show her not to humiliate me again. She will never want to show herself in public either, by the time I finish with her, the bloody bitch!"

Mr Grey ran off to the workshop to ask the men who were working to vacate the place and he gathered the items Henderson requested, placing them on the side, next to the vice, closing the workshop as he left.

Lester, Adisa and Esme were on a high, riding back on the wagon through the odours emitted by the pitch lake. They knew what it was this time. The light was beginning to dim, and the retiring sun cast an array of colours from red to orange and pink. It was a gorgeous warm evening as they dissected the day's events, shared emotions, ways in which to make a difference, the need for compassion and understanding and for the laying down of weapons.

"Sadly, I fear there are some who will be too quick to take up guns and resort to torture for some sense of satisfaction. I pray they will see the error of their ways before too much senseless killing takes place." Adisa pondered.

"I agree. The more we can hold meetings like today, to draw our people along to hear, to get the correspondents on our side and not to inflate their own agenda, and report things honourably, then we can make progress." Lester added.

"I had not thought of that Lester, but you're right. Do you think there were any correspondents there today?"

"Yes, I saw two from the Trinidad Courant and one from the San Fernando Echo, whom I know is on our side. He once gave me great coverage. I think he may do the same for you. I think he will be blown away by your presentation."

"Oh, do you think so?" Adisa asked.

"I have no idea, it depends on what happens tomorrow in the world of news. Other events may take precedence and we may not even get mentioned. We'll have to wait and see."

"Chil', I have never heard you speak so well as you did today. I see you in a new light. I knew there was something very special about you when we met under those terrible circumstances. You're a decent person Adisa and I feel very proud of you."

"Thank you Esme. That means a lot to me."

The trio rode on in silence taking in the sense of freedom they enjoyed being away from the plantation, knowing that it would not last much longer.

Brodie went back to his office and reached for the near empty bottle of rum and poured what was left into a tumbler. He sat down ruminating on the humiliation at Adisa's words. She had made him a figure of loathing, or so he felt. He had to teach her a lesson. He drank the shot in one go and stared out, into the distance, sweat pouring down his brow. His heart was beating rapidly.

In the distance, he saw the wagon approaching. Saw a smiling Adisa, that man Lester and what was Esme doing there?

Lester dropped Esme off at the house first, by the tradesman's entrance. She made her way back inside. Lester, made sure the horse was harnessed to the fence and the wagon removed and placed in the barn, secured and out of the way. It was dark despite the moon emerging from a cloud.

The plantation was eerily still. In the distance a flock of birds flew off into the night sky as if troubled by something. Brodie noticed. Lester and Adisa were unaware, only focusing on each other and still discussing the days' events.

The evening air smelled warm. Mr Grey was walking towards them and asked Lester if he could meet both of them in the workshop presently. He was curt and Lester wondered if something had gone wrong. This didn't feel right.

"Something wrong sir? It's late!" It was ignored. "Sir, I'll just walk Miss Adisa back to the dormitory and will return. Would that be reasonable for you?"

"You're wasting time. Go there now and take her with you!" Mr Grey shouted. Adisa did not like his tone. She did not like him either, but realised something was wrong and it frightened her. Lester looked at her, this was odd behaviour even for Mr Grey.

"Bear with me, it won't take long." He said.

"I'd feel safer with you. Thank you." Adisa whispered and both headed off towards the workshop. Mr Grey was almost there as he met with Brodie Henderson and the two walked in, letting the door shut after them. Lester stood still, trying to take stock of the situation. This was odd. No sign of anyone else working there. He walked in front of Adisa as they entered. Mr Grey on one side of the bench, Mr Henderson the other side as Mr Grey went to block their exit. Lester stood still with Adisa immediately behind him for protection.

"Is there something I've done Sir? Something wrong? Lester asked.

"Give me the girl." Henderson barked. His anger was real. "Give me the bitch!"

"Why do you need her?" Lester asked. A scuffle broke out and Mr Grey managed to grab Adisa as she screamed. He threw her on the bench.

Brodie grabbed her right arm and inserted it into the vice, as Adisa screamed. Lester stood still, a gun was held to his back.

"Stay where you are, boy, this doesn't concern you." Brodie barked at him. Adisa struggled and bit him on the lower left arm that she drew blood. Surprised by this, Brodie hit back at her as Mr Grey went to help restrain her. This moment gave Lester sufficient time to grab a nearby machete, swiping at Mr Grey, ripping across his chest, and driving it straight through Brodie Henderson's thigh, twisting it as he removed it, tearing through muscle and tendons.

Both men were rendered motionless as they realised they were bleeding profusely. Lester released the vice and it let go of Adisa.

"Run. Run!" He shouted at her.

Brodie looked at his bloodied right hand and slowly reached into his jacket, looking for his pistol. A gun went off, followed by silence. Then another shot.

Everyone looked to where the sound came from. A tall silver haired man stood, with his gun pointing in Brodie's direction. Its owner looked at the body now lying on the floor. Brodie tried to speak, but all that he could emit was a bloodied gurgle. He had been shot in the neck and the dirt floor under him was getting darker and darker with the blood as the body became paler and paler. Mr Grey looked on at his boss and the intruder who fired the shot. He reached for Brodies pistol and a second bullet ended his life.

Adisa hid behind Lester once again.

"Sir! Who are you?" Lester asked. Adisa looked at the man; his features somewhat familiar.

"My name is Florian. I own the Conquerabia Plantation in Caroni. I came here to find my daughter." Adisa came out from behind Lester, disbelief in her eyes.

"Surely, I must be dreaming". Adisa was shaking. "Never in my imagination could I have foreseen this. Lester Pearce, this is my father. Florian Dottin. I have not seen him for more than 8 years. Master Dottin, this is Mr Lester Pearce. My friend.

“Mr Dottin. I cannot thank you enough. You have saved us. They wanted to amputate Adisa’s hand and probably would have killed me first, for trying to stop them. I can’t think why they were so compelled to hurt her.”

“Let’s just say, I don’t think Brodie Henderson was very impressed with your speech earlier today. I think you may have said more than enough to embarrass such a man as him, intent on ruling with fear.

“I’ve been looking for you for a long time, Adisa. I can't believe I've finally found you." Adisa and Florian stood not knowing how to react to each other. “I saw you give your talk this afternoon and when I saw Brodie leave in anger, I put two and two together. He was enraged and with Tante hearing two women talking about someone who looked like you, I headed to his plantation and now I’ve found you. I have known Mr Henderson for some time. He's a despicable man. This is providence. God brought us together." Overawed by emotion Florian ran to hug Adisa, who returned the gesture with tears.

"We must call on the local constabulary. I think they will be most interested to find Mr Henderson and Mr Grey dead. They’ve been trying to charge Brodie for some time. They will need to take statements and, don't worry, I'll let them know it was I who killed both. You'll be safe now Adisa."

Chapter 35

The Chief Justice Mr Nathaniel Douglas had listened to all evidence presented by the witnesses, including constables' statements pertaining to other illicit indiscretions by Brodie Henderson and Mr Grey.

"It is my understanding that Mr Brodie Henderson, aided and assisted by Mr Grey, his friend and manager, had the presence to take the law into his own hands, to seek personal satisfaction and retribution. Certain evidence suggests that Mr Henderson was responsible for the death of more than 26 men and women, most of whom were negroes. This means that some cases need to be reopened due to possible miscarriages of justice. We also take into consideration reports from Mr Henderson's time in Santo Domingue which bear remarkable similarities to his conduct here. It is fair to say Mr Henderson has something of a track record where crimes are concerned.

Justice Douglas continued. "It is my opinion that in the conviction of Messrs Gideon Johnston, Pauly Newell and Scipio Alvarez, were scapegoats for Mr Henderson who sought to exact vengeance towards Mr Toby Frederickson, son of Mr Aubrey

Frederickson, who had entered into a relationship with one of his mulatto housemaids Miss Mimi Okiro, whose body was found near the Pitch Lake, having been strangled and eviscerated."

"What is clear is that Brodie Henderson and Mr Gray were once known supporters of Governor Thomas Picton, whose rule based on 'projections of elite masculinity' are no longer supported here. They used their presence and position to intimidate and rule by fear and carry out their own form of law and order. Their version allowed plantation owners' right to use and abuse negroes. It is possible to appreciate why he may have met his end in such a violent manner."

Aubrey sat at the back of the hearing, listening to the Coroner give his conclusion on the events on the night that Brodie, alongside his manager, Mr Grey, had Toby Frederickson killed in such a gruesome manner. He felt the visceral pain of those events as strongly as before, learning how his son died and by whose hands. Therese was at his side and as soon as the assessment was given, sobbed. Aubrey thought it best to leave the courtroom and Therese welcomed his decision.

On hearing a commotion, Lester turned around to see Aubrey and Therese leave. Having heard the summation he too left to join Florian and Adisa who remained sat outside the courtroom, neither wishing to relive the details of that fateful night once again, stood when they saw who left the courtroom. Neither acknowledged them, but as Aubrey left, Adisa saw a broken man. She moved towards them but Lester stopped her, shaking his head.

Therese helped Aubrey descend the steps of the courthouse as he shielded his eyes from the bright sun and turned to look behind him. He saw Adisa's attempted gesture and contemplated its meaning. He nodded in acknowledgement.

Time had passed and both had grown. Seeing how much he had aged Adisa wished there was something she could do or say. She returned to her seat, and bowed her head in silent prayer.

The courtroom doors opened again, as everyone rushed out. Florian looked for Adisa in the melee and went up to her. Their solicitor found them and informed them of the news.

"We are cleared of any wrongdoing. We will not be charged and are free to go!" Adisa looked at him in disbelief. "Isn't that good news? Florian added.

"That is such great news," added Lester. "We are all free and face no further charges." Adisa, without thinking, hugged Lester.

"Do you know why Aubrey and Therese left the courtroom? What do you think was the cause? Do you know?" Adisa asked the solicitor.

"Yes, further eye witness reports suggested that Brodie Henderson was behind the murder of Toby. Not the negroes, who were convicted and hung. Which also means that Scipio Alvarez was more than likely innocent. Brodie Henderson had a history of violence. He was a nasty man according to those reports in there, taking the law into his own hands and meting out his law as it suited him. He ruled his plantation like a brute. A lot of people lived in fear of him. I now understand why he was so anti-abolition. He feared retribution."

"I personally know that. It wasn't nice behaviour at all and I know I should not feel or say this, but I'm glad he's gone!" Adisa looked at Florian to see his reaction. He nodded in agreement.

"We all behave differently when we have something to lose, Father. It's how we behave to those closest to us that matters. It's time to understand and forgive. Our thoughts should be with Mr Aubrey. I do think we need to extend an olive branch to him. As soon as possible. We need to let him know we can forgive." Adisa added.

"Yes. We should do this right away. I'll arrange for the carriage to take us to Aubrey. He may be staying with Therese and the children. What a time to reinforce the importance of family eh? Lester, would you be happy to take the coach back to Conquerabia? I think this should just be the two of us paying Aubrey a visit." Florian handed him his purse.

"Very good Mr Florian. I understand. I wish you both God speed." Lester left, placing his hat on his head to protect him from the late afternoon sun and went to book a stagecoach.

Florian and Adisa rode in the hired buggy in silence. Relieved that this part of their ordeal was finally over. The wooden wheels rattled along the dirt road.

"I'm so glad it's all over. I do regret how Mr Henderson and Mr Grey met their end, but after hearing all that … What makes someone so horrid, so determined to kill and take another life?" Adisa puzzled over the recent events. "I think where I was concerned, he was afraid. Afraid of the possible influence I could have over other negroes.

"I recall the day I gave my speech in the Church in San Fernando, how many other people, not negroes, not black people, were nodding in agreement with me. Father, do you think that a woman, who knows right from wrong, could understand another person's desire for power over others and how that can unintentionally bring out the weakness in another?" It was a rhetorical question as Adisa pondered over the questions. "I know the bible says 'an eye for an eye', but if we all behaved like that, how many more of us would be maimed and killed? Where will it all end? Where's the empathy and understanding? If we are all made in His image, was God black or white? Was God a man or woman? I feel as if I'm beginning to doubt my bible. Doubt my faith, father!"

Florian took Adisa's hand and began to weep, trying to make sense of her current world. She slumped into his arms and cried.

"I think you're being tested or rather, we're being tested. We have to find our strengths and beliefs. If we still have our faith, will we not go wrong? You may not know this Adisa, but out of a sense of duty, I came to Trinidad for my own mother, your Grandmother Mabel. Do you remember her?" Adisa nodded. "I was looking to join the Royal Navy to serve, when my mother wrote to me saying that father was dying. I put my faith in God, even when I so much wanted to return to England and the Navy, but I could not leave my mother and all that my own father had created here. I could have ignored all the problems that Trinidad was experiencing. It took time to learn how to manage and make Conquerabia profitable. There was no way I could leave my mother, newly widowed, alone to run our home, at a time when women could not be seen to own and run a plantation. She was a remarkable woman, you know. She had more strength than I gave her credit for! In hindsight, she's shown me by example and I believe you have inherited a lot of that strength and determination from her."

The journey continued in silence and contemplation. Adisa's tears stopped and she managed to compose herself as the carriage reached Therese's home by Savannah Grande.

"Are you ready for this father?" Florian nodded and alighted from the cab, to help Adisa down, and the pair walked towards the house where they saw Therese on the verandah.

"Mr Dottin. Miss Adisa. Good day to you both!" She was curt and her eyes red from crying.

"Miss Therese, we come in peace and wish to speak with Aubrey to extend our condolences and forgiveness. I think it's time. Is he available?" Florian enquired. Therese was unsure if she should call her father, but common sense prevailed.

"I can ask, but I can't promise. It's been a hell of a day. Please sit down. He's been resting. I'll go and tell him you are here." Florian and Adisa sat on the verandah, in the shade looking towards the parkland. By the post, supporting the roof, desert honeysuckle grew and a hummingbird sought its sweet nectar. Adisa watched it hover then fly to the next flower and back. She was amazed by the pretty bird and the sight of it gave her a sense of calm. In the distance she heard children playing and singing and the gentle hubbub of work taking place. Adisa looked towards her father to reassure him they were doing the right thing.

Therese arrived with a tray of lemon water and four glasses, some homemade biscuits and slices of orange under a net to protect the delicious treats from the flies. She was followed by a frail Aubrey. Florian and Adisa stood to greet him, unsure of their reception.

"A … Aubrey, I have been thinking … " Florian was afraid of his reaction, but followed his conviction. "It's time we put the past behind us and focus on what's important? Today was the beginning of the end and Adisa and I realise we have all been through a lot. It's time for forgiveness. I miss my friend!"

Aubrey had not expected such kindness. As a proud man, he tried to stop his tears. He signalled to Florian and Adisa to sit and took a seat himself. Therese gently rubbed her father's back as he began to sob.

"I am not proud of what I have done and have repented many times. I know that I am human! I know I'm not the best and have let alcohol get the better of me. I say this not to excuse myself but to recognise my own failings. I continue to seek forgiveness from God, and hoped that one day, I would have the strength to ask forgiveness of you Florian and Miss Adisa. I went far beyond the line of decorum, and it has ruined me."

Florian and Adisa sat listening intently. Therese decided she needed to leave them alone to speak freely.

"But what about you Miss Adisa? Can you forgive the stupid and alcoholic behaviour of an elderly man?" He looked towards Adisa, his head bowed, struggling to make eye contact. Adisa got up from the table and walked to where Aubrey sat and took his hands in hers.

"Mr Aubrey. In James verse five it tells us 'we must confess our sins and to pray for each other so we may be healed. The prayer of a righteous person has great power.' We all strive to be decent people every day. There is too much sadness on this island for us to be at battle with our neighbour. I understand you were not yourself that night, the alcohol was to blame, and can see that you have been through so much; that you're making amends with yourself and God. I cannot lie, it's been a rough journey but you have my forgiveness." Florian was touched by Adisa's wisdom and placed a reassuring hand on her shoulder.

"I don't deserve such kindness from either of you. I am heartened that you have taken the bold step to forgive me and I don't take that lightly. You have every reason not to. Aubrey could not say the words for weeping so hard.

"Before we go Aubrey, I would like it very much if you and Therese and her husband would join us for lunch one Sunday. When our feelings have calmed down and you feel you would like to join us. I think it would be a wonderful opportunity to start making amends. You decide the day." Florian offered. "Well, I think we have taken up enough of your time Aubrey. Kindly pass on our gratitude to Therese and thank you for your kind hospitality. It means a lot.

Adisa took Aubrey's hand as he began to weep once again. Florian walked towards him, to shake his hand, but as he reached out once again, Aubrey hugged his friend tightly. "Thank you, for being the bigger man, Florian. I should have been the one, but I am pleased you did.

Florian and Adisa rode off in the carriage in silence, absorbing what just happened. Florian turned to Adisa and said. "You are a remarkable young lady and I'm proud to call you my daughter. When did you get to be so wise? I never thought of it in that way, but you're right. The evil money makes us do. Well, I never! My daughter has become a teacher." Adisa smiled at her father. "I really don't deserve you but I know I'm better off with you in my life. You have brought me riches no money could ever buy.

Chapter 36

Adisa had a fitful night's sleep and was homesick. Her nerves were beginning to jangle. She rose, stretched and walked to Esme's room. Esme was already awake and reading her bible. Adisa let herself in as Esme sat up. They hugged each other.

"Good morning chil'. Let me say a prayer for today. Will you join me, Adisa?"

"Yes, of course." Adisa sat back down on the bed as Esme opened the page she was reading. When she closed it, she signalled to Adisa to join her in the Lord's Prayer. They knelt beside the bed and recited the prayer, closing with an 'amen' and the sign of the cross.

"The Honourable Brandon Pearce will be here today about 12:30 to collect us and take us to Jordan House. I'm so nervous Esme, I feel quite sick. Did he have to say it's an 'historic talk' today? Why can't I just go back to bed?" Adisa was irritable.

"Adisa, you need to draw on what brought you here in the first place. As you said last night at dinner, you've been driven to seek equality and the justice that abolition of slavery could bring. You can't turn your back on us now. We need you now, more than ever."

Adisa had accepted an invitation from Brandon Pearce, a distant cousin of the Quaker MP Joseph Pearce. Brandon had taken an interest in Adisa and had been following the career of this extraordinary young woman whose vision he felt was in alignment with that of the Quakers, and as sponsor he extended an invitation to her to speak at the Jordan's Meeting House in Buckinghamshire, England.

It was to be a unique event, the biggest the meeting house ever held and the first time for an international speaker. It was a heavy burden for Adisa.

"Esme, I'm so glad you're here. I don't think I could do any of this without you. You have been my rock." Adisa became weepy. "It has recently occurred to me what a lonely path I've chosen. At times, I wish I didn't have to do it. Why can't someone else do it? I know that sounds foolish but right now, I doubt my calling."

"I've put my trust in Him, I know what I'm talking about, I've got all my facts up to date, as best as I can get," Adisa could not stop crying and threw herself onto Esme's bed.

"You are not a quitter, Adisa. This is your calling. At each talk you gave, what was your motivation before you opened your mouth. You need to remember what gave you the courage to make that first step onto the stage. Embrace that now. You feel fear, out there you speak to me, out there, when you see everyone, imagine them replicas of me. I'm on your side. Remember that. Most importantly, you need to do this for Lester, Tante and Elders, without whom you would not be here today!" Esme's voice was a little too harsh.

"You're right. I do owe them. I'll dedicate this talk to them. I do wish they were here today to help support me."

"Adisa, they are in spirit here with you today. As is Mr Florian. You can feel shaky, that's understandable. You know what you have to say, and you've delivered many like this before. I know you can do it and have every faith that it will be very special." Esme kissed Adisa on the forehead. "I'm going to the kitchen to make some tea. Would you care to join me?"

"Yes, of course and Esme …" Adisa reached out to her. "Thank you so much for being with me. I don't think I could do this without your friendship and support. You're very special to me and I'm thankful."

"I also have to thank you for inviting me to be a part of this wonderful new adventure in your life. Come on. Let's get ready." Said Esme who gave Adisa the biggest smile she could and headed off to the kitchen.

Brandon was on time. He asked the cab driver to wait whilst he called on Adisa and Esme. They too were ready and waiting for him to arrive. It had just started to rain and the temperature had dropped as a result. Adisa was grateful for the use of the rug to throw over her and Esme's legs in the cab.

"How are you feeling? Nervous?" Brandon asked.

"Yes, very nervous but I like the challenge it offers. I think I'm prepared."

"That's good to hear. It shouldn't take us more than one hour to get to Beaconsfield? I'm sorry about the rain." Brandon was also feeling very nervous and started talking rapidly. "I'm sorry. I'll stop talking now. Forgive me." Adisa smiled, comforted by the fact someone else was as nervous as her. It was a good distraction.

She looked out the window to the people and streets they passed. Right now she longed for the sunshine and cloudless skies of her home. Her heart ached. She then realised one more thing. She missed Lester terribly and recalled that day in the workshop when he presented her with the trinket box and wooden heart. She did not realise until now how powerful her love was for him. More than anything, she wanted Lester by her side.

Staring out the window in silence, Adisa saw on the other side, walking towards the direction of Adisa, a young lad, perhaps no more than 12 or 13 years with soot covering his face and the familiar chimney brush resting over his right shoulder. Despite the dirty face, Adisa could see what a handsome lad he is. He walked as if he had no care in the world.

It was oddly silent as the trio rode in the carriage. As instruction was given to the driver Brandon saw Adisa clasp both hands over what he believed was her bible in her purse, close her eyes and prey. It was a solemn moment in which he felt he could not speak so he averted his eyes to look at the world passing by.

Some time elapsed and Adisa collected her thoughts and asked Brandon about how many he was expecting.

"We've allocated all the tickets for tonight's event. I think we could have filled the space more than thrice over." Esme looked at Adisa with wide eyes. "Yes, we have had so many people wish to attend. This has to be one of our most popular events and, once again, I am thankful to you for accepting the invitation."

"It is my pleasure, but I really don't feel worthy of such an invitation since I have been reading about the work of Elizabeth Heyrick, a remarkable woman, whom I feel more worthy of this than I." Brandon smiled at such humility.

"I have to say .." Adisa continued. "The women's movement here has been exceptional. I do admire the hard work Mrs Heyrick has been carrying out. She's a woman after my own heart. If only I had as much courage as she …". Adisa's voice trailed off.

"Yesterday I was reading that during the 1790s, women were actively encouraged to boycott slave-produced goods such as sugar and rum to add economic weight to the abolitionist campaign. This is extraordinary. I was unaware that women, together, were so instrumental in bringing about such a change."

"Then don't be surprised Mrs Heyrick and others like her turn up tonight. I know she was keen to attend if she could make it down from Leicester." Adisa gasped in shock.

"I would feel honoured to meet her. Do let her know if she turns up, as I personally would like to thank her for her work. However, I fear you have made me more nervous than I was."

As they arrived, turning through the gates Adisa saw the Flemish Bond brick building as the carriage stopped and they alighted. Then she saw the placards and the protestors. Signs saying "Go Home" and "Half Castes Not Wanted Here" and worse. Chants not dissimilar. It was unreal and unnerved Adisa and Esme.

The protesters jostled with those who wanted to attend. As Brendon led her and Esme to a side entrance, a protester ran to her and spat, missing Adisa but hitting Esme on her face.

Brandon quickly took his handkerchief and gently wiped it away and saw her eyes welling up with tears.

"I'm so terribly sorry … so very sorry Esme …". Brandon whispered with embarrassment.

More shouts could be heard as the trio scurried away from the fray. The mayor entered the room and made his apologies for the behaviour and placed himself at Adisa's disposal. Also embarrassed by the action of some of the protestors.

A young woman, smartly dressed, knocked on the door calling for Brandon.

"Mr Pearse? Mr Pearse?" She called out. Brandon stood by the door and she tried to enter, his foot preventing the door from opening too wide. "Oh Mr Brandon, I have a writer here from the Bucks Gazette and another from The Times. They're asking for Adisa's reaction to the protestors?"

Brandon shook his head in despair. "I will be with you momentarily." He replied, holding his hand up to stop her entering. She backed away from the door sufficiently for Brandon to open it and exit. "Miss Dottin is not giving any interviews before the talk. I need to make sure she's safe and that there will be no untoward behaviour or she does not speak at all. Is that understood?" Brandon's voice was muffled amid the chatter and excitement of the event. Adisa was impressed with how he handled the situation.

"Esme I'm so sorry. I had no idea that we would get a reception like this. I think I should cancel, who knows, somebody may get hurt out there if, as Brandon says, the risk of harm is strong!" Esme's eyes welled up, she took a deep breath and stood up, walking towards the opaque window, turned and looked at Adisa.

"Surely you are the reason why they are here? What you say, along with the other members of the abolitionist movements, locally and nationally are the reason these protesters are here? If you don't give your well rehearsed, informed speech, you are giving them a greater voice and all the work done to get to this point will be for nothing. Nothing! You owe it to me and those of us brought from Africa to parts of the world with no choice. Traded as animals at markets. Beaten, physically beaten so we had no voice. Worked harder than most domestic animals for the white man's gain. If you don't speak, you will help reverse all the good work that has got us and those whom you represent, here today. Most of all Adisa, you owe it to Lester and your father. And, ultimately yourself. Never have I believed so much that this is your calling and your duty. How dare you even think you can't speak tonight?"

Adisa looked at Esme and her words hurt. She never imagined her close friend had the words to cut her short and it stung. As each word struck Adisa felt the urge to cry but she also knew Esme was right.

"Adisa, remember you have something many of us don't. Privilege and opportunity."

Adisa could not look Esme in the eye. It was an uncomfortable moment. The sound of the hubbub outside had gone and Adisa could hear her blood coursing through her body with each thump, thump, thump of her heartbeat.

"Esme you are right. Perhaps I have lost myself with this trip and was expecting it to be plain sailing. I never once thought that I could be hated in this way, to be silenced in this manner. thanks to people like Anthony Benezet and Elizabeth Heyrick, I also have the ability to add my voice to their hard work …". A knock at the door broke the tension. It was Brandon.

"Ladies, is everything well here? I sense the mood has changed."

"She was a little concerned by what happened and I've just reassured her that I'm fine. It was a shock for a while, but Adisa knows she cannot let the likes of those protestors silence her." Esme looked sternly at Adisa as she stood up to speak to Brandon.

"I think it is what is termed as a 'wobble'. Adisa added with a forced smile.

"Of course it is to be expected. Do you need anything … ?" Brandon looked calm. "We have five more minutes and then you will be introduced. Adisa walked to Brandon and took his outstretched hand.

"Mr Pearse, one moment please. I would like to thank you personally for all that you have done to make tonight happen and I hope I don't disappoint you in any way. I would like to say that now in case I don't get a chance afterwards. The work you and the Quakers have done is immeasurable. I consider myself honoured to speak," she looked at Esme who was smiling warmly now. "Honoured to have such a platform from which to speak. Thank you."

Brandon felt himself choke. He had no words and bowed to both women closing the door behind him. Adisa walked over to Esme and the women hugged in mutual respect and love.

As Adisa stood on the dais, she saw the Meeting Room packed with people. Some of the placards leaning against the white walls. She bent her head down and caught sight of the red Brick floor, momentarily studying its pattern gave her time to compose her thoughts.

"Ladies and gentlemen, distinguished guests … Thank you for inviting me to speak here this evening. A dear friend pointed out that any discourse cannot reject what one doesn't wish to hear. An argument has two sides and it is very easy to hear that which we favour. However, it is important that we hear that which we do not!" With that statement men and women packed into the meeting room, stood up and cheered.

Chapter 37

The sun was squinting through the curtains, heralding the early morning. It was, oddly, silent bar, the occasional buggy or pedestrian on the street below. She got up to look through the window as the light dazzled her eyes. Through the mullioned glass window she saw the spire of the church of St Mary and All Saints in the distance and the graveyard beyond the small lea. It was a pretty sight, one that would be etched into her mind forever.

In the distance she saw Brandon walking towards the house with a large parcel under his arm. He had a spring in his step. Adisa decided it was time for her to get up and gently nudged Esme awake too.

"Good morning Adisa. How are you today?" Esme stretched and smiled.

"I'm well Esme how about you?" Adisa sat on the edge of her friend's bed and hugged her once again.

“Last night feels like it was a dream, that it did not really happen, but I know something did. Tell me, what did you think of it? How did my talk go down?”

“Chil’, I can honestly say last night you made Mr Florian proud. You conducted yourself in a very dignified manner and they sat up attentively. Don’t you recall the standing ovation you received at the end, not just after your opening remarks?”

“I don’t know if you recall one of the protestors, one who was standing close to the carriage as we alighted, shouting at us to ‘go home’, came up to me and told me how much your words made her rethink how she treated others. You really got through to her, not just her. I think it has to be one of the most powerful talks you have delivered and I was proud to be there Adisa.” The church bells chimed and Esme looked out the window. “I think it must be nearly time for breakfast. It would be rude of us to make them wait, especially on our last day.” As the pair descended the stairs, Brandon was there to greet them with his parents. He was beaming.

“Good morning ladies, I trust you both slept well? You may recall my parent’s from last night. Lord Elgin Pearse and Lady Tabitha Pearse.” Both shook hands with Adisa and Esme and invited them to sit.

“Please call me Bertie.” Brandon’s father stated. “I don’t really like the formality of titles. Tell me, did you sleep well?” As polite conversation took place over breakfast, and the housemaid served the various courses, breakfast overran. It was such a genial affair Adisa did not want to leave. She imagined herself living in a village such as Beaconsfield. It was steeped with history and it stimulated her imagination.

"Oh, do let me show you the front pages from the papers …". Branden walked into the hall where he left the papers, returned and shared them amongst the diners. "I have to say, I'm very pleased with your reception. And the newspapers seem to agree." Headlines such as "Mixed Race Slave Delivers Persuasive Talk" and "Pretty Slave Defies Protestors".

"The gentlemen from the The Times and the Weekly Despatch said their editorial will not appear until the weekend so we have to wait for those and the representative from the local Female Society was so taken by you Adisa, she said they were going to put you on the cover of their next month's issue.

"I feel Brandon is trying to give me something of a rather large head with all this praise." Everyone laughed.

"You gave a very compelling speech Miss Adisa. I for one was quite moved." Lady Pearse added. "We have heard so much about you from Brandon and now we understand why he was so eager to sponsor you. My husband and I wholeheartedly agree it was the right decision to make. We think you have many of us, from both sides of the fence, thinking long and hard about what you said. You won an awful lot of people over and I commend you for that. You're a rather extraordinary young lady."

"I would not be here if it were not for your son, Mr Pearse. I am heartened that he became aware of my work so far away in the West Indies. If my words have helped one person to see the light then it will have been worth it." Adisa said.

"It is almost tangible, the wave for the abolitionist movement. I have never experienced such a change in the mindset of many of our people and particularly through the work of the women's movements and societies. It is seeing some of their work, petitioning and fundraising, that convinced me that you would be the ideal person to help persuade others to the cause and judging by these headlines, we are not wrong."

Adisa sat listening to all that was being said with a strong sense of pride and realised she longed to speak with Florian and Lester. Her deep desire for Lester was stronger than she had ever known and she felt a longing to just be with him.

To tell him all about her trip and show him the headlines. Adisa excused herself and headed up to her room.

"Oh dear." Brandon said. "I do hope we have not said anything to upset her."

“No Mr Brandon. I think she has found the whole experience rich, but overwhelming. She just needs a little bit of time to herself. At what time is our carriage? Esme enquired.

-o0o-

I think your Grandmother would be so proud of you, Adisa.” Rayne was helping to pin up her friend’s hair. “We used to have such good times together. I remember the first time we met in the small town of Peutie. She was a stunning looking woman. Quite serious at the time, but once Cecily and I got to know her, she came out of her shell. She had a remarkable talent for painting too. Did you know that?” Rayne looked at the reflection of Adisa in the mirror.

Adisa recalled the early days of tending to Mabel and how in turn she was mistreated by her. She could not declare that part of Mabel’s life to Rayne. “I did not know that she was an accomplished painter. How I would love to hear you talk more of her and her early days. Florian rarely speaks of her and I’m unsure why.”

“It’s not easy sending your only child away to boarding school, so far away, but it was the best thing for Florian when they moved here. It broke her heart to send him away so young. I recall how she doted on him. It would be another 14 years before she set eyes on him again. Don’t get me wrong, they did exchange letters, so Mabel said in her letters to me. But that was hard.” Adisa contemplated what Rayne said and realised that it could explain a lot about the strained relationship between them. She smiled kindly at Rayne.

There was a knock on the door and Esme answered it, coyly poking her head around. When she realised it was not one of the menfolk, Adisa invited her friend in.

"Your carriages are here, ready to take you both to church." She said, "I think your mother would be so proud of you today. You look so beautiful."

"As do you Rayne. Shall we go?" As soon as the two women departed, Conquerabia became a hive of activity as the food and partying preparations were finished in readiness for the wedding parties.

Florian was most proud to be able to walk his first born down the aisle as is proper, and to be best man to Aubrey, Esme was Matron of Honour to Adisa as Therese was for Rayne. Baxter and Isobel were Best Boy and Bridesmaid for both brides.

As he accompanied Adisa up the aisle, Lester turned around to witness his future wife's arrival, allowing himself a tear or two; he never imagined that he would see such a day, or even be part of it. As Lester raised the veil Adisa looked across at her father. Florian saw her and smiled reassuringly. The wedding ceremony commenced.

The End

But me, not destined such delights to share

My prime of life in wandering spent and care, Impelled, with steps unceasing, to pursue

Some feeling good, that mocks me with the view; That, like the circle bounding earth and skies, Allures from far, yet, as I follow, flies;

My fortune leads to traverse realms alone, And find no spot of all the world my own.

(Goldsmith).

BIBLIOGRAPHY:

- Spanish Trinidad, Ottley, X700/7098,SBN582763134 - http://caribbeanhistoryarchives.blogspot.com/2007/12/royal-cedula-of-1783.html?m=1
- The History of the West Indian Islands of Trinidad & Tobago. Carmichael, G. Redman
- Scandal of Colonial Rule: Power and subversion in the British Atlantic during the Age of Revolution. Epstein, James. Cambridge University Press.
- A History of Modern Trinidad 1783-1962. Brereton, B. Heineman. 0435981161.
- The History of The West Indian Islands of Trinidad & Tobago. Carmichael, G. Alvin Redman Ltd, 1961
- Aboriginal and Spanish Colonial Trinidad. Newson
- The Plantation Negroes of Trinidad 1783 -1816. A Mathematical and Demographic Enquiry. Meredith John, A. Cambridge.
- Memoirs of Lieutenant-General Sir Thomas Picton, Volume1. Robinson. H, B. (https://books.google.co.uk/books?id=sZDEDAAAQBAJ&pg=PT15&dq=Thomas+Picton&hl=en&sa=X&ved=0ahUKEwiR4qft-O_TAhXCKMAKHSjsD4M4ChDoAQgyMAM#v=onepage&q=Abercromby& f=false)

- Political Account of the Island of Trinidad: From its Conquest by Sir Ralph Abercrombie, in the Year 1797, to the Present Time, In a letter to his grace the Duke of Portland. Unknown Author. Forgotten Books.
- An Introduction To The Postal History of the British West Indies. L E Britnor. The British West Indies Study Circle 1959.
- Yellow Jack and the Worm: British Naval Administration in the West Indies, 1739-1748. Crewe. Duncan. Liverpool University Press.
- Naval Leadership and Management 1650-1950. Edited by Doe, Helen: Harding, Richard. Boydell Press.
- Tobago "Melancholy Isle" Volume One 1498-1771. Archibald, Douglas. Westindiana Ltd
- Trinidad. A Philatelic History to 1913. Eds: Marriott, J; Medlicott, M; Ramkissoon, R. A. The British West Indies Study Circle/The British Caribbean Philatelic Study Group.
- The Transport Revolution. Bagwell, Philip. S. Routledge.
- The Ordeal of Elizabeth Marsh: How a remarkable woman crossed seas and empires to become part of world history. Colley, L. Harper Perennial
- The Black Jacobins. James, C.L.R. Penguin History.

- Saltpetre used in cooling liquids in the 18th Century - https://regencyredingote.wordpress.com/2013/08/09/saltpetre-regency-refrigeration/
- http://www.pla.co.uk/Port-Trade/History-of-the-Port-of-London-pre-1908
- A Vindication of the Rights of Women. Wollstonecraft, M. Digireads.com. 2018.
- The rise of a free coloured plantocracy in Trinidad 1783-1813. Campbell. Carl.

Milton Keynes UK
Ingram Content Group UK Ltd.
UKHW021942070824
446675UK00010B/220

9 781917 36776